PETER HALLBERG

Old Icelandic Poetry
Eddic Lay and
Skaldic Verse

Translated with a foreword by

Paul Schach and Sonja Lindgrenson

UNIVERSITY OF NEBRASKA PRESS

LINCOLN AND LONDON

© 1962 by Peter Hallberg

Translation copyright © 1975 by the University of Nebraska Press

All Rights Reserved

Library of Congress Cataloging in Publication Data
Hallberg, Peter.
  Old Icelandic poetry.
  Translation of Den fornisländska poesien.
  Bibliography: p.
  Includes index.
  1. Icelandic and Old Norse poetry—History and
criticism. I. Title.
PT7170.H313   839'.6'1009   74–27186
ISBN 0–8032–0855–3

MANUFACTURED IN THE UNITED STATES OF AMERICA

151516

Contents

Foreword   vii

1   Snorri Sturluson's Poetics   1

2   Eddic Lay and Skaldic Verse: General Characteristics, Meter, and Style   11

3   Eddic Lay   27

4   Skaldic Verse   105

5   Christian Poetry in the Forms of Eddic Lay and Skaldic Verse   173

6   Rímur: Icelandic Form Tradition   185

Text Supplement   191

Bibliography   199

Index   209

Foreword

As a glance at the annual bibliographies in the *Publications of the Modern Language Association* and in *Scandinavian Studies* will reveal, interest in Eddic and skaldic poetry and in the closely related Old Norse prose works has increased appreciably in recent years, not least of all in English-speaking countries. Of the titles listed in the selected bibliography of this volume, over 40 percent were published during the past decade and a half, either for the first time or as reissues or new editions of older works. Especially welcome is the growing emphasis among scholars on the distinctive artistic merit of these remarkable poems of ancient Norway and Iceland. To be sure, Eddic and skaldic poetry continue to be examined as sources of information about Germanic mythology and heroic legend; but a major emphasis of such perceptive scholars as Ursula Dronke, Peter Hallberg, Jón Helgason, Sigurður Nordal, Einar Ól. Sveinsson, E.O.G. Turville-Petre, and others has been the interpretation of these poems as works of creative literature. The genuine enthusiasm for and the keen appreciation of Eddic lay and skaldic verse as unique forms of literary art that inform the writings of such scholars have been contagious, not only among colleagues and students but also among laymen—how widely contagious can be judged by the fact that translations of Eddic lays by Paul B. Taylor and W. H. Auden have recently appeared in such journals as the *Atlantic Monthly*, the *Massachusetts Review*, the *New York Review of Books*, and *Quest*. And the Windhover Press in 1968 brought out a deluxe bilingual edition of *Völuspá: The Song of the Sybil*, the most profound poem in the Old Icelandic language.

Since the publication in 1962 of the revised edition of Lee M. Hollander's *Poetic Edda*, two new translations of this corpus have been made available to English readers. *Poems of the Vikings*, translated by Patricia Terry, appeared in print in 1969. It contains translations of most of the Eddic lays discussed in the present volume. The following year witnessed the publication of *The Elder Edda*, translated by Paul B. Taylor and W. H. Auden, containing sixteen Eddic lays. *The Northmen Talk*, an anthology of Old Icelandic prose and verse in English translation by Jacqueline Simpson (1965), includes six poems of the *Edda* and excerpts from six more as well as ten Icelandic ballads. The Eddic lays have been rendered in an alliterative verse in the form of the Border ballads; the original verse forms of the Icelandic ballads have been retained. And the translation of the *Poetic Edda* by Henry Adams Bellows, first published in 1922, continues to be reprinted, the fifth printing coming in 1966. It is from this volume that most of the translations of Eddic poems contained in the present volume were taken. There is thus no dearth of translations of Eddic poetry, and readers of this volume may find it interesting to compare the Bellows translations with some of the other ones.

Translations of skaldic poetry are less easy to come by. Hollander's book on the skalds and his translation of *Heimskringla*, with its over 600 skaldic verses, are the most fruitful sources of such translations. Other important sources are the translations of such sagas as contain considerable amounts of this type of verse—notably sagas about poets.

The Prose Edda of Snorri Sturluson: Tales from Norse Mythology, selected and translated by Jean I. Young, which was first published in Cambridge in 1954, was reprinted by the University of California Press in 1964. The older translation by Arthur G. Brodeur continues to be reprinted as needed; it is by far the most popular book ever published by the American-Scandinavian Foundation. And in 1970 Mrs. Cynthia King, inspired by the Bellows and Brodeur translations, re-created the tragic story of the Old Norse gods: *In the Morning of Time: The Story of the Norse God Balder.*

A real boon to beginning students in this field as well as to students and scholars in other disciplines who desire to gain some knowledge of Eddic and skaldic poetry are recent bilingual editions of Old Icelandic texts and translations accompanied by texts in the original language. Of importance for the study of this poetry are the *Hervarar saga ok Heiðreks, Gunnlags saga ormstungu,* and *Völsunga saga,* all in the Nelson series. In this connection attention should be called to the two recent editions with German translations of the *Nibelungenlied,* the monumental Middle High German epic whose sources were similar to some of the heroic lays of the *Edda,* although many readers will probably prefer to use the excellent English prose translation by A. T. Hatto. By far the most helpful book for those who wish to read Eddic poems in the original is Mrs. Dronke's edition, which in addition to its complete scholarly apparatus and splendid literary analysis, includes a close English rendering of the poems. The bilingual edition of *Völuspá* mentioned above is obviously helpful to the student spelling his way through this poem for the first time.

It is hoped that the present volume will be of use not only to students and scholars but also to an ever growing circle of lay readers of Old Norse poetry. Hallberg's approach to this poetry is rather similar to that of Jón Helgason in his *Norges og Islands digtning,* to which he gratefully acknowledges his indebtedness. The focus of attention throughout is on literary interpretation. *Völuspá,* for instance, is not interpreted as a system of mythology, which it is not, but as a symbolic vision poem, which it is and was intended to be by its author. Problems of sources, authorship, time and place of composition, etc., are dealt with adequately, but they are never permitted to detract from the main purpose of the book. Hallberg's exposition is fresh, clear, and succinct, whether in reviewing the ideas of other scholars or in setting forth his own. The careful selection and arrangement of the poems and poets to be discussed contributes significantly to the attainment of the aim of the book.

In this translation of the second revised edition of *Den fornisländska poesien* (published in 1964 by Svenska bokförlaget: Bonniers as volume 20 of the Verdandis skriftserie), no substantive changes have been made. A few minor additions have been made, several at the suggestion of the author and the others with his kind permission. The footnotes and bibliography have been expanded somewhat for the purpose of bringing them up to date and making them more useful for English readers. The English prose renderings of Icelandic poetry are my own, and do not differ significantly from Hallberg's Swedish translations. Mrs. Sonja Lindgrenson made a literal rendering of the Swedish text of this book and read both my first and my final revisions of it. Responsibility for errors is mine alone.

As already stated, most of the translations of Eddic lays used in this volume are those of Bellows. Several are from Hollander's *Old Norse Poems* and a few are from his *Poetic Edda*. The skaldic verses are from Hollander's *The Skalds* and from his translation of *Heimskringla*. Although I did not tamper with any of the translated skaldic verses, I made a few slight changes in several of the Eddic lays in order to bring them closer in meaning to the Icelandic text. Where this did not seem to be feasible, I supplied a close English rendering of the Icelandic poem in addition to using the English verse translation. I also followed Hallberg's practice of providing literal renderings of a number of skaldic verses. Such renderings not only are useful to beginning students of Old Icelandic, but serve to point up for the nonspecialist the extreme difficulty of turning skaldic verse into faithful verse interpretations in other languages. For the few poems for which appropriate English translations were not available, I furnished prose renderings. Professor Hollander had planned to make verse translations of these poems for me, but death prevented the carrying out of this plan.

The problem of the spelling of Icelandic proper names is ever with us. The orthography in the verse translations has been retained. Throughout the text and in the index I have used the Modern Icelandic forms since they appear less awkward to readers of English. In the quotations, however, I retained the Old Icelandic form. Thus we find such variants as Gunnar and Gunnarr; Eiríkur, Eiríkr, and Erik; Rögnvaldur, Rögnvaldr, and Ragnvald, etc. For the genitive case I followed Hallberg's practice. Thus Eirík's, Harald's, and Gunnlaug's are the possessive form for Eiríkur, Haraldur, and Gunnlaugur, respectively. Personal names ending in -ir, however, were treated like those in -ar: Grettir's, Gunnar's, etc.

A few words need to be said about pronunciation. All names and most words are stressed on the initial syllable. The acute accent serves to mark vowel length, not stress (for example, *Guðrún*). The vowels *a, e, i, o, u* have approximately the same value as in German. Most consonants have the same value as in English except that *s* is always voiceless, *g* is always a stop as in *go,* and *h* before a consonant is always an aspiràte. The letters *ð* (edh) and *þ* (thorn) represent the sounds of *th* as in *this* and *thin,* respectively. The diphthongs *au, ei,* and *ey* are like those in *house, they,* and French *paysan.* The vowels *y* and *ý* are similar to those in German *Hütte* and *Hüte,* or French *une* and *sûr.* The digraphs *æ* and *œ* stand for vowel sounds as in *hair* and *slur.* The vowel *ö* (= *ǫ*) is pronounced like the *ö* in German *Götter.*

Grateful acknowledgement is made to the following

publishers for permission to use English verse translations in this volume: the American-Scandinavian Foundation (*The Skalds* and *The Poetic Edda* [Bellows]), the Columbia University Press (*Old Norse Poems*), and the University of Texas Press *(Heimskringla* and *The Poetic Edda* [Hollander]). I also wish to express my grateful appreciation to Mrs. Dorothy Henderson for her patient and prompt typing of the manuscript of this book. And finally, it is a pleasure to acknowledge my gratitude to the American Philosophical Society for a grant which made it possible for me to immerse myself in Eddic and skaldic poetry while working on the book in Iceland.

PAUL SCHACH

CHAPTER 1

Snorri Sturluson's Poetics

SNORRI STURLUSON's *Edda* (or the *Prose Edda,* as it is usually called in English) provides a self-evident point of departure for all subsequent accounts of Old Icelandic poetry. With this treatise Snorri laid the foundation for the analysis and characterization of verse forms, figurative language, etc., and codified the terminology in this field—a contribution which may perhaps not be unrelated to European scholastic *artes poeticae* and *artes rhythmicae.* Within its relatively narrow sphere his *Edda* enjoys an authority comparable to that which the *Poetics* of Aristotle has for the study of ancient Greek literature. It is therefore by no means merely a pious tribute to Snorri if we dwell for a while upon the *Prose Edda* even though this work is more than seven hundred years old.

Like all other works of Old Icelandic literature, Snorri's *Edda* has not been preserved in its original form. We do, however, have four complete or almost complete manuscripts as well as several manuscript fragments. The only manuscript that gives us direct information about the title and author of this work is the Codex Upsaliensis, housed in the university library at Uppsala: *Bók þessi heitir Edda. Hana hefir samansetta Snorri Sturlu sonr eptir þeim hætti sem hér er skipat.* (The name of this book is *Edda.* It was composed by Snorri Sturluson in the form in which it is here presented.) This manuscript, which is thought to date from about 1300, is the oldest. The so-called Codex Regius in the Royal Library in Copenhagen, written around 1325, is generally regarded as the most distinguished. The other two complete manuscripts of the *Prose Edda* are the Codex Wormianus from around 1350, also located in Copenhagen,

1

and the Codex Trajectinus, a paper transcript (about 1600) of a medieval codex, which is located in Utrecht.

Snorri's *Edda* consists of four distinct parts: the *Prologue, Gylfaginning, Skáldskaparmál,* and *Háttatal.* Although the original arrangement of the four sections is not immediately apparent, recent research has succeeded in reconstructing the probable genesis of the work. The last section is the oldest. Upon returning to Iceland from a visit to the Norwegian court (1218–20), Snorri composed a laudatory poem in honor of both King Hákon Hákonarson and Earl (later Duke) Skúli Báðarson. The form of this poem, which was completed during the winter of 1222–23, is noteworthy: it consists of 102 stanzas in 100 different meters and is therefore correctly named *Háttatal* ("List of Meters"). To a certain degree the ambitious and demanding metrical design may well have contributed to the fact that the content of this poem is even more meager than is usually the case in such court poetry. But the poet doubtless regarded virtuosity itself as a fitting expression of homage to those whom he wished to eulogize. He wanted King Hákon and Earl Skúli to know that they were celebrated by a true master of the ancient skaldic art. It is also probable that from the very outset Snorri was pursuing a pedagogic purpose with his unique experiment. Evidence to support this belief is provided by the prose commentary which he intersperses throughout the poem and with which he characterizes and designates not only the forms of metrical composition in a narrow sense but also poetic diction in general. *Háttatal* is an instructional poem for skalds.

In order to practice the skaldic art or even to appreciate it as a reader or listener, however, one also needed to have a rather profound insight into the esoteric diction and figurative language of this kind of poetry. Snorri supplies such guidance in *Skáldskaparmál,* which makes up approximately half of the entire *Prose Edda.* The word *skáldskaparmál* means "poetic diction," and this part of the work

2

furnishes a compilation of the rich and varied store of *heiti* and *kenningar*, that is, designations and circumlocutions peculiar to skaldic poetry. (More about these two concepts in the following chapter.) Snorri inserted the information that he wished to impart into a little novelistic setting.

Ægir, who is skilled in the magic arts, comes to Ásgarður (the residence of the gods) for a visit. The gods (*Ás*, pl. *Æsir*) invite him to a banquet, where he is seated beside Bragi, the god of poetry. Bragi entertains the guest with a story about the gods. He relates how the giant Þjazi abducted the goddess Iðunn and stole her magic apples, which could confer eternal youth—all of this seemingly without any connection with the main purpose of this section of the book. But Ægir asks a question regarding the origin of that *íþrótt* (art, skill, accomplishment) that the Æsir call *skáldskapur* (poetic composition). Bragi replies by telling a story, which can be summarized as follows.

The Æsir had been at war with a race of people known as the Vanir. A peace meeting was held, at which both parties, as a token of their reconciliation, stepped forth and spat into a vat. When they parted, the gods preserved the spittle and created from it a man who received the name Kvasir. He was so wise that he could answer any and all questions that were put to him. Once Kvasir was invited to visit some dwarfs, Fjalar and Galar, who took him aside, killed him, and let his blood run into the cauldron Óðrerir and two tubs, named Són and Boðn. They blended honey with the blood; everyone who drinks that mead becomes a skald and a discerning man. After slaying a giant couple, the two dwarfs fell into the hands of the giant Suttungur. He took them out to a skerry that was inundated at high tide, and to ransom their lives they had to surrender the precious mead to him. Suttungur brought the drink to Hnitbjörg, where he put it in the safekeeping of his daughter Gunnlöd.

These events are the reason why the skaldic art is called

3

Kvasir's blood, the drink of the dwarfs or Óðrerir's drink, or Són's or Boðn's liquid. Since the mead saved Fjalar and Galar from being drowned on the rocky islet, it can also be named the craft of dwarfs. Finally, it becomes Suttung's mead or the Hnitbjörg-liquid.

Ægir finds such designations for the skaldic art obscure and asks how the Æsir got hold of Suttung's mead. Bragi willingly answers by telling another story.

Assuming the name Bölverkur, Óðinn seeks employment with the giant Baugi, Suttung's brother, and stipulates that he is to get a draught of the Suttungur mead as wages. When at the end of the summer he appears together with his master at Suttung's home, however, Suttungur bluntly refuses to part with a single drop of his mead. Then Óðinn resorts to cunning. He has a hole bored through the rock into Hnitbjörg. In the shape of a snake he squeezes through and then sleeps three nights with Gunnlöd. She promises him three draughts of mead. With his first draught he empties Óðrerir, with his second Boðn, with his third Són, and thus he has acquired all of it. Then he assumes the guise of an eagle and flies away. But Suttungur, who has discovered the treachery, also assumes the form of an eagle and sets out in pursuit. When the Æsir see Óðinn flying toward them, they place their tubs in the yard and he regurgitates the mead into them as soon as he has reached Ásgarður. But at that moment Suttungur has almost caught up with him, and Óðinn lets some of the mead escape backward. That portion is not saved. Anyone who wishes to can help himself to it, and it is called the lot of the poetasters (skáldfífl). Óðinn gave Suttung's mead to the Æsir and to those men who can compose poetry. That is why the art of poetry is called Óðinn's booty, find, drink, or gift, or the drink of the Æsir.

It is of course impossible to say how original or how widespread these concepts about the origin of the art of poetry can have been. But in the Eddic poem *Hávamál*, for example, there is an allusion to Óðin's encounter with the giant Suttungur. Quite generally the drink of poets is associated with preterhuman beings endowed with supernatural powers: dwarfs, giants, gods. And the basic substance of the drink is Kvasir's blood, the essence of life itself. However, Snorri does not reproduce the myth primarily for its own sake. It is intended above all to provide a key to the many diverse kennings that the skalds have used throughout their esoteric art. With no understanding of the myths behind them, the young adept stands perplexed when confronted with such circumlocutions as "boat of dwarfs" or "Suttung's mead," and cannot himself vary them in his own poetry.

After introducing the kennings of the poem as such, Snorri systematically pursues his instruction with examples from a number of other conceptual spheres; in doing so, moreover, he soon drops the fiction of the dialogue between Ægir and Bragi. How is one to paraphrase the names of the various gods, heaven, earth, the sea, mankind, gold? Numerous examples from authentic skaldic poetry serve as illustrations. All told, more than sixty poets are quoted by name in *Skáldskaparmál*, some of whom would have sunk completely into oblivion by now had it not been for Snorri's reference to them. But all the while kennings are explained; the pedagogical objective is never lost from view. Why, for instance, is gold called Ægir's fire, Sif's hair, otter's ransom, Fróði's meal, Kraki's seed? About these matters Snorri provides good information, and his commentaries often tend to take shape as little gems of narrative art. To illustrate the expression "otter's ransom" the whole story of Sigurður Fáfnisbani is told, the matter of which is so important for many of the heroic lays in the *Poetic Edda*. For the kenning "Fróði's meal" reference is made to the famous poem *Gróttasöngr*, which tells about the Danish king Fróði and his slave girls Fenja and Menja, who were placed in the mill called Grótti to grind gold and happiness for their master, but who ended by grinding out misfortune and death for him. "Kraki's seed" finds its explanation in the story of how on the Plains of Fýris near Uppsala Hrólfur kraki strewed gold from a horn in front of the pursuing Swedes.

Snorri devotes the latter part of *Skáldskaparmál* to *heiti*, which, in contrast to the kennings, are not compounds of two or more members, but more or less unusual synonyms for various concepts. Each word, then, as a rule emphasizes a special aspect or nuance of the object in question, as in the following series of heiti for *woman: víf, brúðr, fljóð, sprund, svanni, snót, drós, ristill, rýgr, feima, hæll, ekkja, mær, kerling,* etc.

As already stated, *Skáldskaparmál* was written for the purpose of instruction in the skaldic art. But since knowledge of the old myths proved to be an indispensable requirement for a proper understanding of the language of the kennings, Snorri often reproduces episodes from Norse mythology. In *Gylfaginning* ("The Deluding of Gylfi"), the second section of the *Prose Edda*, these rather sporadic beginnings are developed into a complete picture of heathen mythology. But at the very beginning of his work, in the *Prologue*, Snorri has provided us with a historical and rational interpretation of the belief in the Æsir.

Snorri tells us that the Æsir are so called because they came from Asia. Perhaps it was this etymology that prompted Snorri to trace the origin of the Æsir to Troy and Turkey. In that region there reigned a renowned royal family within which a certain Trór, "whom we call Þór," distinguished himself. He took possession of Thrace, "which we call Þrúðheimur," and married the seeress Síbil, "whom we call Sif." A descendant of Þór in the eighteenth generation was "the one we call Óðinn." He learned by virtue of his prophetic gift that his name would come to be especially revered in the northern regions of the world and therefore he set out for the North with a magnificent retinue. Wherever they traveled in all their splendor, they seemed to people around them more like gods than human beings. From Óðin's offspring are descended well-known royal dynasties such as the Völsungs in Central Europe, the Skjöldungs in Denmark, and the Ynglings in Sweden.

The frame story of *Gylfaginning* relates that wise King Gylfi in Svíþjóð (Sweden), who was also skilled in magic, wished to discover the secret of the Æsir's sources of power. For that purpose he assumes the appearance of an old man and sets out for Ásgarður. But the Æsir are alert and receive him with optical illusions. At the entrance to a magnificent palace Gylfi introduces himself as Gangleri (One Who Is Tired from Wandering) and requests sleeping quarters for the night. He is shown into the castle and placed before three high seats, each one higher than the last. On them are seated, from the lowest to the highest, Hár (High), Jafnhár (Equally High), and Þriðji (the Third). Gangleri is offered food and drink, but he says that he wants to know first if there is anyone within who is well informed. Hár replies that Gangleri will not leave safe and sound unless he is even more knowledgeable, "and stand forward while you ask: he who replies shall sit."

Then there follows a long series of questions from Gangleri, such as: What is the origin of the world, and what existed before that? Where is the road that leads from Earth to Heaven? Who is the greatest or oldest of all the gods? Which of the Æsir are men obliged to believe in? Who owns the horse Sleipnir and what can be said about him? What can be told about Ragnarök? He receives his answers in turn from Hár, from Jafnhár, and from Þriðji. In their pronouncements they retell large parts of *Völuspá*; but also other Eddic lays such as the gnomic poems *Vafþrúðnismál* and *Grímnismál* are quoted. On the other hand, it would naturally have seemed too obvious an anachronism in this connection to quote the poetry of skalds mentioned by

7

name. At times the answers expand to more epic breadth as in the well-known stories about Þór's journey to Útgarða-Loki or about Baldur's death and the punishment of the malicious Loki.

Finally, after a description of the birth of the new world after Ragnarök, Hár concludes the audience. Gangleri hears a tremendous roar from all directions. Looking about more closely, he finds himself standing in the open air on a level field. He does not see a castle any longer. Thus his whole adventure turns out to have been a deception by the Æsir. "He goes on his way and returns to his kingdom and relates what he has seen and heard, and after him these stories have been told from one man to the other."

Afterward the Æsir assemble in council and agree to transfer to themselves and their surroundings the names that had been mentioned in the stories they told Gangleri, a deliberate deception for the purpose of increasing their power and reputation. Thus Snorri here applies the type of explanation for the existence of the gods that is known as euhemerism (after Euhemeros, ca. 300 B.C.): the Æsir were originally mortal sovereigns who gradually and only after their deaths became objects of religious worship.

Snorri's account of the genesis of the belief in the Æsir is far from being unambiguous and confronts the student of myth and religion with many problems. But if, as is the case here, Gylfaginning too is studied primarily from the viewpoint of its significance for poetics, these problems can simply be ignored. In any case this rich description of the world of the Æsir should comprise an abundant source of kennings of skaldic poetry. In a passage in Skáldskaparmál Snorri himself tells us his pedagogical aim and at the same time adds a warning and an expedient reservation: "This is now to be said to the young poets who wish to learn the language of the skaldic art and to acquire a stock of ancient poetic words, or who desire to comprehend what is darkly woven into the poems—then may they learn to understand this book for knowledge and pleasure. One must not forget or doubt these stories to the extent that one removes from the art of poetry the old kennings that the great skalds have employed. Yet Christian people should not believe in pagan gods or in the truth of these stories other than in the manner indicated at the beginning of this book."

In this way Snorri has freely and frankly asserted the indispensability of the old mythology for poetry, but at the same time as a good Christian he has definitely repudiated the heathen heresy as religious dogma and theology. Snorri's appeal especially to young poets supports the supposition that he wanted to encourage a renaissance of the difficult art of the old poets. It also seems as though skaldic poetry actually experienced a kind of Indian summer in the wake of the *Edda*. For Icelandic prosody Snorri's work has remained a guide down to our own times.

The name *Edda* itself has not yet been explained satisfactorily. The word is otherwise known only in the meaning "great grandmother," which hardly seems applicable here. According to one hypothesis the book title is said to be derived from the name of the estate Oddi, where as a young man Snorri was educated at the home of the aristocrat Jón Loptsson, in a milieu that was literarily stimulating: *Edda*, "the book from Oddi." More attractive perhaps is the explanation that *Edda* is a derivation of the word óðr, which in addition to "soul," "mind," can also mean "poetic gift." According to this plausible interpretation, which can be supported by linguistic parallels, *Edda* would consequently mean "principles of poetic composition." But it is more prudent to leave the question open.

CHAPTER 2

Eddic Lay and Skaldic Verse: General Characteristics, Meter, and Style

Verse Forms and Poetic Diction

OLD ICELANDIC POETRY is generally divided into Eddic and skaldic verse. This distinction has come to be accepted even though neither designation is especially appropriate. After all, "skalds" were also involved in the composition of Eddic poetry. These two kinds of poetry are so different from each other that they should properly be treated separately; and, indeed, this will be done further on, where the two main sections of this book will be devoted to a discussion of these two genres. Here at the outset there will be given only a rather summary definition of Eddic and skaldic poetry. In addition, their verse forms and poetic diction will be illustrated, for despite their discrepancies, they have many characteristics in common.

The Eddic lays deal with material from Norse mythology and Germanic heroic legend. Without exception the authors of such poems remain anonymous. Skaldic verse, on the other hand, generally bears a more topical impress and treats definite situations from the poet's own times. Many skaldic poems are encomiastic and are dedicated to some ruler or other. All skaldic poetry is to a high degree the creation of practitioners who were keenly conscious of their mastery of the art. The names of many skalds are known, both Norwegians and, above all, Icelanders. In contrast to the Eddic lays, their work can often be dated quite accurately.

In form, too, one can distinguish characteristic differences. To be sure, in both genres alliteration is an essential, fundamental prosodic principle, as indeed it is in all older Germanic poetry. But the meters of the Eddic lays are substantially simpler than those of skaldic verse. Eddic poetry is not by any means completely lacking in poetic words and circumlocutions, but on the whole it is very straightforward. By contrast, the skalds (in the narrower, more specific sense of the word) often make a virtue of their endeavor to avoid the direct expression, a penchant that sometimes transforms their poems into veritable rebuses.

Eddic Meters

The two chief metrical verse forms of Eddic poetry are *fornyrðislag* ("old story" or "epic meter") and *ljóðaháttr* ("song" or "chant meter"). The former is a stanza of eight lines, each one of which has two stressed syllables (lifts) and a somewhat varying number of unstressed syllables. The lines are joined together to form couplets by means of alliteration. In the second line of such a couplet the alliteration is always borne by only one word, (*höfuðstafr*, "headstave"), usually the first lift. In the first line generally both lifts alliterate (*stuðlar*, "props" or "staves"). As an example let us take the third stanza from *Völuspá* ("The Prophecy of the Seeress"); the alliterating words are here written in italics:

Ár var *alda*	Of old was the age
þats *ekki* var,	ere anything was,
vara *sandr* né *sær*	sea nor cool waves
né *svalar* unnir;	nor sand there were;
iörð fannsk *æva*	earth had not been,
né *upphiminn,*	nor heaven above,
gap var *Ginnunga,*	but a yawning gap,
en *gras* hvergi.	and grass nowhere.

12

As this example demonstrates, alliteration can be either consonantal (*gap-Ginunga-gras*) or vocalic (*Ár-alda-ekki*). In the first case it is a rule that a single consonant can alliterate only with itself; similarly, the consonant combinations *sk*, *sp*, and *st* can alliterate only with the exactly corresponding combinations. All initial vowels (including *j*), on the other hand, alliterate together. According to Snorri's commentary in *Háttatal*, however, vocalic alliteration sounds more pleasing if the alliterating vowels are of a different quality (*á-a-e* and *i-æ-u* in the stanza above). These rules regarding alliteration have general validity and thus hold true also for the other main verse form, ljóðaháttr.

Ljóðaháttr differs from fornyrðislag through the fact that its second and fourth couplets are replaced by a so-called full line. Thus this verse form has six rather than eight lines, and the long lines alliterate within themselves, as in the following stanza from Hávamál:

Vin sínum	To his friend a man
skal maðr *vinr* vera,	a friend shall prove,
þeim ok *þess* vin;	to him and the friend of his friend;
en *óvinar* síns	but never a man
skyli *engi* maðr	shall friendship make
vinar vinr vera.	with one of his foeman's friends.

As a variant of ljóðaháttr Snorri distinguishes *galdralag*, a verse form that can be illustrated by the following stanza from *Skírnismál*:

Heyri jötnar,	Give heed, frost-rulers,
heyri hrímþursar,	hear it, giants.
synir Suttunga,	Sons of Suttung,
sjálfir ásliðar,	and gods, ye too,
hvé ek fyrirbýð	how I forbid
hvé ek fyrirbanna	and how I ban
manna glaum mani,	the meeting of men with the maid,
manna nyt mani!	the joy of men with the maid.

13

The deviation from regular ljóðaháttr consists in the circumstance that the half stanza, as can be seen, is augmented by an additional full line; particularly characteristic is the final line of the stanza which, with only a slight variation, repeats the preceding one. With its parallelisms and repetitions—giants, frost ogres, and Suttung's sons are, of course, all the same thing—the entire stanza has the typical form of sorcery; and this accords well with the term *galdralag*, since *galdr* means "sorcery," "magic formula," "magic song." In *Skírnismál* this kind of stanza occurs only now and then. It seems quite likely that galdralag was employed mainly to achieve a heightening affect, but seldom in a long sequence of stanzas.

Although a certain differentiation can be observed in the use of fornyrðislag and ljóðaháttr for various forms of Eddic poetry, one can scarcely speak of a completely consistent distribution of these verse forms. Thus ljóðaháttr is preferred for use in mythical lays of a didactic nature (*Hávamál, Vafþrúðnismál, Grímnismál*) and in poems that consist entirely of dialogue (*Skírnismál, Lokasenna*).

As already mentioned, alliterative verse is a phenomenon common to the Germanic languages. An old representative from the continental German area is the *Hildebrandslied,* which was written down in a monastery around the year 800. Its subject matter is from native heroic legend. In the great Old Saxon epic *Heliand,* which was written early in the ninth century, alliterate verse is enlisted in the service of Christianity; in close to six thousand alliterating long lines (i.e., lines of four lifts) the life of Jesus is related. The famous Old English epic *Beowulf* was composed as early as around the year 700; it treats motifs from indigenous Scandinavian heroic legend, but with Christian elements and with Virgil as a literary model. Other well-known examples of Old English alliterative poetry are the elegy *Deor's Lament*, probably from the end of the seventh century, and the approximately contemporary *Widsith*

("The Far Traveler"), with its catalogues of names of renowned rulers, heroes, and tribes. From Denmark and Sweden ancient alliterative poetry is known only from runic inscriptions. As a very old example of Norse alliteration the inscription on one of the two famous golden horns from Gallehus in South Jutland, dating from the beginning of the fifth century, is frequently mentioned. In its Primitive Norse form it runs as follows: "ek *H*lēwagastiR *h*oltijaR *h*orna tawiðo" (I, Hlégestr from Holt, made the horn). The Swedish Rök stone from the ninth century includes among other things a correctly constructed stanza in fornyrðislag about Theodoric the Great, king of the East Goths, who lived during the latter part of the fifth and the beginning of the sixth century. As an incontestably original example of this verse form the runic inscription of the Rök stone may be regarded as unique.

The division into stanzas, which characterizes all Eddic poetry, seems furthermore to be a distinguishing characteristic of Scandinavian alliterative verse; otherwise it is extremely rare in the Germanic area. An exception to this rule is the above-mentioned *Deor's Lament*. But the contrast should not be overstressed. There are also Eddic lays, such as *Völundarkviða* and *Atlakviða*, in which an absolutely regular division into stanzas has not been carried out. It has therefore been suggested that the strict normalizing of fornyrðislag into eight lines is secondary and results from influence from the specifically Norse skaldic poetry, in which the eight-line stanza was a strict rule.

Also in another respect skaldic poetry seems to have influenced Eddic meter. As already stated, the line in fornyrðislag has two lifts, or stressed syllables, whereas the number of unstressed syllables in the sinking can vary. In his systematic running commentary in *Háttatal* Snorri distinguishes *málaháttr* as a special verse form; it differs from fornyrðislag only in that it permits a few more unstressed syllables per line. The difference can be studied in the two

Eddic poems *Atlakviða* and *Atlamál*. The former is in forn-yrðislag while the latter, which treats the same material more broadly, is in málaháttr. But the line that can be drawn between them is less than razor sharp. In a half stanza like the following from *Atlakviða* it would be necessary, according to Snorri's criteria, to designate the first two lines of four syllables each as fornyrðislag and the last two, with six syllables each, as málaháttr:

Atli sendi   Atli sent
ár til Gunnars   of old to Gunnar
kunnan segg at riða,   a keen-witted rider,
Knéfrøðr var sá heitinn.   Knefröth did men call him.

In English and especially in German alliterative poetry the number of syllables is consistently greater than it is in Eddic poetry. As already mentioned, one can perhaps view the reduction in number of unstressed syllables in Old Norse poetry as a consequence of the influence of skaldic meters with their very strict counting of syllables.

Old Norse alliterative poetry deviates metrically quite radically from meters of later times with their regular alternation of stressed and unstressed syllables. Stated differently, alliterative Germanic poetry was accentual rather than syllabic. Snorri's poetics knows nothing of concepts such as iamb and trochee, anapest and dactyl. Fornyrðislag must have its two lifts per line, but their distribution in the line varies; the rhythm can therefore be both rising and falling. The alliteration must always be heavily stressed and must be carried by essential words. At times the unstressed syllables can be completely missing, and the verse is compressed entirely into the two obligatory lifts, which then acquire a very special weight: "Deyr fé." This kind of poetry often impresses one as being matter-of-fact and harsh. It does not flow smoothly with a gently swaying rhythm, nor does it seek euphony as such. To our ears it may sound somberly earnest and darkly conjuring. Yet alliteration often lends itself with equally good effect to the expression of bitter irony and of playful jesting.

It is not known how Eddic poetry was presented to an audience, i.e., whether it was spoken or possibly sung or chanted. The poems themselves reveal scarcely any clues in that respect. Most of them have been classified either as *mál* or as *kviða*. The latter noun is related to the verb *kveða*, which, to be sure, may sometimes refer to some kind of song, but usually means "to tell," "to recite (a poem or stanza)," or simply "to say." It is not possible to come to a definite conclusion on the basis of this word.

Skaldic Meters

Eddic meters are employed now and then also in the verse of court poets. Thus, for instance, Eyvindur skálda-spillir's *Hákonarmál* alternately uses ljóðaháttr and forn-yrðislag. A meter that is closely related to these is *kviðu-háttr,* a sort of regularized fornyrðislag, in which odd lines have three syllables and even lines four. It was used in such well-known poems as *Ynglingatal,* ascribed to the Norwe-gian poet Þjóðólfr hvinverski, and in Egill Skalla-Gríms-son's *Sonatorrek.* The following verse is from the last-named poem:

Mik hefr marr	Much the sea
miklu rœntan,	from me hath taken:
grimmt er fall	cruel to count
frœnda at telja,	my kinsmen's loss
síðan's minn	since from me
á munvega	on fair-paths went
œttar skjöldr	mine own son,
aflífi hvarf.	our sib's strong shield.

The meter *par préférence* of skaldic poetry, however, is *dróttkvœtt,* a form which intrinsically carries a valuation: "suitable to be recited before a *drótt,*" that is, the court of

17

a ruler. This verse form can be illustrated by a stanza by Sighvatur Þórðarson, a court poet of Ólafur Haraldsson; the content refers to the king's meeting with Earl Hákon Eiríksson in Sauðungssund:

Ríkr kvað sér at sœkja	Declared the king, of fame most
Sauðungs konungr nauðir,	covetous, that needs in
fremðar gjarn, í fornu	Sauthung Sound, the ancient,
fund Hákonar sundi.	seek he must Earl Hákon.
Strangr hitti þar þengill	There, the thewful ruler
þann jarl, es varð annarr	that earl met who, although
œztr ok ætt gat bazta	youthful, had to no one yielded
ungr á danska tungu.	yet in rank and high birth.

It is a strictly regulated verse form. Dróttkvætt is virtually a syllabic meter; normally a line consists of six syllables, three of which are stressed. The last two syllables always form a trochee (*sœkja, nauðir, fornu*, etc.), but otherwise the rhythm can be varied. The stanza has both alliteration and assonance, whereby alliteration as usual binds the lines together into pairs, while assonance occurs within the same line. The alliteration is formed by two "supports" in the first, odd line (*sér, sœkja*) and a "main staff" in the second (*Sauðungs*). Since the second, even line of the verse pair must not have anacrusis and the main syllable comes on the first stressed syllable, the alliterative word most always begins the line (*Sauðungs, fund, þann, ungr*). The assonance or internal syllabic rhyme is arranged so that each verse has two rhyming syllables, the second of which must always come on the last syllable but one of the line, while the place of the first can vary. As a rule the odd lines have half assonance or impure syllabic rhyme (*skothending*), that is, the vowels of the two rhyme syllables are different, but the following consonant or consonants are alike (*Rík-/sœk-; gjarn/forn-; Strang/þeng-; æzt-/bazt-*); the even lines, however, have full assonance or pure syllabic rhyme (*aðalhending*) with both vowels and consonants identical (*Sauð-/*

nauð-; fund/sund-; þann/ann-; ung/tung-). The inclination to make out of the half verse, *(vísu)-helmingr,* a well-defined syntactic unit, which is often quite evident in fornyrðislag, has been practically elevated to a rule in dróttkvætt.

Skaldic poetry is notorious for its often extremely complicated word order, which, rightly or wrongly, has been regarded as a deplorable consequence of the strict constraint of the dróttkvætt meter. Let us take a look at a half stanza by Skáld-Refur or Hofgarða-Refur, as reproduced by Snorri in his *Edda:*

> Opt kom (iarðar leiptra
> es Baldr hniginn skaldi)
> hollr at helgu fulli
> Hrafnásar mér (stafna).

In prose word order these lines read as follows: "Opt kom hollr mér at helgu fulli Hrafnásar; stafna iarðar leiptra Baldr es hniginn skaldi." With retention of the kennings they can be rendered thus: "Often the good man brought me to the raven god's holy cup; Baldur of lightning flashes of the land of prows has died from the skald." The good man *(hollr)* signifies the poet's foster father. The raven god *(Hrafnáss)* is Óðinn and his holy cup *(heilagt full)* the drink of poetry. (Compare Snorri's tale, related on page 4.) The land of prows *(iörð stafna)* is the sea, and its glowing flashes of lightning *(leiptr)* is gold; the kenning can probably be traced back to the legend of the Niflung treasure, which was sunk into the Rhine. The Baldur of gold, then, is a circumlocution for man and here means the above-mentioned foster father. And finally the skald is, of course, the poet Refur. Reduced to plain prose, the half stanza means: "My good foster father often instructed me in the art of poetry; he has now passed away from me."

As we can see, not only are the two sentences and statements encapsulated in each other. In addition, the kenning *iarðar stafna leiptr* has been split as completely as possible:

it begins in the first line but is not completed until the last word of the fourth line. A prerequisite for making such a linguistic picture-puzzle understandable is, of course, the grammatical structure of the Icelandic language. With its rich system of inflections it permits a considerable latitude in word order without risking a confusion or misconstruing of syntactic and semantic relationships. Perhaps one should also imagine that the poet, while reciting, may have varied the pitch, strength, and tone of his voice for different passages and figurative sequences in order to distinguish and contrast them more clearly. In any event it is certainly rash to regard the sometimes almost grotesquely tortured word order of the skalds merely as an outcome of the metric tyranny of the dróttkvætt stanza. When everything is taken into consideration, this word order must be understood basically as an expression of a definite stylistic ideal; it bears witness to a desire to create surprise and to tease the intellectual activity of the listener. The Norwegian scholar Hallvard Lie formulates his opinion as follows: "Genuine skaldic verse strives for tension, desires resistance for its own sake; it wants to force the listener into states of psychic frustration from which he suspensefully seeks escape, finally to reward him with the joy of solution and release by letting that which was fractured and torn asunder at last converge and fuse consciously into the logical whole that is the sober, factual content of the stanza."[1] Such a psychological interpretation of skaldic style could profitably be applied to the four lines by Refur quoted above. In the first line he bewilders us with the incomprehensible combination of the two nature concepts earth and lightning *(iarðar leiptra)*. The reward for the attentive and discerning reader comes, as already mentioned, only with the last word *(stafna)* of the half stanza, which gives the key to the kenning and thus to the complete meaning of these lines. The effect is that of a conscious artistic technique in the hands of a true virtuoso.

Heiti and Kennings

The most prominent devices for achieving artistic effect in Old Icelandic poetry are designated by Snorri in the *Prose Edda* as heiti and kennings. Heiti are the less unique of the two; they can be found in poetry from all over the world. They are simply selected and unusual appellations for common concepts. Several different types can be distinguished. First, there are archaisms, old Germanic words which may perhaps have been preserved only in poetic diction: the common word *eldr*, "fire," for example, can be replaced by *funi, furr,* or *hyrr*. Second, there are words that are used in everyday speech but are endowed with a special meaning in poetry. An example that is often cited is *brúðr*, "bride," which the poets are fond of using for woman in general. For the sea, which plays such a vital role in this Viking poetry, one can find a wide variety of heiti, each of which emphasizes a special aspect of the concept and bears witness to a keen observation of nature. In this category can also be counted the many synonyms for names of gods, especially Óðinn; the Eddic lay *Grímnismál* provides a long list: *Gangleri, Herteitr, Hjalmberi, Sanngetall, Svipall, Þekkr, Þundr,* etc. A third kind of heiti consists of poetic neologisms, usually compounds or derivatives. Thus the sun is called *eygló*, "the ever glowing one," or *fagrahvél*, "shining wheel"; both words occur in the Eddic poem *Alvíssmál*. Less common types of heiti are, fourth, loan words—Kormákur Ögmundarson uses the Irish word *díar* for the gods— and, fifth, so-called half kennings. An example of this kind is the designation of a woman simply as *Hlín* (the name of a goddess) without a qualifying attribute, which is required in a regular "full" kenning such as *gulls Hlín* (Hlín of gold).

Here, then, we see the essential difference between a heiti and a kenning; in the former there is no attribute, while the kenning always consists of a main word *(stofn)* plus a modifier in the genitive case *(kenniorð)*, which are sometimes welded together to form a compound noun. This is also the reason for the term *kenning*: it is derived from the verb *kenna* in the meaning of "to characterize," "to define"; a heiti, on the other hand, is *ókennt*, as Snorri says. Several attempts have been made following Snorri, but with a more modern conceptual apparatus, to arrange systematically the vast wealth of kennings. In his detailed and extensive investigation, Rudolf Meissner goes the furthest in this respect. He classifies the material partly according to more formal criteria, partly according to the objects or the subject matter that the kennings designate: sea, wind, fire, battle, sword, blood, man, woman, gold, etc.[2]

One group of kennings thus distinguished consists of those in which a personal name is replaced by a designation of the person's ancestry or other relationship. Thus Baldur is called "Frigg's son," Óðinn "Baldur's father," and Þór "Sif's husband." A ruler is often named in relation to the country or people he rules over: "king of Jutland," "lord of the Trönder." Such a kenning is virtually a sort of definition.

Another very common type of kenning, mainly for persons, has as a stem word a *nomen agentis* that characterizes some sort of activity. A warrior is "the feeder of the raven," "brandisher of the sword," "destroyer of shields." A ruler can be described as "commander of the battle," "suppressor of discord," "promoter of wisdom." Within this otherwise rather uniform category the poets excel above all in the art of searching out unusual words or of creating new ones.

A third category of kennings comes closer to a metaphoric manner of expression than the two mentioned above. If blood is called "the fluid of swords" *(hjörlögr)* or the sea "the path of breakers" *(brimleið)*, the main word on the whole retains its customary meaning. Here one is still talking about a fluid and a path, albeit in a special sense.

But if instead of that one talks about blood as "sweat of the sword" *(sœfis sveiti)* or about the sea as "boatshed of lobsters" *(humra naust)*, both *sveiti* and *naust* have lost their normal acceptations and have become metaphors. Here there arises a tension, a more or less pronounced antithetical relationship between the main word and the total meaning of the kenning: the sea is anything but a shed. But this fourth type of kenning, too, is far from unique. The metaphorical appellation of the camel as "the ship of the desert" is quite common. Just as it did for the first three categories, Old English poetry yields examples of the fourth one, such as "stallion of the breakers" *(brimhengest)* for ship or "jewel of the head" *heafodgim)* for eye. But there is no doubt that Old Norse poetry has cultivated this kind of kenning with an intensity that seems to be unknown in the literature of other climes. It is metaphors such as these that probably offer the most interesting study by far for the person who wishes to delve deeply into the artistic principles of skaldic poetry. It is here that we encounter that predilection for poetic rebuses, antithesis, and contrastive effect which strikes us as having to such a high degree left its imprint on the stylistic ideal of the ancient skalds.

The examples thus far considered can be characterized as simple kennings, i.e., those that consist of only two elements, the basic word together with its modifier. But often one or both of the elements are a new kenning whose elements may possibly also be split up. Thus the resolution of "the swan of the sweat of the thorn of wounds" *(sára þorns sveita svanr)* is as follows: the thorn of wounds is the sword, the sweat of the sword is blood, and the swan of blood, finally, is the raven, the bird of the battlefield. One can even encounter an example like the following: *nausta blakks hlémána gifrs drífu gimslǫngvir.* Here *nausta blakkr* is "the horse of the boatsheds" = ship; *hlémáni* of the ship, "the lee moon of the ship," protective moon = shield; the *gifr* of the shield, "the troll of the shield" = sword; *drífa* of the sword, "storm of the sword" = battle; *gim* of the battle, "fire of battle" = sword; *gimslǫngvir*, "brandisher of the sword" = warrior. In this interpretation the various elements have been neatly arranged in their logical sequence before the main word. But one can well imagine the complication that arises when a garland of words such as this must be fitted into the demanding scheme of the dróttkvætt meter. Small wonder that the word order can become entangled. This complicated kenning is, of course, an extreme case.

We find the typical kenning style fully developed in the oldest examples of skaldic poetry that have been preserved. In view of its complex, artistic nature, it seems highly probable that skaldic style represents the outcome of a long period of growth, but this is something that remains unknown. Nor are the hypotheses that have been advanced regarding the origin of the kenning itself very convincing. Among other things reference has been made to certain taboo-conditioned expressions among primitive hunters and fishermen who in their occupations feel themselves to be constantly surrounded by dangers and powers that must not be provoked through being mentioned by name. An appellation of that kind is *grayleg* for wolf. But there is a wide gap, difficult to bridge, between the primitive background of such taboo concepts and the aristocratic craft of the skalds. More compatible with skaldic poetry would be a sacral taboo language, connected with religious rites. Unfortunately, however, we lack factual evidence of the existence of a ritual use of language in Norse religious cult. And whether one reckons with secular or sacral taboo language or both, it does not suffice to explain the specifically artistic style of skaldic kennings freed from practical or magical aims.

An interesting attempt to interpret the style of the skalds psychologically, on the assumption of a uniform stylistic ideal, was made by Hallvard Lie, who was mentioned above. He assumes an intimate connection between skaldic poetry and the pictorial art of the viking era, with the latter as the source of inspiration for the former. "The viking belonged to a cultural milieu," he says, "where a thoroughly anorganic, anaturalistic stylistic ideal was all-prevailing; where 'art' primarily meant keeping nature at a distance."[3] This formal principle, which came to be realized in poetry with the dróttkvætt style, already dominated other kinds of art from the Viking Age. Now it merely conquered another area. Lie finds support for his hypothesis in the fact, well worth considering, that some of the earliest and most pronounced skaldic poems consist of descriptions of series of pictures that the poet had before his eyes, for instance, the decoration of a shield. He is not unsympathetic to the idea that the dróttkvætt style might even have begun as an attempt to create a direct poetic correspondence to contemporary pictorial art. Lie envisions Bragi the Old—the oldest poet we know, from the first part of the ninth century—confronted with the task of composing his *Ragnarsdrápa* about the mythical pictures on the shield he has received as a gift. Bragi, Lie believes, had no poetic models before him. He seized upon the expedient of transposing into poetry not only the content of the pictures but even their mode of artistic expression. This was something new. Eddic poetry, which in Lie's opinion is naturalistic, was not regarded as real art by the old peoples of the North, not as *íþrótt* or *list*—Icelandic terms for acquired skills in various fields—but as *skemmtan*, "entertainment," or *fræði*, "knowledge," similar, in this respect, to the realistic Icelandic sagas. But with the dróttkvætt style there was introduced into literature as well a real *íþrótt*, practiced by highly self-confident artists.

Lie seeks to demonstrate his views on the basis of an analysis of the kennings of the *Ragnarsdrápa*. Sometimes his interpretation of details may seem somewhat too subtle. But it is stimulating to observe his consistent endeavor to see the unique poetic art of the old skalds from within as an expression of a definite artistic purpose, and not as a mere curiosity, some sort of uninspired feat of metric acrobatics. Lie's contribution is rather in line with our contemporary revaluation of baroque poetry, which was formerly in such bad repute and which, furthermore, shares certain points of similarity with the art of the Old Norse skalds.

Finally it might be well to note that the frequency of kennings obviously varies greatly from one poet to another. There are poets who employ them with considerable moderation and restraint. On the other hand, the Eddic lays are not entirely free of kennings. They occur most frequently in the mythological poem *Hymiskviða* and in the heroic lay *Helgakviða Hundingsbana I*. The latter also resembles the genre of court poetry by virtue of the fact that it is an encomiastic poem.

Notes

1. Hallvard Lie, *"Natur" og "Unatur" i skaldekunsten* (Oslo 1957), p. 33.

2. Rudolf Meissner, *Die Kenningar der Skalden* (Bonn 1921). An excellent, highly concentrated analysis of kenning types and their poetic function is provided by Einar Ól. Sveinsson in his article "Dróttkvæða þáttur," *Skírnir* 121 (1947): 5–52.

3. Hallvard Lie, "Skaldestil-studier," *Maal og Minne* 44 (1952): 3.

CHAPTER 3

Eddic Lay

Name, Age, and Origin

ORIGINALLY the name *Edda* was applied only to Snorri Sturluson's previously discussed treatise on mythology and prosody; and as already mentioned, the meaning of the word is still much disputed. That the same designation should later come to be applied to what we now call Eddic poetry is evidently based on a misunderstanding. In 1643 the Icelandic bishop Brynjólfur Sveinsson came into possession of an old codex containing poems about gods and heroes, the one that is now housed in the Royal Library in Copenhagen and bears the title Codex Regius. The bishop seems to have taken this anthology to be the work of his famous fellow countryman, the historian Sæmundur fróði (1056–1133); the quotations from the same poems in Snorri's *Edda* then appeared to be only extracts from Sæmund's supposedly older work. Although this association is completely unjustified, the appelation *Edda* (*Sæmundar Edda*) for the newly discovered manuscript became conventional. To distinguish it from Snorri's work it is nowadays usually referred to in English as the *Poetic Edda*. Also classified as Eddic poetry are a number of poems which are not found in Codex Regius but belong to the same genre.

The Codex Regius, the main source of our knowledge of Eddic poetry, is thought to date from the end of the thirteenth century. But characteristic scribal errors reveal that the famous manuscript must be a copy of an older original that is no longer extant.[1] A large number of Eddic poems are also referred to and cited in Snorri's *Edda*, completed about 1220. This is as far back as the manuscript tradition goes. But it is obvious that many Eddic lays must have been preserved through oral tradition for a long period of time before they finally were recorded on parchment. Even if nothing else happened to them, they must have been quite roughly used in several cases. Clearly the collectors and scribes in the thirteenth century did not always completely understand the poems, which had been worn and damaged by time.

Much ingenuity has been devoted to trying to establish a chronology for Eddic poetry—if not an absolute one, then at least a relative one. Scholars have endeavored to distinguish an older and a younger group, to arrive at an internal chronology. Here, of course, one must take into consideration many uncertain factors and be content with more or less probable conclusions. Among the criteria that have been applied are the relation of various poems to: (1) the development of the Scandinavian languages, (2) archeological facts, (3) the Scandinavian landscape with its flora and fauna, (4) historical events, and (5) Christian thoughts and beliefs.[2]

It is obvious that such touchstones can be used only with the utmost care. For example, one or two conspicuously archaic linguistic forms need not be interpreted as evidence that the poem in question is especially old. It can just as well be a matter of intentional archaism. Furthermore, our knowledge of the growth of language during the viking era is for obvious reasons rather vague, especially when it comes to chronological criteria.

The fact that some of the heroic lays of the *Edda* retain blurred memories from the time of the Great Migration should not mislead one to the conclusion that the poems as such originated during that era. The material may have existed in oral tradition century after century before it was cast into the form of Eddic poetry.

On the other hand it must be admitted that the uniquely Icelandic landscape in *Völuspá*—among other things a volcanic eruption seems to have been part of the poet's experience—is a strong reason for linking this powerful vision poem with Iceland. This would mean that *Völuspá* can hardly be older than the tenth century, a date that can also be supported on several other grounds. When, on the other hand, one stanza in *Hávamál* compares the man whom no one loves to a lonely pine on a hill, without the protection of bark and needles, the picture seems to point away from Iceland. That poorly wooded country with its sparse birch vegetation has, as far as we know, never provided soil for pines. A poet can, of course, know and talk about many things that are not part of his immediate environment; Icelanders from the first centuries after the settlement, after all, seem to have been constant travelers. Nevertheless, one has the feeling that a stanza like the one about the man and the pine, which comes close to being an adage, should rather be connected with an intimate, everyday experience. And then a reasonable conclusion would be that a picture like that was probably created in Norway, before Iceland was colonized, or possibly by some emigrant with vivid recollections of his native land.

The most certain possibility of dating Eddic lays seems to be afforded if they can be connected with skaldic poetry. Thus Eyvindur skáldaspillir's (ca. 910–90) *Hákonarmál* contains what seems to be an obvious quotation from *Hávamál*: "Deyr fé, deyja frændr." Since Eyvind's poem celebrates the last battle of Hákon the Good, his slaying and arrival in Valhöll (Valhalla), it seems likely that it was written in connection with the king's death in 961. That provides a terminus ante quem for *Hávamál* or, to express it more cautiously, for the quoted passage from the poem. (More recently, on the other hand, an Eddic scholar has maintained just the opposite: he regards it as probable that *Hávamál* has borrowed the passage in question from *Hákonarmál*. On this see p. 45).

Nowadays scholars agree on the whole that the genesis

of the Eddic lays covers a considerable period of time, perhaps from about 800 to 1300. Whereas some poems create an archaic impression, there are others that are, all things considered, the work of collectors and learned men. But whatever share the other Nordic peoples may possibly have had in the creation of this poetry, it is a fact of literary history that it is in Iceland, and only there, that it has been preserved.

Mythological Poetry

The poems in the Codex Regius are arranged according to a definite plan. First there are poems about the ancient Norse world of the gods, and then there are poems with themes from heroic legend. The former category includes the following poems: *Völuspá, Hávamál, Vafþrúðnismál, Grímnismál, Skírnismál, Hárbarðslióð, Hymiskviða, Lokasenna, Þrymskiða, Völundarkviða, Alvíssmál.* In this series of mythologic and didactic poems, however, *Völundarkviða* seems a little out of place. This poem about the imprisonment and revenge of the skilled smith Völundur belongs certainly not among the poems of gods, but hardly among the heroic poems either. Perhaps that is why the editor of the Codex Regius felt uncertain as to where it should be inserted. It would seem to be more consistent if *Völundarkviða* and the mythologic-didactic *Alvíssmál* could have exchanged places so that the former would have come to be right between the two main types of Eddic lays.

In addition to the poems about gods in the Codex Regius, there are in other sources a number of poems of a similar kind which generally are incorporated into editions of the *Edda. Baldrs draumar* or *Vegtamskviða* is found in a fragmentary collection of Eddic lays from the beginning of the fourteenth century. *Hyndluljóð* is included in the well-known codex *Flateyjarbók* from the end of the same century; *Rígsþula* and *Gróttasöngr* are included in different manuscripts of Snorri's *Edda*, which, as we know, also quotes other Eddic poetry abundantly. *Grógaldr* and *Fjölsvinnsmál*, finally, are found only in manuscripts from the seventeenth century.

Of the two major genres of Eddic poetry, the mythological poems stand out as specifically Nordic, to judge from the extant material; the heroic poems, on the other hand, have counterparts in other Germanic literatures.

Völuspá. It is self-evident that *Völuspá* ("The Prophecy of the Seeress") deserves its initial position in Codex Regius. The creation of the world, the dissolution of world order, the destruction of the world, and the emergence of a new world make up the theme of the most universal of all Eddic poems. It received its name from the *völva* who speaks in the poem, an aged seeress who remembers the ancient destinies of the world and with her vision penetrates the veils of the future. In prophetic tones she invokes the attention of all listeners: "Listen to me, all / holy descendants / haughty and humble / sons of Heimdal." The seeress then relates what she knows about the great events in the world. Many things she says are vague, and perhaps they are meant to be. Other things have eventually become obscure because we no longer know the circumstances or understand the concepts to which she alludes.

But the main line is clear. First there is a description of the great void before the creation of the world. Then the thriving green earth, the *Miðgarður*, the common home of men and gods, is raised out of the abyss. The heavenly bodies are assigned their places: sun, moon, and stars. Morning, day, and night are given names so that time can be told. The Æsir meet at the Iðavöllur, where they devote themselves diligently to handicrafts and engage in merry games. Finally three of them breathe life into the first pair of humans, Askur and Embla, who correspond in Norse

31

mythology to Adam and Eve in the Bible. According to Snorri's *Edda*, which often elucidates and supplements the description of the *Poetic Edda*, Askur and Embla were created from two tree trunks. The former name is identical with the name of a tree (*askur* = ash tree); the interpretation of the latter is less certain.

An essential and majestic element in the vision of the seeress is the picture of the world tree, the ash Yggdrasil, which spreads its enormous crown over the earth. From its foliage dew falls into the valleys. It stands like a guardian of our whole existence. At its foot are seated the three Norns Urður, Skuld, and Verðandi, "maidens / mighty in wisdom." . . . "Laws they made there, / and life allotted / to the sons of men, / and set their fates." Then there follows that part of the poem which is most difficult to interpret. It is suggested that the Æsir have slain a sorceress and then broken agreements and oaths. The condition of innocence is past. After a series of ominous mythological allusions, centered around the death of Baldur, there occurs for the first time the evil-foreboding refrain:

Geyr Garmr mjök	Now Garm howls loud
fyr Gnipahelli,	before Gnipahellir,
festr mun slitna,	the fetters will burst,
en freki renna;	and the wolf run free;
fjölð veit hon frœða,	much do I know,
fram sé ek lengra	and more can see
um ragna rök	of the fate of the gods,
röm sigtíva	the mighty in fight.

Among human beings moral corruption will prevail, as the seeress beholds it:

Brœðr munu berjask	Brothers shall fight
ok at bönum verðask,	and fell each other,
munu systrungar	and sisters' sons
sifjum spilla;	shall kinship stain;

32

hart er í heimi,	hard is it on earth,
hórdómr mikill,	with mighty whoredom;
skeggöld, skálmöld,	axe-time, sword-time,
skildir ro klofnir,	shields are sundered,
vindöld, vargöld,	wind-time, wolf-time,
áðr veröld steypisk;	ere the world falls;
mun engi maðr	nor ever shall men
öðrum þyrma.	each other spare.

This moral dissolution portends doom and destruction. All ethic bonds will break. The air itself will be envenomed with treachery. Giants and other terrifying creatures will be abroad. The wolf Fenrir will burst his fetters, the monster that will kill Óðinn, the father of the gods. The ash tree Yggdrasil will tremble and groan. Finally there will come the inevitable end of all this anxiety and agony, this weltering chaos: the destruction of the world, *ragnarök* "the extinction of the powers." The fire demons will reach the world tree, the sustainer of life *(aldrnari)*, and cause it to burst into blazing flames:

Sól tér sortna,	The sun turns black,
sökkr fold í mar,	earth sinks in the sea,
hverfa af himni	the hot stars down
heiðar stjörnur;	from heaven are whirled;
geisar eimi	Fierce flares the heat
við aldrnara,	'gainst the life-feeding tree,
leikr hár hiti	till fire leaps high
við himin sjalfan.	about heaven itself.

It is difficult to imagine a more magnificent symbol of *ragnarök* than the world tree blazing like a torch against the vastness of space while the waning stars hurtle down from the firmament. This could have been the end of the poem. But it is not the last word from the seeress. She beholds a new creation still further in the future:

Sér hon upp koma	Now do I see
öðru sinni	the earth anew
iörð ór ægi	rise all green
iðjagrœna;	from the waves again;
falla forsar,	the cataracts fall,
flýgr örn yfir,	and the eagle flies,
sá er á fjalli	and fish he catches
fiska veiðir.	beneath the cliffs.

The simplicity and freshness in such a description is remarkable. The language is objective and factual. Except for the matter-of-fact *iðjagrœnn*, "eternally green," there are no descriptive adjectives or adverbs in the stanza. Things and actions must speak for themselves, devoid of decorative or evaluating attributes, and it is precisely for this reason that they create such a vivid effect: an archaically style-pure picture of a landscape in the morning of creation. In this new world the Æsir will meet again on the plain called Iðavöllur, where they will find in the grass their golden draughtsman from former times and take up their game anew. And good people will enjoy eternal happiness.

The poem ends with a picture of the flying dragon Niðhöggur with corpses in its wings. The last line of the stanza runs: "Nú mun hon sökkvask" ("Now she will sink"). These final words have been interpreted as referring to the seeress; also in other passages she talks about herself in the third person. Before disappearing from the scene, she finally directs her farseeing eyes still farther into the future and conjures up a frightening symbol for conditions in the world in the form of a dragon.

Immediately preceding this concluding stanza, however, a half stanza has been preserved which has caused scholars a great deal of puzzlement, primarily because the latter part of the stanza has been lost—"the most deplorable lacuna in *Völuspá*,"[3] it has been said:

Þá kömr in ríki
at regindómi
öflugr ofan,
sá er öllu ræðr.

There comes from on high,
all power to hold,
a mighty lord,
all lands he rules.

A stumbling block here is the word *regindómr*, understood as an expression for "god's judgment," "the great judgment," "the last judgment." It seems strange, indeed, that the innocent conditions prevailing in the newly created world should give cause for a reckoning of that kind. For this reason the above quoted half stanza has been judged to be "false" in *Völuspá*, a later interpolation of purely Christian origin. But *regindómr* can be interpreted quite differently, as "highest power and authority." In that case the poet is merely alluding in general terms to the arrival of a lord of the world. It would not necessarily imply any direct contradiction of the mythology of the poem as a whole.

But undoubtedly reference to the mighty being "from above" directs one's thoughts toward Christianity—as perhaps other details in *Völuspá* do also. Thus when reading this poem, a modern reader can hardly help recalling the biblical descriptions of the creation and the destruction of the world in Genesis and the book of Revelation. There are scholars who are of the opinion that the poet of *Völuspá* himself believed in the Æsir, that he knew something about Christianity and had been influenced by it. His poem might even be a magnificent endeavor to vindicate the sublimity and authority of the old faith in its struggle against the new doctrine. Iceland officially adopted Christianity by a resolution of the General Assembly in 1000. But there were some Christians even among the first immigrants at the end of the ninth century, and the Icelanders maintained active relations with the Christian peoples of Europe. The basic tenets of Christianity may thus have been quite well known in Iceland long before the year 1000. Sigurður

Nordal has devoted an extensive monograph to *Völuspá*, characterized both by perceptive and penetrating analysis of detail and by broad historic-cultural perspectives. He emphasizes the fact that apocalyptic apprehensions reached a high point in Christendom just before 1000. People believed or at least generally feared that the completion of the first Christian millennium would bring the end of the world. Nordal reckons with a reflection of this mood of doomsday in *Völuspá*, and this—together with other factors—would suggest that it should be dated shortly before the year 1000.

But however the question of possible Christian influence and details in *Völuspá* is judged, the work as a whole has an unmistakably Norse stamp in both form and content. Lofty, pure, austere are several attributes that come to mind when one tries to describe one's impression of this poem. With a majestic arch it spans existence from the beginning to the end of time, from creation to creation. With the same sovereign artistry the calm and quiet of peace and the din and tumult of strife are given poetic form. It must have been a noble culture that nurtured the poet of *Völuspá*. And it is not merely the probable time of the poem's origin that indicates that his home was in Iceland. In the description of *ragnarök*, as already mentioned, one can discern characteristics of a volcanic eruption. What Northman could be closer to impressions of or hearsay about such a natural catastrophe than an Icelander? Nor is it very probable that a Norwegian would have chosen the picture "vara *sandr* né sær" ("there was neither *sand* nor sea") as an expression for the great void before creation. On the other hand, it would be quite natural on the south coast of Iceland, with its enormous bare expanses of sand against a vast, open sea horizon.

In various ways the cosmology of *Völuspá* is supplemented in several other Eddic lays. Most important among these are two poems in ljóðaháttr in which Óðinn, the father of the gods, plays the principal role. Disguised and under the assumed name Grímnir—one of his many quick-change performances—he holds forth in a king's hall on the world of the gods and other elevated subjects *(Grímnismál)*. On another occasion he conquers the giant Vafþrúðnir incognito in a dramatic duel of wits *(Vafþrúðnismál)*. In both poems the creation of the world from the body of the giant Ymir is described, though in greater detail in *Grímnismál*:

Ór Ymis holdi	Out of Ymir's flesh
var iörð of sköpuð,	was fashioned the earth,
en ór sveita sær	and the ocean out of his blood;
björg ór beinum,	of his bones the hills,
baðmr ór hári,	of his hair the trees,
en ór hausi himinn.	of his skull the heavens high.

En ór hans bráum	Mirthgarth the gods
gerðu blíð regin	from his eyebrows made,
Miðgarð manna sonum,	and set for the sons of men;
en ór hans heila	and out of his brain
vóru þau hin harðmóðgu	the baleful clouds
ský öll of sköpuð.	they made to move on high.

This poem also gives an account of the dwellings of the various Æsir and describes the huge dimensions of Valhöll, the abode of those who have fallen in battle and have been resurrected after death, the *einherjar*:

Fimm hundruð dura	Five hundred doors
ok umb fjórum tögum,	and forty there are,
svá hygg á Valhöllu vera;	I ween, in Valhall's walls;
átta hundruð einherja	eight hundred fighters
ganga ór einum durum,	through one door fare [go.
þás fara við vitni at vega.	when to war with the wolf they

Here we also meet such mythic beings as Óðin's two ravens with the symbolic names Huginn (He Who Thinks) and Muninn (He Who Remembers), which bring him messages from all corners of the world; the immortal boar Særímnir, slaughtered every day for food at the feasts of the warriors in Valhöll; the squirrel Ratatoskur, which runs up and down the world tree Yggdrasil and carries messages from the eagle in its crown to the serpent Niðhöggur, which gnaws its roots. A long alliterating catalogue of names of rivers is presented, all of which have their source in the well Hvergelmir and flow through Miðgarður towards Hel, the realm of the dead. And so on. Óðin's cross-examination of the giant in *Vafþrúðnismál* culminates in the following exchange of words, in which the lord of the Æsir at last pikes his opponent on a question in connection with Baldur's funeral:

Óðinn kvað:	Othin spake:
Fjölð ek fór,	"Much have I fared,
fjölð freistaðak,	much have I found,
fjölð of reyndak regin,	much have I got from the gods:
hvat mælti Óðinn,	what spake Othin himself
áðr á bál stigi,	in the ears of his son,
sjálfr í eyra syni?	ere in the bale-fire he burned?"
Vafþrúðnir kvað:	Vafthruthnir spake:
Ey manni veit,	"No man can tell
hvat þú í árdaga	what in olden time
sagðir í eyra syni;	thou spak'st in the ears of thy son;
feigum munni	with fated mouth
mæltak mína forni stafi	the fall of the gods
ok of ragnarök.	and mine olden tales have I told."

But in spite of occasional superb passages, poems such as *Grímnismál* and *Vafþrúðnismal* deal mostly in minute detail with questions of mythological lore without ever approaching the powerful, visionary completeness of *Völuspá*.

Perhaps to an even higher degree this appraisal is true of *Alvíssmál*, which is also in ljóðaháttr. In this poem Ása-Þór interrogates the dwarf Alvís (He Who Knows All) and delays him so long that the sun rises before he can disappear, and the dwarf is therefore turned into stone—a metamorphosis well known from folk tales. For once Þór appears as the clever fellow; generally he is described as the man with a strong back and a rather dull mind. His questions to Alvís concern the various names of thirteen different phenomena, which are, in turn: earth, heaven, moon, sun, cloud, wind, dead calm, sea, fire, forest, night, grain, and beer. In every other stanza the dwarf answers with a list of six different expressions used, respectively, by men, gods, giants, dwarfs, and other creatures. For human beings, who are always mentioned first, the conventional word is employed throughout, whereas the rest of the beings generally are allowed to use more unusual or poetic appellations. Thus the Vanir, using regular kennings, call the cloud *vindflot*, "that which floats on the wind"; the giants call the sea *álheimr*, "the world of the eel" (or perhaps rather "the world of the currents"); the gods call the forest *vallarfax*, "the man of the field." The names given by the elves are often lyrically descriptive and full of feeling: the earth is *gróandi*, "growing," "fertile"; the sky *fagra-ræfr*, "shining roof"; the sun *fagrahvél*, "shining wheel"; the forest *fagrlimi*, "beautifully branched"; the night *svefnga-man*, "joy of sleep." *Alvíssmál* is consequently a kind of catalogue of names—and indeed, a sonorous one and one that stirs the imagination, where the name rigmaroles themselves open wide vistas over existence. Perhaps this should be regarded primarily as the expression of a poet's delight in words, his joyful cataloguing of the possibilities of language.

Hávamál. *Völuspá* has a sacral character and treats questions that do not occupy the human mind every day. But the *Edda* also offers less exacting practical wisdom. Coming from *Völuspá* to the next poem in the collection, *Hávamál*, is like stepping from a festive to the workaday world, from great expanses in time and space to the confined and crowded place of here and now.

Yet such a characterization does not apply to the entire poem which bears the name *Hávamál* in Codex Regius. For in its preserved form this is the longest poem in the *Edda*, and it was compiled from various parts which, it seems, can no longer be distinguished with certainty. Among them we can discern fragments of several poems in which Óðinn himself relates his fortunes, as, e.g., the story of how he managed to get possession of the poetic mead among the giants; or the remarkable description of how he hung for nine nights in a tree, surrounded by moaning winds, wounded with a spear, sacrificed to himself by himself. Obviously it is primarily such passages as these that have given the entire poem its name—"The Words of the High One (= Óðinn)"—and which determined its position in the collection. But such mythological or ritual passages have only slight or superficial connections with the rules of life that are usually associated with the name *Hávamál*. It is primarily this gnomic verse—it comprises by far the major part of the poem—that we are going to consider here.

Near the beginning of the poem we read the assertion: "Wits must he have / who wanders far." *Hávamál* offers good common sense in abundance and coins it in sentences that often have the forceful brevity and graphic clarity of the proverb. Again and again throughout the poem we catch glimpses of realistic pictures of ancient Nordic daily life.

If "much practical wisdom" (*Mannvit mikit*) is the wanderer's best travel ration, then conversely "too much beer" is the worst. Moderation is praised, and not only in food and drink. Throughout the poem the ideal of the golden mean is proclaimed. Not least of all one should guard one's tongue and above all see to it that one never talks too much. Nor should one be overly wise, nor create too many cares and concerns for oneself; the golden mean is best, here as in other cases: "Moderately wise / a man may be, / never too wise."

In *Hávamál* much thought is devoted to the question of how to get along with one's fellow men. In the very first stanza the virtue of precaution, or rather distrust, is stressed:

Gáttir allar Within the gates
áðr gangi fram ere a man shall go,
of skoðask skyli, full warily let him watch,
of skyggnask skyli; full long let him look about him;
óvíst er at vita, for little he knows
hvar óvinir where a foe may lurk,
sitja á fleti fyrir. and sit in the seats within.

One must listen and be on one's guard so that one does not fall into the many pits that others dig in one's way. It is necessary for a man to have his weapons within reach; he can never know when he will feel the sudden need for his spear while in the open field or on the distant road. Treachery must be repaid—or better yet, forestalled—with cunning and lies. In an evil and hostile world there is all the more reason to cultivate one's ties of friendship; and about this there must be no uncertainty.

Vin sínum To his friend a man
skal maðr vinr vera, a friend shall prove,
þeim ok þess vin; to him and the friend of his friend;
en óvinar síns but never a man
skyli engi maðr shall friendship make
vinar vinr vera. with one of his foeman's friends.

Despite his misanthropy, however, the poet is well aware that "man is the joy of man," that human beings need each other; as a marked contrast to his somewhat cynically sober reflections on friendship there is his elegiacally touching picture of the misfortune of loneliness and isolation:

Hrörnar þöll,	On the hillside drear
sú er stendr þorpi á,	the fir-tree dies, [bark;
hlýrat henni börkr né barr;	all bootless its needles and
svá er maðr,	it is like a man
sá er manngi ann,	whom no one loves,—
hvat skal hann lengi lifa?	why should his life be long?

Hávamál is a strongly earth-bound poem. There is no hint there about a life after death. This philosophy of life completely lacks the heroic perspective. It is not a matter of the hero's choice between all and nothing, his contempt for death and the imperishable fame won by meeting death bravely. The demands of life are reduced:

Haltr ríðr hrossi,	The lame rides a horse,
hjörð rekr handar vanr,	the handless is herdsman,
daufr vegr ok dugir;	the deaf in battle is bold;
blindr er betri,	The blind man is better
en brendr sé;	than one that is burned,
nýtr manngi nás.	no good can come of a corpse.

After being treated to such skeptical practical wisdom for more than seventy stanzas, one is quite surprised at being confronted with the following lines, some of the most magnificent in the whole *Edda*:

Deyr fé,	Cattle die,
deyja frændr,	and kinsmen die,
deyr sjalfr hit sama;	and so one dies one's self;
ek veit einn	one thing I know
at aldri deyr:	that never dies,
dómr of dauðan hvern.	the fame of a dead man's deeds.

Alliterative poetry has seldom achieved such monumental weight and force as in this verse, where the words stand as though chiseled in stone. This stanza also reveals that, after all, not even the poet of *Hávamál* can stop at

42

the practical needs of everyday life. He finally directs his view to that which transcends the life of the individual: the judgment passed upon him by posterity.

In later years the adages and maxims of *Hávamál* have often been claimed to be a kind of collective expression of the practical life wisdom of our Scandinavian ancestors. As is normally the case with proverbs in general, it has not been possible to trace the individuality of a poet behind the sayings in *Hávamál*. They generally seem to correspond rather well to the picture of the ancient milieu and mentality one gains, for instance, from the Icelandic sagas. But perhaps one should not be too eager to generalize uncritically the experiences expressed in *Hávamál*. The possibility cannot be excluded that at least some of the adages in the poem may have been based on individual experiences and express a purely personal view of life. To be sure, one usually does not risk attributing too much significance to the fact that the adages are often expressed in the first person, a form which is otherwise not common for proverbs and general maxims. But in some cases the formulation strikes us as so personal and the situation as so unique that we feel certain that we can discern the contours of an individual:

Ungr vark forðum,	Young was I once,
fórk einn saman,	and wandered alone,
þá varðk villr vega;	and nought of the road I knew;
auðigr þóttumk,	rich did I feel
er ek annan fann,	when a comrade I found,
maðr er manns gaman.	for man is man's delight.

Váðir mínar	My garments once
gafk velli at	in a field I gave
tveim trémönnum;	to a pair of carven poles;
rekkar þat þóttusk,	heroes they seemed
er ript höfðu;	when clothes they had,
neiss er nökkviðr halr.	but the naked man is nought.

An aged man looking back, a man with a broad and deep experience, not least of all of the lonely life of the wanderer, a man who has dried his drenched clothing at many a strange hearth and sat on many strange benches, a man without illusions either about himself or about others?

Of course one can find counterparts to the didactic poetry of *Hávamál* in other parts of the world. One probably thinks first of all of the book of Proverbs and Ecclesiastes in the Old Testament. Also in these works the edification bears to a large extent the imprint of a skeptical, worldly wisdom. Good common sense is praised, foolishness is castigated. There is a warning of the harmful effect of wine on judgment. At times individual formulations bear a striking resemblance to those of *Hávamál*. Corresponding to the counsel in the Norse poem to be reasonably wise there is this passage in Ecclesiastes: "Be not righteous overmuch, and do not make yourself overwise. Why should you destroy yourself?" (7:16). And the reflection that "the blind man is better / than a burned man is, / a corpse is no use to anyone" also has its counterpart in Ecclesiastes: "A living dog is better than a dead lion" (9:4). A decided difference, however, is the fact that the biblical texts presuppose religious sanctions ultimately even for a seemingly quite worldly philosophy of life. Ecclesiastes ends with a reference to God's judgment on good and wicked deeds. In *Hávamál* everything points to the concept that the judgment of the dead is completely of this world; it belongs to one's fellow men and to posterity.

In several respects the rules for the conduct of life in *Hávamál*, both in line of thought and in formulation, exhibit striking similarities with the so-called *Disticha (Dicta) Catonis*, an anonymous collection of versified maxims in Latin from the third or fourth century A.D. This poetic work achieved great popularity during the Middle Ages. It was diligently used in Latin instruction and was translated into many languages, including Icelandic, where it received the title *Hugsvinnsmál* ("The Words of the Wise One"). It is difficult to establish the date of the Icelandic translation; the thirteenth century seems to be a generally accepted approximation. But it may be older, and recently (1972) quite good reasons were advanced to demonstrate that certain locutions in *Hávamál* were derived from *Hugsvinnsmál*, and some of them perhaps directly from the *Disticha Catonis*.[4] Should this be the case, these borrowings would belong to a late stage in the genesis of *Hávamál*, close to the final composition of this composite poem.

Rígsþula. Whereas *Völuspá* and *Hávamál* deal, respectively, with the fate of the world as a whole and with the condition of our coexistence as human beings, *Rígsþula* treats of the origin and structure of human society. (*Rígsþula* means the "Lay of Rígur"; *þula* = "list [of names]," "enumeration.") Rígur is another name for the god Heimdallur. The poem relates that, while on a journey, Rígur visits three different farms and that the housewife in each of them gives birth to a child, a boy, nine months later. At the first place the boy is named Thrall, at the second Karl, and at the third Earl. *Rígsþula* thus gives poetic form to a myth about three social classes and affords an interesting glimpse into what is considered typical in appearance, food, and occupations for the different estates.

Thrall has coarse fingers, a crooked back, and long heels. Karl is red-haired and has a ruddy complexion and alert eyes. Earl has light blond hair and eyes as piercing as those of the serpent's brood—a sign of noble birth and heroic spirit. At the first farm Rígur comes to—where Thrall is later born—they set on the table "a coarse loaf of bread, / which was heavy and thick, / full of husks" and to go with that "a bowl of broth." In the home where Earl grows up they treat the guest Rígur to "browned pork / and well-cooked birds" and "wine from a flagon." And the

45

occupations? When Thrall becomes strong enough, he binds bast and makes bundles, carries home brushwood the whole day. It is heavy, monotonous labor. Karl represents the independent farmer, the basis of ancient Scandinavian society, and he can devote himself to occupations that are more creative—equally useful and necessary, but more stimulating and developing. He tames oxen, makes wooden plows and wheelbarrows, builds houses and sheds, guides the plow. Earl, finally, occupies himself only with work that is not connected with the necessities of life—practice with weapons, hunting, and sports:

fleini at fleygja,	Spears he loosened,
frökkur dýja,	and lances wielded,
hestum ríða,	horses he rode,
hundum verpa,	and hounds unleashed,
sverðum bregda,	swords he handled,
sund at fremja.	and sounds he swam.

Last but not least, by his father, Rígur, Earl is eventually initiated into the knowledge of the art of runes, which, endows him with wisdom and power. Earl and his wife have twelve sons: the youngest is called *Kon unge*, with a name symbolism that can easily be interpreted as *konungur*, "king." Thus *Rigspula* has sketched the social hierarchy from thrall to king.

In this sketch there is no noticeable criticism of the social order. If there is any tendency at all, it rather reveals a certain degree of sympathy for the aristocratic ideal. *Gróttasöngr*, on the other hand, preserved and commented on in two manuscripts of Snorri's *Edda*, has at least in modern times been interpreted as an expression of social indignation. As is well known, Victor Rydberg in *Den nya Grottesången* has applied the old myth to the epoch of industrialism and capitalism, a picture of cynical contempt for human beings and ruthless exploitation. There is, of course, no corresponding perspective in *Gróttasöngr*. But the point of view is that of the oppressed. It is they who speak, though only for their own sake and with no intention of criticizing society. According to Snorri's prose introduction, the Danish king Fróði in Sweden had gotten possession of the two enormously strong female slaves named Fenja and Menja. He made them turn a mill whose stones were so huge that no one else was strong enough to handle them. The mill, named Grótti, had an extraordinary quality: it could grind forth whatever the owner wished for. According to the words of the poem, the slaves first grind gold and happiness for King Fróði and peace in his kingdom; that is the famous period of the peace of Fróði. They sing while they toil at their heavy task:

"Auð mölum Fróða,	"Gold and good hap
mölum alsælan	we grind for Fróthi,
mölum fjölð féar	a hoard of wealth,
á feginslúðri;	on the wishing-mill;
siti hann á auði,	he shall sit on gold,
sofi hann á dúni,	he shall sleep on down,
vaki hann at vilja.	he shall wake to joy:
þá er vel malit.	well had we ground then!
Hér skyli engi	"Here shall no one
öðrum granda,	harm his neighbor,
til böls búa	nor bale-thoughts brew
né til bana orka,	for others' bane,
né höggva því	nor swing sharp sword
hvössu sverði	to smite a blow,
þótt bana bróður	though his brother's banesman
bundinn finni."	bound he should find."

But Fróði yields to the temptation of exploiting his slaves too greedily and ruthlessly. He begrudges them their sleep. He does not allow them to sleep longer than the cuckoo rests or than it takes him to recite a verse of poetry.

Protest begins to stir within the slaves and they remind each other that they are descendants of giants, a fact that Fróði does not know. Their tremendous feats of strength in an earlier existence are described menacingly, when they hurled rocks, bridled bears, and broke through battle lines of warriors clad in mail coats. One of the slave women sees a beacon flaming in the distance; there is an enemy army approaching Fróði's castle. The oppressed rise from their debasement. Instead of gold and happiness they will now grind out vengeance and destruction over the tyrant:

Mólu meyjar,	The mighty maidens,
megins kostuðu,	they ground amain,
vóru ungar	strained their young limbs
í iötunmóði	of giant strength;
skulfu skaptré,	the shaft tree quivered,
skauzk lúðr ofan,	the quern toppled over,
hraut hinn höfgi	the heavy slab
hallr sundr í tvau.	burst asunder.

There is a powerful intensification in this poem which is reminiscent of the apocalyptic vision in *Völuspá*.

Poems about individual gods: Óðinn, Þór, and others. A number of Eddic poems present more individualized portraits of the gods. Foremost among the Æsir is Óðinn, the ruler of Ásgarður. He reveals himself in many guises and forms. He is the lord of battle and the battlefield; in his abode slain combatants are gathered for eternal battle games and feasts. But he is also the god of wisdom and the art of poetry. Through cunning he stole the mead of poetry from the giant Suttungur. And to win his secret knowledge he had to pawn one of his eyes to another giant; since then Óðinn has been one-eyed.

Óðinn reveals several of his typical characteristics in various sections of *Hávamál*, which, we remember, also takes its name from him. It is true that it is most uncertain whether he is to be regarded as the speaker in that part of this heterogeneous poem which is generally named for the otherwise completely unknown Loddfáfnir; the latter is apostrophized in a series of secular maxims of about the same kind as those in the gnomic main section. But elsewhere in *Hávamál* Óðinn himself does refer to one of those amorous escapades that are such characteristic episodes in his biography. He has been seized with desire for Billing's maiden, who is as fair as the sun, and she pretends to be willing to have a rendezvous toward evening. But when Óðinn arrives, full of expectation, he finds a band of warriors with blazing torches guarding Billing's house and has to go away, his purpose unaccomplished. When at daybreak he makes another visit, the inhabitants of the house are fast asleep, but on the desired woman's bed he finds only a bitch tied fast. This ignominious outcome motivates reflections about the untrustworthiness of women. In several other sections of *Hávamál* one finds Óðinn in more impressive roles than that of the frustrated Don Juan. In the final group of stanzas of *Hávamál*, often called *Ljóðatal*, the speaker—who quite likely is Óðinn—enumerates a series of *ljóð*, "magic songs," numbered from one to eighteen: "That I can do for the seventh," "That I can do for the twelfth," etc. He does not reveal the words of the *galdrar*, but only their effect. They are magical expedients in varying situations, with power, for example, to dull the weapons of the enemy, to still storms at sea, to lead witches astray, or to call a hanged man back to life.

In *Ljóðatal* we encounter Óðinn in one of his central functions: as the master of runes, the lord of secret wisdom. Several other stanzas in *Hávamál* evidently refer to the same capacity, and in this case the god speaks in person; they are found in the section immediately preceding the concluding portion of the poem:

Veitk at ek hekk	I ween that I hung
vindgameiði á	on the windy tree,
nætr allar níu,	hung there for nights full nine;
geiri undaðr	with the spear I was wounded,
ok gefinn Óðni,	and offered I was
sjálfr sjálfum mér.	to Othin, myself to myself.

Við hleifi mik sældu	None made me happy
né við hornigi;	with loaf or horn,
nýstak niðr,	and there below I looked;
namk upp rúnar,	I took up the runes,
œpandi nam,	shrieking I took them,
fellk aptr þaðan.	and forthwith back I fell.[5]

Thereupon Óðinn relates that he has gained possession of nine *fimbulljóð*, "mighty songs," and tasted a drink of the "precious" mead of poetry. He began to thrive and to grow wise: "I searched out / words out of words, / one deed led to the other." Then runes are mentioned, "very great runes, / very strong runes," and the god asks:

Veiztu, hvé rísta skal?	Knowest how one shall write,
Veiztu, hvé ráða skal?	knowest how one shall rede?
Veiztu, hvé fáa skal?	Knowest how one shall tint,
Veiztu, hvé freista skal?	knowest how one makes trial?
Veiztu, hvé biðja skal?	Knowest how one shall ask,
Veiztu, hvé blóta skal?	knowest how one shall offer?
Veiztu, hvé senda skal?	Knowest how one shall send,
Veiztu, hvé sóa skal?	knowest how one shall sacrifice?

The tree, surrounded by sighing winds, on which Óðinn says he was hanging for nine nights, is evidently identical to the ash tree Yggdrasil. Its name actually means Ygg's (= Óðin's) horse, that is, gallows. This strange hanging ritual has been interpreted as a link in the god's endeavor to attain insight into the deepest secrets of existence. The idea that various forms of sacrifice, self-torture, and asceticism help to achieve such magic goals is far from unique in the conceptual world of the *Edda*. Furthermore, it is found in other passages in connection with Óðinn. Thus, as we know, he sacrificed one of his eyes to the giant Mímir to acquire a portion of his wisdom. In a poem already mentioned, *Grímnismál*, a king called Geirröður has the disguised and anonymous father of the Æsir placed between two fires to be tortured and brought to speak. His fur cloak has already begun to smolder. "I have sat between the fires / for eight nights, / and no one has given me to eat," complains Grímnir—this is a situation which reminds one somewhat of his torment on the gallows of the world tree, except that this time it was not self-inflicted. It is not entirely out of the question that torture here should be regarded as a sort of prerequisite for the spiritual strength and the mythological insights that Grímnir develops.

In the dialogue poem *Hárbarðsljóð*, in which Óðinn and Þór are played off against each other, the former is characterized in a much lighter vein. As so often, Óðinn is here in disguise and uses an assumed name, Hárbarður. He stands by his boat on one side of a strait, pretending to be a ferryman, and has the pleasure of seeing Þór coming down the opposite bank on his way home from one of his expeditions against the giants in the Baltic. Þór calls and wants to be ferried over. Hárbarður replies with taunting remarks, makes fun of the traveler's clothing, his misfortunes with his enemies the giants, etc. The exchange of words degenerates into bragging, insults, and abuse between the two Æsir. Óðinn boasts, typically enough, of his success as a charmer of women. But much to the indignation of the straightforward Þór, he also boasts of his cunning and magic skills. On top of that he portrays himself as the aristocratic war chieftain who loves strife for its own sake and spurs kings to battle. Sarcastically he remarks: "Óðinn gets great men / who fall in battle, / but Þór gets the race of slaves"—thus pointing out that his opponent is the representative of more plebeian raw strength. Against Hárbarð's

51

The runestone by the Altuna church in Uppland. In the lower part, on the narrow side of the stone, we see a picture of Þór fishing for the serpent. He has just hooked the *Miðgarðsormur* and is holding his hammer aloft in his right hand, ready to deliver the deadly blow. In the struggle with his quarry Þór has chanced to thrust one of his feet through the bottom of the boat. See the text on p. 54.

provocations and sneering word play Þór is hopelessly in-
adequate. His retorts are clumsy, and in despair he threat-
ens his antagonist with his hammer. He does not perceive
that Hárbarður is Óðinn in disguise. The conflict is one
between skillful verbal sophistry and sluggish strength.

The humor in *Hárbarðsljóð* is quite coarse, yet there
is an irresistibly amusing characterization in the situation
and in the spicy rejoinders. Moreover, one frequently has
occasion to smile or chuckle when Þór makes his appearance in the Eddic poems. In two of them he is the indisputable protagonist. *Hymiskviða* relates that Ægir is going
to give a drinking party for the Æsir. But in order to procure for him a cauldron sufficiently large to brew the beer
in, Þór sets out, accompanied by his brother Týr, on an
expedition to the home of the giant Hymir. Here they meet
first of all two female creatures: one is the monstrous wife
of the giant, and Týr's grandmother, with nine hundred
heads; the other is her beautiful gold-and-jewelry-bedecked
daughter, who is Týr's mother; his father is, of course,
Óðinn, who, to be sure, did not disdain amorous adventures
with giant maidens. The master of the house turns up
from out-of-doors with icicles in his beard. As is easily
understood, he is not very pleased to find Þór, the heredi-
tary enemy of the giants, in his home. The columns behind
which the guests are concealed burst asunder before his
furious gaze. In a dark mood he prepares supper. Of the
three bulls that have been slaughtered and cooked, Þór all
by himself consumes two before he goes to bed. Hymir ob-
serves resignedly that they will probably have to go fishing
for supper the following evening, and Þór willingly agrees
if only the host will supply him with bait. Þór himself goes
out into the forest and tears "the high fortress of both
horns," i.e., the head, from a completely black bull—a
drastic act that does not exactly improve Hymir's mood.
Out on the sea the giant hauls up two whales at a single
cast; but with the bull's head as bait, Þór almost succeeds

53

in making a still more remarkable catch, the Miðgarður serpent itself:

gein við öngli,	There gaped at the bait
sús goð fía,	the foe of the gods,
umbgjörð neðan	the girdler of all
allra landa.	the earth beneath.

Dró djarfliga	The venomous serpent
dáðrakkr þórr	swiftly up
orm eitrfáan	to the boat did Thor,
upp at borði;	the bold one, pull;
hamri kníði	with his hammer the loathly
háfjall skarar	hill of the hair
ofljótt ofan	of the brother of Fenrir
úlfs hnitbróður.	he smote from above.

Hraungölkn hrutu,	The monsters roared,
en hölkn þutu,	and the rocks resounded,
fór hin forna	and all the earth
fold öll saman;	so old was shaken;
sökðisk síðan	then sank the fish
sá fiskr í mar.	in the sea forthwith.

Þór's astounding achievement makes Hymir still gloomier, yet he cannot resist challenging the guest to demonstrate new feats of strength. Þór is given the choice of carrying the whales home to the farm or of making fast their boat. He seizes the boat at the prow, lifts it with the bilge water still in it, and carries it to the farm with oars and all—including, presumably, the two whales. But Hymir stubbornly persists. He declares that he is not impressed with Þór's strength if he cannot crush a certain goblet in the room. On his first attempt Þór hurls the glass against a stone column, which shatters whereas the goblet is brought back intact. Then Týr's mother and Óðin's sweetheart, "the fair friend," advises him to throw it against Hymir's head. This time he is successful: the goblet breaks in two, but the giant's head remains undamaged. Finally Þór lifts the huge beer cauldron, which he and Týr have come to get. He breaks right through the floor in the effort, but heaves it up onto his head. On their way back they are pursued by Hymir and a large band of giants. But Þór puts down the cauldron, swings his hammer, and slays them all.

Formally *Hymiskviða* is characterized by an abundance of kennings that is remarkable among Eddic mythological poems, but they never exceed more members than a main word plus an attribute or qualifying noun and throughout are quite easily understandable. Generally they are applied to the main character himself, who is called Sif's husband, Móði's father, Óðin's son, lord of goats, slayer of giants, the causer of the giantess's tears. The boat is called stud of rollers (rollers were round logs which were placed under the keel to haul the boat over land), water goat, sea stallion, surf swine. Otherwise the poem has nothing in common with the artistic style of skaldic poetry; the narrative, in fornyrðislag, is brisk and straightforward.

The comedy, which in the eyes of the modern reader plays over several situations in *Hymiskviða*, can scarcely be regarded as completely unintentional. And in *Þrymskviða*, the other lay in which Þór is the central figure, the poet's humorous vein is quite obvious. Moreover, one's attention is drawn to the striking parallels between these two poems about Þór. Even the titles with their giant names correspond closely to each other. In both cases Þór with a companion journeys to the giant world in an attempt to procure or regain an object that the Æsir consider absolutely necessary (the cauldron, the hammer). After several exciting episodes with Mymir and Þrymur, respectively, the expedition ends in complete success with a massive slaughter of giants. But in *Þrymskviða* the plot as a whole is more concentrated and dramatic, the composition exceptionally firm, and the theme shaped with greater precision and finesse both in general and in detail.

Þrymskviða relates that the giant Þrymur has gained possession of Þór's hammer and demands Freyja as a wife in return for it. But the goddess of beauty refuses point-blank to make herself available for such a barter. In reply to Loki's direct request to adorn herself in bridal linens and to accompany him to the giant world, Freyja answers with a magnificent outburst of fury:

Reið varð þá Freyja	Wrathful was Freyja,
ok fnasaði,	and fiercely she snorted,
allr ása salr	and the dwelling great
undir bifðisk,	of the gods was shaken,
stökk þat hit mikla	and burst was the mighty
men Brísinga:	Brisings' necklace:
"Mik veizt verða	"Most lustful indeed
vergjarnasta,	should I look to all
ef ek ek með þér	if I journeyed with thee
í Jötunheima."	to the giants' home."

Now good counsel is sorely needed, for the fearful weapon of the thundergod is the Æsir's strongest and best protection against the giants. At a general discussion of the matter among the gods Heimdallur comes up with the proposal that Þór himself play the role of Freyja and have himself smuggled into Þrym's house as his bride:

"Bindum Þór þá	"Bind we on Thor
brúðar líni,	the bridal veil,
hafi hann hit mikla	let him bear the mighty
men Brísinga.	Brisings' necklace;
Látum and honum	"Keys around him
hrynja lukla	let there rattle,
ok kvenváðir	and down to his knees
of kné falla,	hang woman's dress;
en á brjósti	with gems full broad
breiða steina	upon his breast,
ok hagliga	and a pretty cap
of höfuð typpum."	to crown his head."

It is a trying ordeal for the manly self-esteem of the powerful god to be dressed in skirts and adorned in bridal linens, but necessity knows no bounds. The cunning Loki, otherwise one of the most malicious adversaries of the gods—it is he who instigates the slaying of Baldur the Good—appears in *Þrymskviða* somewhat surprisingly as their quick-witted helper. In the guise of a bridesmaid he accompanies Þór in the wagon drawn by goats. With burlesque situation comedy the well-known action at the abode of the love-sick giant Þrymur is then developed. It is only by conjuring up all his inventiveness that the bridesmaid Loki manages to explain away the carryings on of the huge bride at the wedding feast—she washes down one ox, eight salmon, and all the dainties intended for the women with three barrels of mead—and her terrifyingly piercing eyes. It is certainly not thanks to Þór that the hammer eventually lands safely in his lap so that he can take revenge for his ignominious role and reveal his true self in the giant's house.

With its succinct character portrayal, its swift narrative art, and light, lucid style *Þrymskviða* constitutes an artistic high point in Eddic poetry.

Nowadays scholars are quite generally in agreement that the poem must belong to the youngest layer of the collection and should perhaps even be dated as late as the thirteenth century. It is a striking fact that the myth about about the recovery of Þór's hammer is not even mentioned in Snorri's *Edda*, where otherwise such great interest is shown for Þór's various adventures. If Snorri had really known *Þrymskviða*, it is difficult to understand why he did not use this most popular of all Eddic poems, which has among other things been transformed into Icelandic *rímur* (cf. pp. 185 ff. below) and Norwegian folk song. On the other hand, it is hardly reasonable to believe that a poem of this kind could have escaped the collector and expert Snorri if it had really existed when his treatise on poetics was written at the beginning of the thirteenth century. Maybe after all Snorri's remarkable silence about *Þrymskviða* is due not to the fact that he was unacquainted with the poem but, on the contrary, to the fact that he knew it only too well. For there are several indications that Snorri himself may have written *Þrymskviða* as a kind of pastiche while he was absorbed in the collection of Eddic poetry for his handbook. If this hypothesis should be true—it can, of course, never be proven definitely—the puzzling absence of *Þrymskviða* from Snorri's *Edda* has a natural explanation. As a mythologist Snorri could not of course adduce a "myth" that he himself had fabricated.[6]

In contrast to *Þrymskviða*, *Skírnismál* impresses one as being archaic. This dialogue poem in *ljóðaháttr* deals with the god Frey's consuming desire for the giant maiden Gerður, whom he has seen at a distance:

Í Gymis görðum	From Gymir's house
ek ganga sá	I beheld go forth
mér tíða mey;	A maiden dear to me;
armar lýstu,	her arms glittered,
en af þaðan	and from their gleam
alt lopt ok lögr.	shone all the sea and sky.

His servant Skirnir calls on the beautiful woman in the giant world—a deed not entirely lacking in risks—to prevail upon her to grant Freyr her favor. The messenger is successful, but only after resorting to the most drastic sorceries and threats. He can return home with the reply that Gerður has promised to meet his master in the sheltered grove Barrey nine nights later. Freyr answers in the last stanza of the poem:

Löng er nótt,	"Long is one night,
langar ro tvær,	longer are two;
hvé of þreyjak þrjár;	how then shall I bear three?
opt mér mánaðr	often to me
minni þótti	has a month seemed less
en sjá hálf hýnótt.	than now half a night of desire."

Certain scholars have interpreted *Skírnismál* as a cult poem, as the text for a fertility rite. Freyr, son of Njörður and brother of Freyja, belongs to the family of the Vanir among the gods. He is the lord of sunlight, vegetation, and procreation. According to the description of the famous heathen temple at Uppsala given by Adam of Bremen (ca. 1070), Freyr figured with Óðinn and Þór as a major god at that place with an enormous phallos as his typical attribute. His cult seems to have had a strongly erotic, sometimes even obscene character. If interpreted as a text for part of a Freyr cult, *Skírnismál* would represent the marriage of the earth goddess (Gerður) to the sun god (Freyr). Their meeting in the grove Barrey would then be symbolic of how the sunlight fructifies the earth in spring.[7]

Just as the Homeric songs do not always depict their gods very respectfully, the Eddic poets do not hesitate to expose the weakness of the Æsir. The altercation between Óðinn and Þór in the already mentioned *Hárbarðsljóð* is comparatively good-natured. The satire in *Lokasenna* ("Loki's Wrangling"), however, is more venomous. Here Loki appears in his traditional role as the scourge of the gods. At a drinking feast in Ægir's hall he takes advantage of the occasion to humiliate the assembled gods, one after the other. The accusations against the Ásynjur, the female Æsir, are always imputations of erotic excess and lust for men; the Æsir are harangued and accused of cowardice and unmanliness. The scene is interrupted only when Þór appears and by threatening to use his hammer drives Loki out. But before leaving Loki also has time to deliver a few sneering remarks about the thundergod's experiences on his journey to Útgarðar-Loki, the story that Snorri relates in prose:

Austrförum þínum	"That thou hast fared
skalt aldrigi	on the East-road forth
segja seggjum frá	to men shouldst thou say no more;

59

síz í hanzka þumlungi   in the thumb of a glove
hnúkðir einheri, [vera.   didst thou hide, thou great one,
ok þóttiska þa Þórr   and there forgot thou wast Thor."

It has been suggested among other things that the author of *Lokasenna* with Loki himself as mouthpiece wanted to censure the insufficiency of the old naive myths of the gods in comparison with more highly developed ethical norms. But it is highly uncertain that the poem should really be interpreted as an expression of such intentional religious criticism. On the whole people have too often been overly inclined to read Eddic lays as a versification of a generally valid mythology, or in other words, to regard them primarily as material for the study of ancient Scandinavian religion. It is certainly prudent to leave a fairly wide margin for the temperament and vision of the individual poets, and thus to recognize the character of Eddic poetry as just that—poetry.[8]

Heroic Poetry

As already stated, it has not been possible to demonstrate direct counterparts to the mythological poetry of the *Edda* outside the Nordic countries. Heroic poetry, however, does have certain parallels. There is, as we know, the German alliterative *Hildebrandslied* (from ca. 800) with material from the time of the Great Migration. A broad epic like the English *Beowulf* (eighth century), with its more than three thousand verses, has a different character than the *Hildebrandslied*, which treats a single event and consists mostly of dialogue; *Beowulf* is based partly on Scandinavian heroic legends, but is, as already mentioned, written from a Christian point of view and with Virgil as a model. The heroic poetry of the *Edda* deals essentially with Germanic characters and themes, sometimes known also from other sources, literature as well as pictorial art.

But in regard to both volume and character this major branch of Eddic poetry is unique as well.

The heroic poems in the Codex Regius are the following: *Helgakviða Hundingsbana I*, *Helgakviða Hjörvarðssonar*, *Helgakviða Hundingsbana II*, *Frá dauða Sinfjötla* ("About Sinfjötli's Death," prose), *Grípisspá*, *Reginsmál*, *Fáfnismál*, *Sigrdrífumál*, *Brot af Sigurðarkviðu* ("Fragment from the Lay of Sigurður"), *Guðrúnarkviða I*, *Sigurðarkviða hin skamma* ("The Short Lay of Sigurður"), *Helreið Brynhildar* ("Brynhild's Ride to Hel"), *Guðrúnarkviða II*, *Guðrúnarkviða III*, *Oddrúnargrátr* ("Oddrun's Lament"), *Atlakviða*, *Atlamál hin grœnlenzku* ("The Greenlandish Lay of Atli"), *Guðrúnarhvöt* ("Gudrun's Incitement"), and *Hamðismál*.

Völundarkviða. Before the actual heroic poetry is discussed, however, we must turn to the archaic and signal *Völundarkviða*, which is difficult to place in either of the two main categories of Eddic poetry (cf. p. 30, above). The skillful smith Völundur is captured by King Niðuður in Sweden. On the queen's advice his knee sinews are severed and he is isolated on an islet, where he is compelled to forge precious treasures for the king. But Völundur broods on revenge. Without being discovered, he manages to cut the heads off the two sons of the king, who have come out of curiosity to view his smithwork. From their skulls, eyes, and teeth he fashions ornaments, which he sends to Niðuð's house, where nobody suspects anything about their origin. The king's daughter Böðvildur comes to him secretly to have a ring mended; she did not dare to tell her parents that it was broken. Völundur puts the girl to sleep with an intoxicating drink and violates her. After that he rises laughingly in flight on a pair of wings which he has evidently created secretly. But before he leaves the place he settles down on the wall surrounding the royal castle and triumphantly boasts to Niðuður about his actions:

61

En ór tönnum	"And from the teeth
tveggja þeirra	of the twain I wrought
slók brjóstkringlur,	a brooch for the breast,
sendak Böðvildi;	to Bothvild I gave it;
nú gengr Böðvildr	now big with child
barni aukin,	does Bothvild go,
eingadóttir	the only daughter
ykkur beggja.	ye two had ever."

The poem ends on an elegiac tone, a stanza in which Böðvildur confesses her misfortune to her father:

Satt er þat, Niðuðr,	"True is it, Nithuth,
es sagði þér.	that which was told thee,
Sátum vit Völundr	once in the isle
saman í holmi	with Völund was I,
eina ögurstund,	an hour of lust,
æva skyldi;	alas it should be!
ek vætr hánum	Nought was my might
vinna kunnak,	with such a man,
ek vætr hánum	nor from his strength
vinna máttak.	could I save myself."

The central character in this archaic poem, the mythic smith Völundur, is also known elsewhere. Thus in the Old English poem *Deor's Lament* there are allusions both to Völund's captivity and to his slaying of the two sons of the king and his violation of Böðvildur. The similarity is further underscored by several striking verbal parallels with *Völundarkviða*. Then there is a picture of Völundur and Böðvildur on an old jewel case of whalebone in the British Museum, called Franks Casket or the Clermont Casket, possibly from the end of the seventh century. These and certain other reminiscences in English tradition could indicate that the poem about Völundur might have come from England to the North. On the other hand, the vocabulary in *Völundarkviða* is considered to reveal occasional traces of German origin; the names of the three leading persons in the drama—Wieland, Midhad, and Baduhild—could point in the same direction. Therefore it has been considered possible that an originally German poem was transferred both to England and to the North. In such Eddic problems we seldom get beyond a well-founded hypothesis. *Völundarkviða* also reveals a general resemblance to the Greek tale about Dædalus, who rose out of the labyrinth where he was imprisoned on wings that he had made himself. That resemblance was observed quite early in the North; in Icelandic a labyrinth is still called *völundarhús*, "house of Völundur."

The grouping of heroic poems in the Codex Regius. The major portion of the heroic poems of the Edda revolve about the champion Sigurður Fáfnisbani, the best-known warrior in the entire cycle of Old Germanic legend. The second greatest hero, the specifically Norse Helgi Hundingsbani, has been connected with Sigurður by being made his older half brother: both are portrayed as sons of a certain King Sigmundur, but of different mothers. In a long sequence of poems, partly linked together and supplemented by short sections of prose, one can follow Sigurð's life from his youthful accomplishments, primarily the slaying of the dragon Fáfnir and the acquisition of his enormous gold treasure, through his connections with the Gjúkungs and his marriage to Guðrún up to the time of his death. In this part of Codex Regius there is, however, a lacuna; there is missing probably a gathering of eight leaves, or about 280 stanzas of eight verses each. At certain points the course of Sigurð's life history can here be reconstructed with the aid of the late Icelandic prose work *Völsungasaga*, a paraphrase of old heroic lays. The poems that follow after Sigurð's death deal mostly with Guðrún's later fate, especially her two subsequent marriages, first to King Atli and then to King Jónakur. The whole bloody chronicle culminates in a description of how Guðrún's three sons with Jónakur are slain.

The heroic poetry in Codex Regius has thus been arranged in accordance with the chronology of the course of events. That is the work of the editor of the collection and has nothing to do with the time when the individual lays were written. This complex of poems obviously includes contributions from the most varied ages, some very old, others perhaps only little older than the collection itself. Along with basic textual criticism, Eddic scholars have also regarded it as a major task to try to establish different chronological layers within this heroic poetry. On certain points results and opinions are generally in agreement, but in other respects they differ widely. In the following survey it has therefore seemed natural to adhere to the order of the *Edda* editor himself. It is intrinsically advantageous not to break the epic line that places the characters and their actions in substantially more distinct relief. Possible questions concerning the ages of various poems, their characteristics in style or meter, etc., will be discussed as they arise.

Helgi Hundingsbani and Helgi Hjörvarðsson. *Helgaviða Hundingsbana I* begins with the birth of the hero:

Ár var alda	In olden days,
þats arar gullu,	when eagles screamed,
hnigu heilög vötn	and holy streams
af Himinfjöllum;	from heaven's crags fell,
þá hafði Helga	was Helgi then,
hinn hugumstóra	the hero-hearted,
Borghildr borit	Borghild's son,
í Brálundi.	in Bralund born.

That this is not the birth of an ordinary child is indicated by the lively activity of the norns:

Snöru af afli	Mightily wove they
örlögþáttu,	the web of fate,
þás borgir braut	while Bralund's towns
í Brálundi;	were trembling all;
þær of greiddu	and there the golden
gollin símu	threads they wove,
ok und mánasal	and in the moon's hall
miðjan festu	fast they made them.

At the age of only one day this son of Sigmundur stands clad in a coat of mail; his sharp eyes testify to a warrior's temperament. At the age of fifteen Helgi takes up arms against the harsh king Hundingur and slays him—for what reason is not said. The sons of Hundingur demand compensation for their father's death from Helgi, but he only challenges them to another battle by the mountain named Logafjöll and slays them all. After the battle he is addressed by a valkyrie—later on she reveals that her name is Sigrún—who complains that her father has promised her in marriage to Höddbroddur, "the cruel son of Granmar." Helgi promises to help her against Höddbroddur at the risk of his own life and at once begins to gather his crew. Their departure and voyage are described in a concrete and stirring manner:

Varð ára ymr	There was beat of oars
ok járna glymr,	and clash of iron,
brast rönd við rönd,	shield smote shield
röru víkingar;	as the ships'-folk rowed;
eisandi gekk	swiftly went
und öðlingum	the warrior-laden
lofðungs floti	fleet of the ruler
löndum fjarri.	forth from the land.

The weather becomes severe and the waves threaten to sink the ship. But Helgi defies the elements, and Sigrún hovers protectively over the water:

Draga baðð Helgi	Helgi bade higher
há segl ofar,	hoist the sails,
varðat hrönnum	nor did the ships'-folk
höfn þingloga,	shun the waves,
þás ógurlig	though dreadfully
Ægis dóttir	did Ægir's daughter
stagstjórnmörum	seek the steeds
steypa vildi.	of the sea to sink.

Upon arrival on the battlefield there develops a kind of comical interlude, a quarrel between Helgi's brother Sinfjötli and one of the leaders of the enemy. The exchanged abuses run to accusations of perverse inclinations and general cowardice. But Helgi puts a stop to the scene with an exhortation to begin the battle and "to treat the eagles." A band of valkyries, Sigrún among them, once more appear as his protectors in the battle. The poem ends with her congratulations to the hero, who now, after his victory, will also receive her as a reward.

It has been suggested that *Helgakviða Hundingsbana I* reveals influence from skaldic poetry. It is constructed very much like a praise poem for a prince, with a decided preference for splendid rhetoric. Here the kennings are used as an ornament more profusely than in any other of the heroic lays of the *Edda*. On their "stay-steered stallions," or "breakers' beasts" or "stags of sail-rings" the host of warriors set off for the battle's "sword-meeting," also called "the storm of grey spears," "the clang of bows," and "the din of shields." The hero is a "friend of wolves" with a hard "acorn of mind" (heart). He swings his "blood snake" or "wound flame," thereby mowing "Hugin's barley" (the raven's food = corpses), to the delight also of "Óðin's bitches" (wolves). These simple kennings, however, are completely free of the heaviness and overloading which so often seem inherent in the skalds' dróttkvætt style, nor do they retard the flow of action. There is swiftness, verve, and splendor throughout the fornyrðislag poem. One feels a fresh, realistic breath of sea voyages and viking life, while at the same time fate-spinning Norns and valkyries eager for battle lend a mythic strain to the description.

Helgakviða Hundingsbana II quotes and refers to *I*, although this does not preclude the possibility that in other parts it may be the older of the two. It is far less uniform than *I*, and among its stanzas there are now and then inserted prose passages that clearly testify to the hand of the collector or commentator. Helgi's and Sigrún's story is chiefly drawn as in *I*, with certain new details, but it is also brought to its tragic conclusion. For Sigrún's brother Dagur is driven by the dictates of family revenge to pierce his brother-in-law Helgi with his spear because he has slain their father. Full of grief, he himself delivers the message about his deed to his sister. Sigrún answers with a long series of dire curses over her brother. May all the oaths that he has sworn Helgi fall back upon him! May his ship never gain speed even with a favorable wind, may his horse not run, even if it is a matter of saving his life from the enemy! May his sword bite nothing but himself! May he be a wolf in the forest with no other food than corpses to eat himself to death on—then Helgi's death would be avenged on him! "You are out of your senses, sister," replies Dagur, who blames Óðinn for having sown discord between kinsmen, and offers her gold and land as redress for her sorrow. But Sigrún continues with ecstatic praise of the incomparable hero:

Svá hafði Helgi	Such the fear
hrædda görva	that Helgi's foes
fíandr sína alla	ever felt,
ak frændr þeira,	and all their kin,
sem fyr úlfi	as makes the goats
óðar rynni	with terror mad
geitr af fjalli	run from the wolf
geiskafullar.	among the rocks.

Svá bar Helgi	Helgi rose
af hildingum	above heroes all
sem ítrskapaðr	like the lofty ash
askr af þyrni	above lowly thorns,
eða sá dýrkalfr,	or the noble stag,
döggu slunginn,	with dew besprinkled,
es efri ferr	bearing his head
öllum dýrum.	above all beasts.

During the evening after Helgi's burial Sigrún's maid-servant espies the slain man riding with many followers to his grave mound on a visit from Valhöll. She informs her mistress, who goes out to meet her husband. Sigrún prepares a bed in the grave mound and rests one last night in Helgi's embrace. There is an intimate and melancholy air over their last hours together which is singular in this heroic poetry. Sigrún remarks that her husband is covered with blood, and Helgi replies that she herself has caused it. She sheds bitter tears before she goes to bed, and each tear falls as blood on his chest. But at this moment Helgi says that he lacks nothing, since Högni's fair daughter rests on his arm. But he cannot tarry long; he must return to Valhöll before the cock Salgófnir summons the warriors to the coming day's battle games. Helgi's last words are the counterpart in Norse heroic poetry to the alba or Tagelied of trouba-dour poetry, the song at the departure from the beloved one at daybreak:

Mál er mér at ríða	Now must I ride
roðnar brautir,	the reddened ways,
láta fölvan jó	and my bay steed set
flugstíg troða,	to tread the sky;
skalk fyr vestan	westward I go
vindhjálms brúar,	to wind-helm's bridges,
áðr Salgófnir	ere Salgofnir wakes
sigrþjóð veki.	the warrior throng.

Helgi disappears forever and Sigrún dies of grief.

Strangely enough, these two poems about Helgi Hundingsbani are separated by a lay about another Helgi, *Helgakviða Hjörvarðssonar*. He is the son of a certain King Hjörvarður and the beautiful princess Sigurlinn. He is initiated into the heroic life by the valkyrie Sváfa, who gives him his name and a sword and becomes his beloved. A tragic complication arises when, during the yule celebration in honor of Bragi, Helgi's own brother Héðinn happens to make the vow that he shall possess the woman that his brother loves. This is a witch's revenge. He is immediately stricken with remorse and sets off to the South to find Helgi and confess his rash act. Helgi takes the matter calmly and declares that he will probably soon fall in battle anyway—a foreboding that soon comes true. Mortally wounded, he asks Sváfa to dry her tears and give her love to Héðinn instead. She refers to her own vow never voluntarily to love an "unknown king" after Helgi's death. The poem ends with a comment in prose: "It has been said that Helgi and Sváfa were reborn."

That remark can be connected with the information in the prose introduction of *Helgakviða Hundingsbana II*. For there it is stated that King Sigmundur and his wife called their son Helgi after Helgi Hjörvarðsson. Maybe one should also imagine that the valkyrie Sváfa is reincarnated in the valkyrie Sigrún. In any event there is certainly a striking similarity between the two couples. It is also remarkable that a place called Frekasteinn occurs both in the two poems about Helgi Hundingsbani and in the lay of Helgi Hjörvarðsson as the scene of a decisive battle—even if in the case of the first hero it has a fortunate ending and for the last-mentioned a tragic one. Maybe these facts indicate a certain fusion of the two Helgi characters in tradition. But what this tradition was originally and what its relation is to historic reality, if there is any—those are problems hardly worth speculating about.

Inserted into the lay of Helgi Hjörvarðsson and Sváfa is a section that must originally have been a separate poem. This is testified to at least by the meter—ljóðaháttr in contrast to the surrounding fornyrðislag. The inserted episode is a dialogue—a quarrel with burlesque and obscene features—between Helgi's trusty follower Atli and the giant daughter Hrímgerður, whose father, Hati, was slain by Helgi. At the end Helgi himself too appears. Hrímgerður suggests that she be allowed to sleep with him for one night—as a compensation for the slaying of her father. But Helgi rejects the erotic invitation. The section ends when one of the two men—probably Atli—announces the dawning day and its fateful consequences for the giant maiden:

Dagr er nú, Hrímgerðr,	It is day, Hrimgerth,
en þik dvalða hefr	for Atli held thee
Atli til aldrlaga,	till now thy life thou must lose;
hafnarmark	as a harbor mark
þykkir hlœgligt vera,	men shall mock at thee, [stand.
þars þú í steins líki stendr.	where in stone thou shalt ever

This *Hrímgerðarmál*, as the episode is usually called, has been compared with the fantastic *fornaldarsögur*, in which battles with giants and similar beings are a favorite motif. The somewhat less than tactful altercation itself also reminds one very much of the corresponding wrangling in *Helgakviða Hundingsbana I* between Helgi's brother Sinfjötli and a man on the enemy side. In both cases the dialogue begins with someone asking to know the name of the leader of Helgi's side. Maybe there is even a direct literary connection here—unless, of course, it is a matter of comparatively general and standardized elements in battle descriptions of this kind.

Sigurður Fáfnisbani. The poetry about Sigurður which makes up the remainder of Codex Regius begins with a prose section in which the hero's ancestry is recounted. As already mentioned, Sigurður is a half brother of Helgi Hundingsbani, son of King Sigmundur and King Eylimi's daughter Hjördís. After Sigmundur has fallen in battle, Hjördís marries king Hjálprek's son Álfur. "This is where Sigurður grew up in his childhood. Sigmundur and all his sons were far superior to all other men in strength and towering stature and in intellect and all accomplishments. Sigurður, however, was the foremost of all; and in the ancient chronicles all call him the most outstanding of men and the noblest among warrior kings."

Thereupon there follows as the first poem *Grípisspá* ("Grípir's Prophecy"), a dialogue of about fifty stanzas in fornyrðislag between young Sigurður and his maternal uncle Grípir. Sigurður has come to his prescient kinsman to learn about his destiny. Grípir is willing enough as long as he can tell about his nephew's early and happy life, replete with achievements and splendor. But as darkness descends over the hero's path, his uncle is reluctant to reveal more to him, and Sigurður has to urge him repeatedly to speak. Little by little Grípir lifts the veil of the future and relates the killing of the dragon Fáfnir, Sigurð's love for Brynhild, his dealings with the Gjúkungs and marriage with Guðrún, Brynhild's revenge and Sigurð's death at the hands of his brothers-in-law, and Guðrún's grief as a widow. But as a kind of consolation, a brighter final vignette to his gloomy view of the future, his uncle adds:

Því skal hugga þik	Ever remember,
hers oddviti,	ruler of men,
sú mun gipt lagið	that fortune lies
á grams ævi:	in the hero's life;
munat mætri maðr	a nobler man
á mold koma	shall never live
und sólar sjöt	beneath the sun
en þú Sigurðr, þykkir.	than Sigurth shall seem.

71

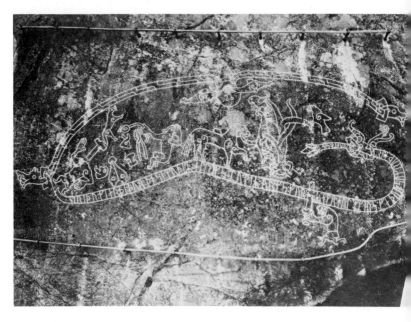

The Sigurðr petroglyph on the Ramsundsberg in Södermanland. The rune master has ingeniously made the runic meander into the dragon Fáfnir, which Sigurðr pierces with his sword from below. Sigurðr can also be seen roasting Fáfnir's heart over the fire. In the tree, to which his horse, Grani, is tied, sit the birds that advise him to slay Reginn. To the extreme left we see Reginn, with his head cut off, surrounded by his smithy tools: anvil, bellows, sledge hammer, and tongs. See the text, pp. 73–75.

Photo by courtesy of Vitterhetsakademiens bildarkiv.

Thus at the very outset we are given a survey of the main events in Sigurð's biography. *Grípisspá* is generally considered to be a very late poem, perhaps composed as late as the thirteenth century and designed as an introduction to a collection of Sigurðr poems. It has, moreover, a certain importance from the standpoint of textual history as a clue to what the much discussed lacuna in Codex Regius may have contained.

Sigurð's exploits as a young man are related in the two poems that are generally called *Reginsmál* and *Fáfnismál* in editions of the *Edda*, but which from the standpoint of textual criticism are a rather tangled skein of alternating ljóðaháttr, fornyrðislag, and prose sections. In the former lay we encounter Reginn, the fosterer of the lad Sigurður, "more skillful with his hands than other men and in growth like a dwarf," "wise, cruel, and skilled in the sorcerer's art." He relates the story about the great golden treasure, which is to play such a fateful role in Sigurð's future. Loki had killed Regin's brother Otur, who used to dwell in a waterfall disguised as an otter, and to expiate this slaughter the trio Óðinn, Hœnir, and Loki had been forced to give an enormous were-gild to Regin's father, Hreiðmar. Not only did they have to fill the otter skin with gold, but they also had to cover it to the last whisker with the same precious metal. Loki had extorted all this treasure from the dwarf Andvari so that the compensation could be paid and the three companions save their lives. But Andvari pronounces a curse on all future owners of the treasure—may it cause the death of two brothers and bring misfortune to eight princes and never be of good use to any human being—and Loki in turn directs similar threats at Hreiðmar. Out of greed for the gold, Regin's brother Fáfnir with a sword slew their father as he slept and then claimed the entire treasure for himself.

At this point the actual events of the poem begin. Reginn tells Sigurður that Fáfnir, disguised as a dragon and with a "helmet of terror" on his head, lies gloating over his gold treasure on the Gnitaheiði. He forges a sword for Sigurður: "it was so sharp that he dipped it into the Rhine and let a tuft of wool drift against it with the current, and it cut the tuft like water." Reginn incites Sigurður to kill Fáfnir. First, however, the poem tells how Sigurður sails off to take vengeance for his father's death by killing Hunding's sons.

73

Fáfnismál relates that Sigurður digs a pit in Fáfnir's path and from there thrusts his sword into the heart of the dragon as it crawls past. But before Fáfnir breathes his last a dialogue develops between him and his slayer. Fáfnir reminds Sigurður of the curse on the gold treasure, and the young hero replies with proud fatalism:

Féi ráða	Some one the hoard
skal fyrða hverr	shall ever hold,
æ til hins eina dags;	till the destined day shall come:
þvíat einu sinni	for a time there is
skal alda hverr	when every man
fara til heljar heðan.	shall journey hence to hell.

Strangely enough, there is also some rather special mythological wisdom inserted into this dialogue, when Fáfnir willingly answers Sigurð's questions.

When the slaying is accomplished, there appears the instigator, Reginn, who up until now has remained in the background. Now he is eager to emphasize his share in the deed, but Sigurður refutes him:

Regin kvað:	Regin spoke:
"Lengi liggja	"Long wouldst thou
létir lyngvi í	in the heather have let
þann hinn aldna jötun,	yon hoary giant hide,
ef sverðs né nytir,	had the weapon availed not
þess es sjálfr gerðak,	that once I forged, [bear."
þíns hins hvassa hjölrs."	the keen-edged blade thou didst

Sigurðr kvað:	Sigurth spoke:
"Hugr er betri	"Better is heart
en sé hjörs megin,	than a mighty blade
hvars skulu vreiðir vega;	for him who shall fiercely fight;
hvatan mann	the brave man well
sék harðla vega	shall fight and win,
með slævu sverði sigr."	though dull his blade may be.

Reginn steps forth and cuts the heart out of Fáfnir. He hands it to Sigurður and asks him to hold it over the fire while he himself lies down to sleep for a while. Then follows in prose: "Sigurður took Fáfnir's heart and roasted it on a wooden spit. When he thought it was fully cooked, and blood frothed from it, he touched the heart with one finger to feel if it was well roasted. He burned himself and put his finger in his mouth. But when Fáfnir's heart blood touched his tongue, he understood the speech of birds. He heard titmice chirping in the thicket." The birds warn him of the deceitful Regin's scheme against him and advise Sigurður to strike off his head. This is done, and Sigurður himself eats Fáfnir's heart and drinks both Fáfnir's and Regin's blood. The birds then urge him to ride and take possession of the gold treasure. They also prophesy his visit to King Gjúki and his marriage to the king's daughter. Finally they tell him about the valkyrie Sigurdrífa, sunk in magic sleep in a golden hall, surrounded by fire, on the mountain Hindarfjall.

A number of concrete details from Sigurð's slaying of Fáfnir, which quite agree with the description in *Fáfnismál*, are reproduced in the famous petroglyph on the Ramsundsberg in Södermanland, made in the eleventh century. This is one of many pieces of evidence that indicate how popular and widely known the legend of Sigurður Fáfnisbani was. On the other hand, the picture itself tells us nothing about the literary form in which the story reached the Swedish artist. It need not necessarily have been in poetic form; we cannot simply assume that it was some "Eddic poem" or other.

Sigrdrífumál—whose title has been included in editions of the *Edda* only from late transcriptions—begins where Fáfnismál ends. On his way southward toward Frakkland, Sigurður comes riding up the mountain Hindarfjall and there finds a sleeping woman in full armor. Her coat of mail fits as though it were grown fast to her flesh. Sigurður cuts it open with his sword. The woman awakens and he asks her her name. Her answer begins with a beautiful invocation, which in its hymn-like quality has no counterpart elsewhere in the *Edda*:

Heill dagr,	"Hail, day!
heilir dags synir,	Hail, sons of day! [now!
heil nótt ok nipt;	And night and her sister
óreiðum augum	Look on us here
lítið okr þinig	with loving eyes, [win.
ok gefið sitjöndum sigr.	that waiting we victory
Heilir æsir,	"Hail to the gods!
heilar ásynjur,	Ye goddesses, hail,
heil sjá hin fjölnýta fold,	and all the generous earth!
mál ok manvit	Give to us wisdom
gefið okr mærum tveim	and goodly speech, [long."
ok læknishendr, meðan lifum.	and healing hands, life-

She tells him that she is a valkyrie and that her name is Sigurdrífa. Óðinn himself has stung her with a "sleep-thorn" and sunk her into a trance in revenge for her having caused a king to fall in battle after Óðinn had promised him the victory. The remainder of the poem is gnomic poetry in both ljóðaháttr and fornyrðislag. Sigurdrífa imparts some mythological knowledge to Sigurður, but also insight into the magic arts, including the art of healing. Finally she gives him some bits of advice, numbered from one to eleven, which are strongly reminiscent of *Hávamál*. As in that great didactic poem, they are sometimes rather trivial: one should not dispute with stupid people, nor with intoxicated warriors, for wine steals many a man's wit. Her last admonition is also a prediction about Sigurður:

Þat ræðk þér ellipta,	Then eleventh I rede thee,
at við illu séir	that wrath thou shun, [friends;
hvern veg at vinum,	and treachery false with thy

langt líf	not long the leader's
þykkjumka lofðungs vita;	life shall be,
römm eru róg of risin.	for great are the foes he faces.

Sigrdrífumál thus has none of the erotic character that one might well expect after the beginning of the poem, with the valkyrie being waked from her magic sleep by the young hero. *Völsungasaga*, however, has preserved in prose the content of several verses which evidently belonged to the end of the poem (see p. 63, above). Sigurður swears to possess Sigurdrífa, and she in turn declares she would prefer him of all men. They bind this promise with oaths.

Right in the epilogue to *Sigrdrífumál* the above-mentioned great lacuna in Codex Regius begins, and with the beginning of the next leaf we are right in the midst of a dialogue about the slaying of Sigurður. There has been extensive discussion as to what was written on the missing leaves, but on the whole their contents can probably be reconstructed from *Völsungasaga*. For the sake of continuity the main events will be recounted here.

Sigurður continues his journey, preceded by his reputation as the great dragon slayer. In a chieftain's castle he meets beautiful Brynhildur, Buðli's daughter, and falls passionately in love with her. But Brynhildur declares that she is a shield maiden and has to take part in battles among warrior kings. Nevertheless, their meeting ends with an exchange of oaths, and Sigurður gives her a ring as a token of his fidelity. The next stage of his journey is King Gjúki's court. Queen Grímhildur would like to have the famous hero and owner of Fáfnir's treasure as a son-in-law, and one night she gives him a drink from a horn and ceremoniously receives him as a son into the family. But after that drink Sigurður no longer remembers Brynhildur. Several years later he marries Gjúki's daughter Guðrún and enters into foster brotherhood with his brothers-in-law Gunnar and Högni.

Grímhildur now urges her son Gunnar to woo Brynhildur. Together with Sigurður and other companions he
sets off for the court of King Buðli. But the latter doubts
that his daughter would care for any man who cannot ride
through the burning fire that surrounds her castle. Gunnar
attempts to do so, both on his own horse and on Sigurð's
Grani, but is forced to retreat. Then Gunnar and Sigurður
exchange appearances—Grimhildur has taught them how
to do this—and Sigurður breaks through the barrier of fire.
He remains for three nights in the castle with Brynhildur.
They lie on the same bed, but Sigurður places his bare
sword between them. When Brynhildur asks what this ritual
means, he answers evasively. Then he rides back through
the fire and once more changes appearances with Gunnar.
Brynhildur is bewildered and asks her stepfather for advice.
She had expected nobody but Sigurður—"the one to whom
I swore oaths on the mountain," "my first husband"—to be
able to accomplish the feat of riding through the fire. Then
the wedding between Buðli's daughter and Gunnar is
celebrated. "And when the feast was over, Sigurður recalled
all the oaths he had sworn to Brynhildur, but nevertheless
he did nothing about it".

The episode about Sigurð's sojourn with the valkyrie
Brynhildur in her inaccessible castle is strongly reminiscent
of *Sigrdrífumál*. It is also evident that *Völsungasaga* has
identified Sigurdrífa with Brynhildur—a version which
might possibly derive from a lost poem in the lacuna.

Once when Brynhildur is wrangling with Guðrún she
learns that she has been deceived: it was not her husband
Gunnar but Guðrún's Sigurður who penetrated the flames
and entered her castle. This discovery awakens a consuming jealousy and desire for revenge in the proud shield
maiden. She begrudges Guðrún the love of the incomparable hero and incites Gunnar to slay his brother-in-law.

Therewith we have again returned to extant Eddic
poetry. *Brot af Sigurðarkviðu* ("Fragment of a Lay of Sigur-

ður") is so called because an undetermined number of stanzas are lacking at the beginning. The remaining twenty stanzas begin with a dialogue between Gunnar and his brother Högni. Gunnar maintains that Sigurður has broken his oaths to him and must therefore die. Brynhildur has hinted—evidently for the purpose of inciting her husband—that Sigurður betrayed him during the wooing. But Högni warns that Brynhildur is pursuing her own goals.

Þik hefr Brynhildr	Thy heart hath Brynhild
böl at görva	whetted to hate,
heiptar hvattan	evil to work
harm at vinna;	and harm to win;
fyrman hón Guðrúnu	she grudges the honor
góðra ráða	that Guthrun has,
en síðan þér	and that joy of herself
sín at njóta.	thou still dost have.

But the course of the tragedy can no longer be checked. With the help of their younger brother Gutþormur, they slay Sigurður, "south of the Rhine," and Högni reports after they have returned home:

sundr höfum Sigurð	Sigurth we
sverði höggvinn,	with our swords have slain;
gnapir æ grár jór	the gray horse mourns
of grami dauðum.	by his master dead.

Guðrún invokes curses on her brother Gunnar, but the poem devotes greater attention to Brynhild's reaction:

Hló þá Brynhildr,	Then Brynhild laughed—
bœr allr dunði,	and the building echoed—
einu sinni	only once,
af öllum hug:	with all her heart;
"Lengi skuluð njóta	"Long shall ye joy
landa ok þegna,	in lands and men,
es frœknan gram	now ye have slain
falla létuð."	the hero noble."

79

It is a laugh that reveals—or perhaps one should rather say conceals—complicated emotions: possibly triumph, but even more so desperation. Her kinsmen are also perplexed by her behavior when a little later she speaks in tears about what she earlier "laughingly asked / her brothers to do." Now she pours her contempt and hatred out on Gunnar, who has been her tool, because he has broken his oaths and betrayed his brother-in-law and unselfish helper. Cruelly and bitterly she at last bears witness—in a matter about which she alone is in position to bear witness— to Sigurð's unswerving loyalty to Gunnar. Now that the murder of the hero is irrevocable, the truth about the sword on the bed between Brynhildur and Sigurður in the castle surrounded by fire must strike Gunnar like a thunderbolt:

Benvönd of lét	The wound-staff, then,
brugðinn golli,	all wound with gold,
margdýrr konungr	the hero let
á meðla okkar;	between us lie;
eldi váru eggjar	with fire the edge
útan görvar,	was forged full keen,
en eitrdropum	and with drops of venom
innan fáðar.	the blade was damp.

In the prose section attached to this poem we have a fine example of how the editor of Codex Regius can reveal himself as a critic of tradition in an almost scientific spirit. Conscientiously he enters into the ledger deviant versions of the story: "Here, in this poem Sigurð's death is described, and here it is related as if they had slain him outdoors, but some say that they killed him indoors in his bed as he slept. But Germans say that they slew him in a forest, and in the old Guðrún lay it is said that Sigurður and Gjúki's sons had ridden to the þing when he was slain; but all agree that they treacherously deceived him in his trust of them and attacked him while he was lying down and unprepared."

80

The following poem, *Guðrúnarkviða I*, places Guðrún in the center of attention. In it the young widow's mute sorrow is described as she sits beside her husband's corpse without being able to weep. It does not seem to have any effect on her when other women try to console her by telling her about their own misfortunes, each one worse than the other. Not until one of them hits upon the idea of lifting the shroud from Sigurð's dead body so that his bloody head is bared does Guðrún's emotional spasm relax, so that she can both shed tears and utter words:

Þá hné Guðrún	Then Guthrun bent,
höll við bolstri,	on her pillow bowed,
haddr losnaði,	her hair was loosened,
hlýr roðnaði,	her cheek was hot,
en regns dropi	and the tears like raindrops
rann niðr of kné.	downward ran.

She praises her husband's heroic figure and touchingly confesses her abandonment: "Now I am as small as a leaf in the willow copse." In the final stanza of this delicate elegy we are given as a contrast a picture of her rival, fiercely observing Guðrún's grief:

Stóð hón und stoð,	By the pillars she stood,
strengdi efli;	and gathered her strength,
brann Brynhildi	from the eyes of Brynhild,
Buðla dóttur	Buthli's daughter,
eldr ór augum,	fire there burned,
eitri fnœsti,	and venom she breathed,
es sár of leit	when the wounds she saw
á Sigurði.	on Sigurth then.

Sigurðarkviða hin skamma and *Helreið Brynhildar* follow Brynhild's story to the end. She does not want to survive the death of Sigurður. The first poem recapitulates what has happened from the time Sigurður arrived at the court of the Gjúkungs and once more describes how he was slain—in this version he is pierced by Gutþorm's sword indoors, in his and Guðrún's bed. But the main character of the lay is Brynhildur. After inciting her husband to commit the evil deed she speaks clearly about her own feelings and her life's tragedy. She distributes jewelry and other gifts among her female attendants and, while dying, gives directions that her body be placed on the funeral pyre beside Sigurð's with a naked sword between them—as they lay side by side once before:

Liggi okkar	Let between us
enn í milli	lie once more
egghvasst éarn,	the steel so keen,
sem endr lagit,	as so it lay
þás vit bæði	when both within
beð einn stigum	one bed we were,
ok hétum þá	and wedded mates
hjóna nafni.	by men were called.

The short poem *Helreið Brynhildar*, as the title indicates, describes Brynhild's journey to the realm of the dead. On her way she encounters a giantess who accuses her bitterly of having brought disaster on Gjúki's house. Brynhildur answers "the very senseless woman" with a review of her life. Among other things she describes her magic sleep, caused by Óðin's wrath, in a way that quite agrees with *Sigrdrífumál*—additional evidence that traditionally Sigurdrífa and Brynhildur were thought to be one and the same person. At the end she looks back over her life on earth without regret, convinced that she and Sigurður will be able to remain together after death:

Muno við ofstrið	Ever with grief
alls til lengi	and all too long
konur ok karlar	are men and women
kvikvir fœðask,	born in the world;

vit skulum okkrum	but yet we shall live
aldri slíta	our lives together,
Sigurðr saman;	Sigurth and I.
søksk gýgjar kyn.	Sink down, Giantess!

Before Brynhildur breathes her last, she predicts much of what is going to happen, among other things that Guðrún will remarry, this time Brynhild's brother Atli—this character is a reflection of Attila, the historical king of the Huns. The marriage between Guðrún and Atli brings about more slaughters and acts of vengeance. In *Guðúnarkviða II* Guðrún is at the court of Atli and gives an account of her life destiny in a single long soliloquy. For three and a half years after Sigurð's death she remained in Denmark with Þóra Hákonardóttir and devoted herself to womanly skills, weaving tapestries of battle scenes. But then there came men from far away, dark-haired and dressed in red cloaks with short coats of mail, to bring her jewelry and to speak kindly to her—clearly Atli's bridal emissaries: "I did not believe them." Guðrún accedes only when her mother, Grímhildur, gives her a drink of oblivion with many remarkable ingredients and, by promising her goods and gold, persuades her to agree to the marriage with Atli—although Guðrún is perfectly aware of what terrible events are going to take place because of that marriage. But to go to one's destruction with seeing eyes is one of the rules of the game in this kind of heroically fatalistic poetry. Toward the end of Guðrún's monologue there is an abrupt change of scene, which indicates a lacuna in the poem. Guðrún is awakened in her bed by Atli and is "full of bitterness / over the death of her kinsmen." It must therefore be assumed that the murder of her brothers Gunnar and Högni has already been accomplished. Atli gives an account of weird dreams which evidently forebode terrible misfortunes in his house. But Guðrún cunningly conceals her plans and gives her husband's dreams a trivial interpretation.

Guðrúnarkviða III, only ten stanzas in fornyrðislag, deals with an episode outside the main story. One of Atli's serving women, his earlier mistress Herkja, has accused Guðrún of adulterous relations with King Þjóðrekur—that is the famous Dietrich of Bern, in history the Gothic king Theodoric—who is a guest at Atli's house. Guðrún denies all guilt and herself suggests a kind of divine judgment in the matter. She thrusts her white arm into a kettle of boiling water and picks up some precious stones from the bottom quite unharmed. Atli is relieved and orders Herkja to submit to the same test:

Sáat maðr armligt,	Ne'er saw man sight
hverr's sáat þat,	more sad than this,
hvé þar á Herkju	how burned were the hands
hendr sviðnuðu;	of Herkja then;
leiddu þá mey	in a bog so foul
í mýri fúla;	the maid they flung,
svafði Guðrún	and so was Guthrun's
sína harma.	grief requited.

The following poem, *Oddrúnargrátr,* is connected even more loosely to the main thread of the story. It is conceivable that it was inserted here because of its erotic motif, which has something in common with the lay of Guðrún's alleged infidelity. With Oddrún, Atli's sister, a new person is introduced into the drama. She visits King Heiðrek's daughter Borgný, who is suffering great difficulties in childbirth. With "biting galdrar" she succeeds in relieving some of the childbearing woman's suffering, and assists at the birth of a boy and a girl. As Borgný's lover and the father of her children an otherwise unknown man Vilmundur is mentioned, who is here described as the slayer of Högni: thus it would seem that he may have been a member of Atli's court. But this situation merely serves as a background to a long monologue by Oddrún about her own unhappy love affair. It became her fate to love Gunnar, as her sister, the valkyrie Brynhildur, should have done but could not. Gunnar offered Atli great fortunes for the hand of Oddrún, but he refused to permit the marriage. Then nothing remained for them but forbidden love—"We had not strength / to resist our desire, / I bent my head / to the chieftain's breast"—and Oddrún bears witness from personal experiences about love as fate and a force of nature:

En mik Atli kvað	Atli said
eigi mundu	that never I
lýti ráða	would evil plan,
né löst gera,	or ill deed do;
en slíks skyli	but none may this
synja aldri	of another think,
maðr fyr annan,	or surely speak,
þars munúð deilir.	when love is shared.

They are discovered and Atli is told. Then Oddrún recalls how the two brothers, Gunnar and Högni, came to visit and how they were murdered; she herself did not succeed in saving her lover from the viper pit. All her *grátr*, "weeping"—a word that could rather be interpreted as "elegy" in this case—ends with several melancholy reflections about her own fate and about the conditions of human life in general:

Opt undrumk þat,	Oft have I wondered
hví eptir mák	how after this,
linnvengis Bil,	serpent's-bed goddess
lífi halda,	I still might live,
es ógnhvötum	for well I loved
unna þóttumk	the warrior brave,
sverða deili	the giver of swords,
sem sjalfri mér.	as my very self.

Satt ok hlýddir	Thou didst see and listen,
meðan sagðak þér	the while I said

mörg ill of sköp	the mighty grief
mín ok þeira;	that was mine and theirs;
maðr hverr lifir	each man lives
at munum sínum;	as his longing wills,—
nú er of genginn	Oddrun's lament
grátr Oddrúnar.	is ended now.

Immediately following *Oddrúnargrátr*, with its tender strains, there follows in Codex Regius as a glaring contrast *Atlakviða*, which, in its archaic wildness and unbridled heroism, is one of the absolute highlights of heroic poetry. Atli sends a messenger to his brothers-in-law Gunnar and Högni with an invitation to his court, evidently to lure them into ambush and to gain possession of the immense gold treasure they have taken from Sigurður. At the same time their sister Guðrún has sent them a sign of warning— a ring with wolf hair twined around it—but they proudly defy the danger. Atli gets them into his power. Gunnar is asked if he wants to ransom his life with gold. Not, he replies, until he holds in his hand Högni's bleeding heart, cut from his living breast with a sword. They cut the heart out of a slave called Hjalli and carry it to Gunnar on a tray. He easily sees through the deception. That cannot be the heart of brave Högni: "it trembles much / there on the tray / it trembled doubly / when it lay in his breast." Then they seize Högni; he laughs when his heart is cut out. And now his brother accepts the proof they present. This is really brave Högni's heart: "it trembles little / there on the tray / it did not tremble more / when it lay in his breast." Triumphantly Gunnar declares that the golden treasure has been sunk in the Rhine, and that after Högni's death no one but he himself any longer knows the place of concealment.

Rín skal ráða	The swift Rhine shall hold
rógmalmi skatna	the strife-gold of heroes,
svinn áskunnum	That once was the gods',

arfi Niflunga,	the wealth of the Niflungs,
í veltanda vatni	in the depths of the waters
lýsask valbaugar,	the death-rings shall glitter,
heldr en á höndum goll	and not shine on the hands
skíni Húna börnum.	of the Hunnish men.

Gunnar is thrown into a snake pit, where he plays a harp as long as his strength lasts. But Guðrún exacts horrible vengeance for her brothers. At Atli's victory banquet she serves her husband a meat dish, and only afterwards reveals what it consists of:

Sona hefr þinna,	Thou giver of swords,
sverða deilir,	of thy sons the hearts
hjörtu hrædreyrug	all heavy with blood
við hunang of tuggin,	in honey thou hast eaten;
melta knátt móðugr,	thou shalt stomach, thou hero,
manna valbráðir	the flesh of the slain,
eta at ölkrásum	to eat at thy feast,
ok í öndugi at senda.	and to send to thy followers.

It is a barbaric scene, reminiscent of a similar settlement between the brothers Atreus and Thyestes in the ancient Greek legend. It even seems as though Guðrún may have told about her deed in even more brutal words than was generally believed and the translation of the cited stanza shows, for one scholar has adduced evidence that the last line, whose meaning has been much discussed, probably means that the food passes its natural way out of the body.[8] With unparalleled cynicism then Guðrún is said to have described to Atli his horrible experience right to his face and with disgustingly bold digestive terms. There is a great gulf fixed between this female furie and the young widow who, in *Guðrúnarkviða I,* sat bowed in mute grief over Sigurð's body. This vast difference also provides a measure for the wide range of emotions expressed in heroic poetry.

87

The tragedy culminates in Guðrún's final act of vengeance when, during the night, she burns her drunken husband and all his followers to death in his castle.

In Codex Regius there is a note in prose attached to *Atlakviða*: "This is told in greater detail in the Greenlandic *Atlamál*." Then there follows this more detailed poem, *Atlamál hin grænlenzku*. Here, then, we are afforded a unique opportunity to study the same Eddic motif in two different versions. The attribute "the Greenlandic" is also given for *Atlakviða* in the collection, but that is generally considered to be due to an error, a slip of the pen. On the other hand, scholars are scarcely in complete agreement as to what the epithet really means as far as *Atlamál* is concerned. For Finnur Jónsson, for example, the matter is quite clear: "That this poem is correctly called Greenlandic is beyond the shadow of a doubt; the entire milieu which it reveals leads definitely in that direction."[9] One can also point to such a striking detail as the fact that Högni's wife dreams about a polar bear. But when the question of the possible Greenlandic origin of *Atlamál* is discussed, more weight is usually placed upon the general character of the poem, somewhat as Björn Collinder did in this formulation of his opinion: the poem "may very well have been written by a Greenlandic farmer who wished to improve on the Atli poem by relating in greater detail precisely what happened."[10]

Not only does *Atlamál* have over twice as many stanzas as *Atlakviða* (105 versus 46); it is the only Eddic poem that employs the fuller meter málaháttr, with more syllables per line than fornyrðislag. With its greater epic breadth it can create the impression of being plebian and wordy in comparison with the tight concentration and laconic character of *Atlakviða*. The difference is further underscored by the fact that the diction of *Atlamál* is often strikingly prosaic. It is just as though the heroic poem had sunk both socially and esthetically to a more common, everyday level. In

Atlakviða Guðrún's horrible revelation about her and Atli's sons evokes wild grief in the castle of the Huns. There is no response from Atli; he has spoken his last word in the poem. In *Atlamál*, however, he is made to make a comment on the message that includes the following words:

| snýtt hefr þú sifjungum, | Thou hast slain thine own kin, |
| sem þú sizt skyldir. | most ill it beseemed thee, |

an understatement that can scarcely avoid making a somewhat comical impression on the modern reader. When Atli lies mortally wounded, a quarrel ensues between husband and wife that degenerates into something resembling vainglorious and faultfinding autobiographies. At the end Atli admonishes his wife at least to provide an honorable funeral for him.

The whole point of the episode in which Gunnar demands that his brother Högni's bloody heart be put in his hand—this climax of inhuman heroism—is completely lost in *Atlamál*. Here the author instead concentrates on the thrall Hjalli and has him appear in a scene of macabre comedy. Howling with terror, the "guardian of the kettle" scurries about trying to escape the knife until Högni, disgusted with his shrieking, or perhaps out of pure sympathy, offers to take the slave's place:

Fyr kveðk mér minna	I would find it far better
at fremja leik þenna,	this knife-play to feel,
hví mynim hér vilja	why must we all hark
heyra á þá skræktun?	to this howling longer?

Guðrúnarhvöt and *Hamðismál*, which comprise the epilogue to the heroic poetry of the *Edda*, are closely related to each other. The prose introduction of the former relates that after Atli's death Guðrún goes down to the sea to drown herself. She cannot sink, however, but floats to the other shore of the fjord to King Jónakur's country. He

89

marries her, and they have three sons, Erpur, Sörli, and
Hamðir. Here Svanhildur, Guðrún's daughter with Sigurður, also is reared. Svanhildur is married to Jörmunrekkur the Mighty. "In his house was Bikki; he gave the
advice that the king's son Randvér should take her. Bikki
told the king. The king had Randvér hanged, but ordered
Svanhildur to be trampled to death under horses' hooves."

The poem itself begins with Guðrún's incitement *(hvöt)*
to her sons to take vengeance for their sister's shameful
death. They ask her to bring helmets and coats of mail
for them. Mounted on his horse and ready to leave, Hamðir
declares that their mother will drink the arvel (funeral
feast) for all of them: "one dead-draught thou / for us all
shalt drink; / For Svanhild then / and thy sons as well."
Then Guðrún begins to weep and sits down to relate the
misfortunes of her life. Quite naturally in this situation,
she dwells on her fair-haired daughter, Svanhildur, a ray
of sunlight in her hall. But at last her thoughts return to
the man she loved most of all in her life—"Matchless among
men / to me was Sigurður." She seems to imagine that
now after many years he will return from Hel, once more
to be laid on the funeral pyre, this time with her:

Hlaðit ér jarlar	Pile ye up, jarls,
eikiköstu,	the pyre of oak,
látið þann und hilmi	make it the highest
hæstan verða,	a hero e'er had;
megi brenna brjóst	let the fire burn
bölvafullt eldr,	my grief-filled breast,
þrungit of hjarta	my sore-pressed heart,
þiðni sorgir.	till my sorrows melt.

The "incitement" is gradually resolved into a soft,
elegiac chord. Thus the poem reflects both the heroically
harsh features and the tender womanly traits of Guðrún.

There is an elegiac mood in the introduction to *Ham-*

90

ðismál, too, in which Guðrún urges her sons to take revenge for Svanhildur and laments that her clan is dying out:

Einstœð emk orðin	Lonely am I
sem ösp í holti,	as the forest aspen,
fallin at frændum	of kindred bare
sem fura at kvisti,	as the fir of its boughs,
vaðin at vilja	my joys are all lost
sem viðr at laufi,	as the leaves of the tree
þás hin kvistskœða	when the scather of twigs
kemr of dag varman.	on a warm day strikes.

But otherwise this lay is completely dominated by the heroic ideal, by the wreaking of vengeance and the fall of the avengers. In the concluding line the poem is named "the ancient *Hamðismál,*" and it really does create the impression of archaic wildness with its abrupt transitions in the action and its grim laconic utterances. Howling with fury, Hamðir and Sörli ride out on their quest for revenge over "the misty mountain." On their way they meet their half brother Erpur. After a quick exchange of words they stab him to death, and the reader cannot see why. Later on they pass by their sister's stepson and lover, hanging on the gallows, "windchilled wolftree / west of the castle." In the final settlement in Jörmunrekk's castle the brothers prove to be invulnerable to spears and cutting weapons, and the king roars to his men through the din of arms to stone them instead. Evidently an unguarded word from Hamðir has revealed to Jörmunrekkur the secret of their invulnerability, for Sörli reproaches his brother for being too talkative. He also regrets the slaughter of Erpur, the battlehardened warrior, whom he would gladly have at his side; the *dísir* goaded them to perform that rash deed. But Sörli's last words reveal no remorse, lamentation, or fear; they testify only to his joy in battle, pride in honor, and unflinching courage in the face of death:

91

Vel höfum vegit,	We have greatly fought,
stöndum á val Gotna	o'er the Goths do we stand
ofan eggmóðum	by our blades laid low,
sem ernir á kvisti,	like eagles on branches;
góðs fingum tírar	great our fame though we die
þótt nú eða í gær deyim,	today or tomorrow;
kveld lifir ekki	none outlives the night
maðr ept kvið norna.	when the Norns have spoken.

In its stark objectivity the final vignette of the poem stands as though chiseled in stone:

Þar fell Sörli	Then Sorli beside
at salar gafli,	the gable sank,
en Hamðir hné	and Hamther fell
at huúsbaki.	at the back of the house.

Echoes of Continental Germanic history in heroic poetry: The Nibelungenlied. It has already been mentioned that certain historical figures can be recognized behind some of the characters in the heroic poetry of the *Edda*. Sigurður Fáfnisbani is altogether legendary as far as we know. But the Gjúkungs have been associated with the Burgundians, a Germanic tribe that had a kingdom on the Rhine at the beginning of the fifth century. The name of their king, in its Latinized form, is *Gundicarius*. According to an old source his kingdom was destroyed and he himself killed by the Huns in 437; Attila the Hun came to be connected with this event. Other royal names are found in a Burgundian legal codex from the beginning of the sixth century, after the remaining Burgundians had settled elsewhere. These laws, namely, contain a regulation that every man shall be free who can prove that his ancestors were free under the kings *Gibica, Godomarus, Gislaharius* and *Gundaharius*. Of these names *Gibica* is in German *Gibich* and in Old Norse *Gjúki*, while *Gundaharius* corresponds to *Gunther* and *Gunnar*, respectively. And in Eddic poetry *Gutþormur* could possibly be a reflection of *Godomarus*.

According to Jordanes, the Hunnish king Attila died in 453, and a Latin source from the beginning of the sixth century relates that he was killed by a woman. A later historian supplements this information with the statement that the woman was a Germanic princess whose father had been slain by Attila.

These scattered names and data obviously show striking similarities to the story of the Gjúkungs in the *Edda*. Guðrún slays Atli in revenge—not for a father, to be sure, but for two brothers. One brother is called Gunnar, like the Burgundian prince slain by the Huns. According to the sources, sixteen years elapsed between the fall of Gundicarius in 437 and Attila's death in 453. In *Atlakviða* the two corresponding events are made to take place on the same day in order to achieve artistic concentration and dramatic suspense.

The last two poems in Codex Regius, *Guðrúnarhvöt* and *Hamðismál*, are believed to contain the very oldest traditions in Germanic heroic poetry and to reflect memories from the beginning of the Great Migration. In his Gothic history, written about the middle of the sixth century, Jordanes tells of a king named Hermanaricus, who had ordered that a woman named Sunilda should be tied to wild horses and torn to pieces because her husband had betrayed the king. But she was avenged by her two brothers, Sarus and Ammius, who slew Hermanaricus with a sword. Not only the constellation of characters and events but also the names themselves are clearly recognizable in the Eddic poems: *Hermanaricus—Jörmunrekkur; Sunilda—Svanhildur*; less transparently in *Sarus—Sörli* and *Ammius—Hamðir*. Furthermore, the course of events in the work of Jordanes may possibly be more legend than history; it has therefore been suggested that Jordanes may have used a Gothic heroic poem as a source. Besides, there are traditions about Jörmunrekkur elsewhere in English and German literature among other places. Thus the *Quedlingburg*

Chronicle from about the year 1000 states that the Gothic king *Ermanricus* was slain by *Hemidus, Serila,* and *Addacarus* as revenge because he had had their father killed; the first two names of the three brothers clearly correspond to *Hamðir* and *Sörli*. And Ermanaric was also known to the English poets who composed *Beowulf, Deor's Lament,* and *Widsith.*

Of course it would be interesting enough in itself to see how the motifs of the heroic lays of the *Edda* have been developed in other literary sources. The first to come to mind is the German epic, the *Nibelungenlied,* which is known with reasonable certainty to have been written in Austria between 1200 and 1205, and has been preserved, completely or in part, in more than thirty manuscripts. In this great work of almost 2,400 stanzas, each consisting of four long lines divided into two parts, the events take place essentially as they do in the *Edda*. The hero, Siegfried, is married to the Burgundian princess Kriemhilde; in the *Edda* that is the name of Guðrún's mother, Grímhildur. He conquers the valkyrie Brünhilde for his brother-in-law Gunther, and is then slain, primarily at the instigation of Brünhilde and the malevolent Hagen—Högni in the Eddic lays. Siegfried's widow, Kriemhilde, is eventually married to King Etzel—alias Atli. Unlike Atli, however, Etzel invites the Burgundians to his court with quite friendly intentions, as a favor to his wife. In the *Nibelungenlied* it is Kriemhilde herself who demands horrible vengeance on her own brothers and Hagen.

The German poem is enormously extensive in comparison with the *Edda,* and this, of course, means a wealth of episodes and details that have no correspondence in the laconic poetry of the *Edda*. It willingly makes concessions to chivalric poetry's taste for brilliant sceneries, festivities, and tournaments with an abundance of beautiful women, knights, pages, and minstrels. Heathen Germanic heroic poetry has thus been transposed into the world of medieval chivalry. The Burgundians go to Mass as good Catholics, and even at King Etzel's Hunnish court it is found offensive that they attend divine services armed and in armor. On the other hand, the poet of the *Nibelungenlied* sometimes reveals a rather plebeian penchant for the comic and burlesque. Unlike Brynhildur in the Eddic lays, Brünhilde is not to be won by a hero who defies the magic fire around her castle, but by a man who defeats her in martial contests. With a scornful smile the muscular Amazon rolls up her sleeves before warriors with a foreboding of evil and prepares to cast the spear that three ordinary men can scarcely lift. During the nuptial night this powerful bride ties up her husband with a belt and simply hangs him on a hook in the wall. There is undeniably more of harsh earnestness, more chilling tragedy in the version of the fateful drama as it is portrayed in the *Edda*.

But to map the ramifications and variations of Germanic heroic legend in greater detail is a task which belongs to the study of legend and folklore rather than to literary history.

Other heroic poetry in Eddic style: Darraðarljód, Hlöðskviða, Hjálmár's Death-Song, Bjarkamál hin fornu. A remarkable poem in Eddic style, preserved outside the Codex Regius, is *Darraðarljóð*. It is found in manuscripts of *Njáls saga* and is connected with the battle of Clontarf near Dublin, which was fought on Good Friday, 1014, between the Irish king Brian and a Norse viking army. Old Brian fell, but his army was victorious. *Njáls saga*, which describes the battle, also relates several omens in connection with it. At Caithness on the morning of Good Friday a certain man sees twelve female figures ride up to a stone hut and disappear inside. Through a chink in the wall he sees them set up a loom of a frightening kind. Woof and warp are human intestines. Instead of stone weights to stretch the web they

95

use human heads. The rods are arrows and a sword serves as a weaver's reed. As they work, the women chant a song, ten and a half stanzas in fornyrðislag. Then, according to the saga, they tear up the web and each keeps a piece of it. Then they mount their horses again and ride away, six to the north, six to the south.

The weaving and singing women are valkyries, and their occupation is a symbolic accompaniment to the battle that is going on; the song contains hints of what is happening. "Vindum, vindum, / vef darraðar," is how three of the stanzas begin. There is an old word *darraðr*, meaning "spear"; *vefr darraðar* "the spear's web," then would be a kenning for battle. But the word *darraðar* has also been explained as the genitive of a name *Dörruðr* for Óðinn, which is supposed to occur in the title of the poem *Darraðarljóð*, although it is otherwise completely unknown. But even if the word is interpreted in this way, the meaning of *vefr darraðar* would be much the same, for "Óðin's web" would also be a fitting kenning for battle. The quoted lines thus mean: "We weave, we weave / the web of the spear-god." This would also agree very well with the idea that the valkyries are the battle god Óðin's companions who intervene in the train of events on the battlefield at his command.

In one respect *Darraðarljóð* resembles skaldic poetry: its theme is a real contemporary event. But on the other hand, the form is characteristic of Eddic poetry. And the song is anonymous, or rather, it is ascribed to mythic beings. We recall the grinding slave women in *Gróttasöngr*, who also sing while performing their heavy work. The weaving valkyries make the impression of Norns, shaping the fates of the combatants at their terrible loom. The poem is informed with enchanting magic, with visionary fantasy in which external nature, the bloody battle, and the song of the valkyries are interwoven into a suggestive whole:

Nú er ógurligt	Now awful is it
um at litask,	to be without,
er dreyrug ský	as blood-red rack
dregr með himni;	races overhead;
mun lopt litat	is the welkin gory
lýða blóði,	with warriors' blood
er sóknvarðar	as we valkyries
syngja kunnu.	war-songs chanted.

Now it is dreadful to look about as bloody clouds move across the sky. The air is colored with human blood when the battle women (= the valkyries) sing.

A poem which was not included in the collection of Eddic poems but which, like *Atlakviða* and *Hamðismál*, has been assigned to an especially archaic layer of Norse heroic poetry, is *Hlöðskviða*. It received its name fairly recently—after one of its chief characters. It is preserved in manuscripts of an Icelandic *fornaldarsaga* from the thirteenth century, *Heiðreks saga* or *Hervarar saga*.

Fornaldarsögur are sagas whose action, as opposed to the classical *Íslendingasögur*, "Sagas of Icelanders," takes place before the Norse settlement of Iceland. They frequently contain fantastic and supernatural features.

The background of *Hlöðskviða* is the death of the Gothic king Heiðrekur at the hands of his thralls. His son Angantýr slays all the perpetrators of the crime and then holds a funeral feast in memory of his father. Angantýr's half brother Hlöður, who is Heiðrek's illegitimate son, hears about this. Heiðrekur had gone south one summer, defeated the Hunnish king Humli in battle, and abducted his daughter Sifka. The following summer he sent her back home. She was then pregnant and gave birth to a son, who grew up at his grandfather's Humli's court. At the beginning of the poem Hlöður appears at Angantýr's court and demands half of the paternal inheritance. Angantýr is willing to share his property and treasures generously, but he is not willing to cut in half the unique sword Tyrfingur, as he says:

Bresta mun fyrr, bróðir,	Your shining shield
in blikhvíta lind	will be shattered, brother
ok kaldr geirr	and by cold spears will be
koma við annan	split many another,
ok fargr gumi	and many a man
í gras hníga	will meet his death
áðr en Tyrfing	before Tyrfing
í tvau deilak	in two I sunder,
eða þér, Humlungr,	or to thee, son of Humli,
hálfan arf gefa.	leave the half of it!

Hlöður is even more deeply affronted by a man in Angantýr's bodyguard who calls him the son of a slave woman, and he returns home enraged. He and his grandfather gather a huge Hunnish army and turn north to attack the Goths. But under Angantýr's leadership the Goths gain the victory and both Hlöður and Humli are slain. After the battle Angantýr inspects the field. He finds his dead brother and utters the following words, which comprise the end of the poem:

Bauð ek þér, bróðir,	Untold arm-rings
basmir óskerðar,	I offered thee, brother,
fé ok fjölð meiðma,	a wealth of gold
sem þik fremst tíddi;	and what most thou didst wish.
nú hefir þú hvárki	As guerdon for strife
hildar at gjöldum	now hast gotten neither,
ljósa bauga	nor lands nor lieges
né land ekki.	nor lustrous rings.
Bölvat er okkr, bróðir,	A baleful fate wrought it
bani em ek þinn orðinn;	that, brother, I slew thee!
þat mun æ uppi,	Will that aye be told.
illr er dómr norna.	Ill's the norns' doom.

This lay has aroused great interest among scholars, primarily perhaps because it is believed that it reflects historic events from the time of the Great Migration. In this the interpretation of a number of place names has played an important role. *Harvaðafjöll*, for instance, has been equated with the Carpathians, the first part of *Danparstaðir* with the Gothic name of the river Dnieper, etc. It is striking that several central characters in *Hlöðskviða*—Heiðrekur, Sifka (whose name does not occur in the preserved stanzas, however), Hlöður, and Angantýr—seem to have a direct correspondence in the very ancient Old English lay *Widsith* (see p. 14, above); in this poem the singer mentions "Heaþoric and Sifecan, Hliþe and Incgenþeow" among the many sovereigns he has visited. It is evident that *Hlöðskviða* retains vague memories of battles between Goths and Huns; but to try beyond that to extract more definite historical associations is probably futile.[11] Poetically it can hardly bear comparison with *Atlakviða*, which is considered by some scholars to reveal influence from *Hlöðskviða*.[12]

In *Heiðreks saga*, and in somewhat more complete form in *Örvar-Odds saga*, there is included another poem in fornyrðislag, ascribed to the Swedish hero Hjálmar inn hugumstóri (the great-hearted). He has won Ingibjörg's love; she is the daughter of the Swedish king in Uppsala. Hjálmar is challenged to a duel *(hólmganga)* by his rival Angantýr. To be sure, he slays his opponent, who is the eldest of twelve brothers, all berserkers and impressive warriors, but he is mortally wounded himself by Angantýr's sword Tyrfingur, forged by dwarfs:

Sár hefi ek sextán	Wounds have I sixteen,
slitna brynju,	is slit my byrnie,
svart er mér fyrir sjónum,	dim grows my sight,
séka ek ganga;	I see no longer;
hneit mér við hjarta	to my heart did hew,
hjörr Angantýs,	venom-hardened,
hvass blóðrefill	Angantýr's sword
herðr í eitri.	slashing sharply.

I have sixteen wounds, a slashed mail-coat; it is black before my eyes; I cannot see to walk. Angantýr's sword pierced my heart, the keen sword-point, tempered in poison.

The dying Hjálmar asks his brother-in-arms Örvar-Oddur to carry his last greeting to his beloved:

Drag þú mér af hendi	The red-gold ring
hring inn rauða,	from my right arm draw,
fœrðu inni ungu	to Ingibiorg bring it,
Ingibjörgu;	in her bower sitting.
sá mun henni	Will yearn for me
hugfastr tregi,	the young maiden,
er ek eigi kǿm	since not e'er after
til Uppsala.	each other we'll see.

Draw the red ring from my arm; take it to young Ingibjörg. Grief will afflict her heart when I do not come to Uppsala.

This swan song ends with a gloomy allusion to the vultures that approach the field of battle:

Hrafn flýgr austan	Flies from the South
af hám meiði,	the famished raven,
flýgr honum eptir	flieth with him
örn í sinni;	the fallow eagle;
þeim gef ek erni	on the flesh of the fallen
efstum bráðir,	I shall feed them no more:
sá mun á blóði	on my body both
berja mínu.	will batten now.

A raven flies from the east from a high tree; an eagle flies after it as a companion. This is the last eagle to which I give corpses; it will gulp my blood.

Örvar-Oddur brings the ring to Ingibjörg, who then takes her own life or, according to *Örvar-Odds saga*, collapses dead in her chair. Hjálmar's death song with its resigned lamentation makes a gentler impression than most of the heroic poetry in the *Edda*. It is usually considered to be comparatively late, about as Jón Helgason interprets it: "Eddic poetry dies away on this soft elegiac tone. The age of the ancient heroic poetry has long since passed, and the more sentimental tones of the popular ballad draw near."[13]

The heroic poetry in Codex Regius has practically all its roots in Central European tradition. In conclusion let us look at an old heroic lay which is not recorded in the *Edda*, but which indubitably is of Norse origin. In his *Ólafs saga helga*, Snorri Sturluson relates that during the night before the battle of Stiklastaðir King Ólafur naps briefly and fitfully, surrounded by his men. He wakes up just as the sun is rising, calls for his Icelandic poet Þormóður, and asks him to recite something for them.

> Þormóður sat up and chanted very loudly, so that it could be heard by the whole army. He recited *Bjarkamál hin fornu*, and it begins like this:

Dagr er upp kominn,	The day has come,
dynja hana fjaðrar.	claps the cock his wings:
Má er vílmögum	'tis time for thralls
at vinna erfiði.	to go to their tasks.
Vaki æ ok vaki	Awake, ye friends,
vina höfuð	be aye awake,
allir enir œztu	all ye best men
Aðils of sinnar.	of Athil's board.
Hár enn harðgreipi,	Hár the hard-gripping,
Hrólfr skjótandi,	Hrólf the bowman,
ættum góðir menn,	men of noble race
þeir's ekki flýja,	who never flee;
vekka yðr at víni	I wake you not to wine
né at vífs rúnum,	nor to women's converse,
heldr vek ek yðr	but rather
at hörðum	to the hard
Hildar leiki.	game of Hild.

Then the men awoke. When the poem was finished, they thanked him for his recital. They liked it very much and thought it very fitting and called the poem *Húskarlahvöt* ("The Inciting of the King's Men").

In his *Edda,* Snorri reproduces three more stanzas from the same poem, but only as examples of various poetic designations for gold. The few glimpses here and in *Ólafs saga helga* do not give any idea of *Bjarkamál hin fornu* as a whole. Its content, however, is preserved in Saxo's great Danish history, written in Latin about the year 1200. Now and then Saxo has his heroes speak in metric language, and in those cases he has probably almost without exception followed Old Norse poetry. In the preface to his history the author mentions specifically that he received much of the material for his book from Icelanders. Concerning his own version of *Bjarkamál* in 298 hexameters, the longest poem in the whole work, he comments that the poem is found in a shorter version in the Norse tongue; in that form it is well known to many men of knowledge. The opinion is widely held that Saxo's knowledge of *Bjarkamál,* too, stems from Icelandic sources.

Saxo's poem in hexameters is inserted into the conclusion of the story of Hrólfur kraki. An enemy army attacks King Hrólfur at night and kills him and all of his followers. Two warriors, Hjalti and Bjarki, are the main characters on Hrólfur kraki's side. They are contrasts in character and disposition. Hjalti is impatient and impetuous; Bjarki is calmer and more experienced. The poem is ascribed to the two of them; they speak alternately to spur on the combatants, to rebuke each other, to describe the course of the battle, to call to mind past events, and to praise King Hrólfur. Finally they are the only ones left of the king's men and they fall by their lord's dead body, Hjalti at his feet, Bjarki at his head.

Through its penchant for ostentatious rhetoric and

abundant variations Saxo's hexameter is, of course, quite different from the more Spartan fornyrðislag of the original poem. As for the content itself, Saxo may well have misunderstood some details and he may have added several out of his own head. Thus in a manner that is characteristic of him he has added color to the beginning of the poem, which otherwise agrees very well with the two preserved stanzas in *Ólafs saga helga*. The brief hint at "fondling maidens" *(at vífs rúnum)*, for instance, has been embroidered by Saxo with a series of sensual details. But otherwise the original tone and object of the old lay has probably been preserved in its Latin version. It is an admonition to the sovereign to be generous to his courtiers, generous with gold and favors, but above all it is an exhortation to his warriors to fight to the death for their lord. No fate can be more enviable for a warrior than to fall by his king's side. Saxo himself talks about his poem as *exhortationum series* (a series of incitements). This agrees splendidly with the name *Húskarlahvöt* in *Ólafs saga helga*. Þormóður Kolbrúnarskáld clearly chooses to chant *Bjarkamál hin fornu* not just as a form of entertainment, but as a forceful exhortation to all the king's men—"it can be heard by the whole army"—to be ready now in the crucial battle to give their ruler the ultimate proof of their fidelity.

If Snorri's description can be considered correct, it is an interesting example of the fact that old pagan heroic poetry could serve a purpose not only as inherited legend and poetic art, but also as inspiration even for Christian warriors.

Notes

1. In an article "Har nordmenn skrevet opp Edda-diktningen," *Maal og Minne* 43 (1951): 3–33, D. A. Seip sought to demonstrate that the Icelandic Codex Regius exhibits so many Norwegian traits in its language that it must be derived from a

Norwegian prototype. This bold hypothesis, however, has not found wide acceptance among Eddic scholars.

2. For a brief critical review of scholarly efforts to date some of the Eddic lays, see Bjarne Ulvestad, "How Old Are the Mythological Eddic Poems?" *Scandinavian Studies* 26 (1954): 49–69.

3. The quotation is from Nordal's *Völuspá*, 2d ed. (Reykjavík, 1952), p. 152.

4. On this see Klaus von See, *Die Gestalt der Hávamál: Eine Studie zur eddischen Spruchdichtung* (Frankfurt/Main: Athenäum Verlag, 1972), and "Disticha Catonis und Hávamál," *Beiträge zur Geschichte der deutschen Sprache und Literatur* 94 (1972): 1–18.

5. For a recent reinterpretation of this rite see Jere Fleck. "Óðinn's Self-Sacrifice—A New Interpretation. I. The Ritual Inversion. II. The Ritual Landscape," *Scandinavian Studies* 43 (1971): 119–42, and 385–413.

6. The hypothesis that Snorri himself composed *Þrymskviða* was developed by P. Hallberg in the article "Om Þrymskviða," *Arkiv för nordisk filologi* 69 (1954): 51–77.

7. On this see Bertha S. Phillpotts, *The Elder Edda and Ancient Scandinavian Drama* (Cambridge, 1920), pp. 38ff.

8. T. Johannisson, "Ett eddaställe och ett ortnamn," *Festskrift till Elias Wessén* (Lund, 1954), pp. 120–32.

9. Finnur Jónsson, *De gamle Eddadigte* (Copenhagen, 1932), p. 314.

10. Björn Collinder, *Den poetiska Eddan* (Stockholm, 1957), pp. 28f. For a detailed and perceptive discussion of *Atlamál* and its relationship to *Atlakviða*, see D. O. Zetterholm, *Atlamál: Studier i Eddadikts stil och meter* (Stockholm, 1934).

11. The futility of such attempts is emphasized by Christopher Tolkien in his critical review of the century-old discussion in "The Battle of the Goths and the Huns," *Saga-Book of the Viking Society* 14 (1955–56) : 141–63.

12. On the influence of *Hlöðskviða* on *Atlakviða*, see Einar Ól. Sveinsson, *Íslenzkar bókmenntir í fornöld,* vol. 1, (Reykjavík, 1962), p. 410.

13. Jón Helgason *Norges og Islands digtning* (Stockholm, Oslo and Copenhagen, 1953), p. 89.

CHAPTER 4

Skaldic Verse

General Observations

THE EPISODE IN WHICH Þormóður Kolbrúnarskáld in a
loud voice chants the *Bjarkarmál hin fornu* in order to
exhort the royal army to perform great deeds in the battle
of Stiklastaðir in the year 1030 shows the court poet at
work. But in connection with this same historic event
Snorri provides us with still another informative insight
into the activities of the skalds. He relates that before the
battle King Ólafur ordered the three court skalds who
were present to enter the phalanx of shields: "You shall
stay here," he said, "and see what happens. Then you will
not have to rely on the accounts of others, but can your-
selves report and compose poems about the battle afterwards."

Here one of the most essential functions of skaldic
poetry is mentioned. Certain skalds held a position that
could almost be considered official, as chroniclers and court
poets whose principal task it was to sing the praise of the
ruler and his deeds. As is evident from the prologue to his
Heimskringla, Snorri was well aware of how valuable the
poetic products of court skalds were as historical documents.
He declares that he believes what is told about the journeys and battles of rulers in such poems as are recited in
the presence of the rulers themselves or of their sons. It
is true, of course, that poets usually express themselves
exuberantly about the prince in whose service or presence
they are at the moment, but no one would dare praise him

105

for exploits and merits which both he and others among the audience knew were pure, unadulterated lies: "That would be scorn and not praise."

A large portion of the skaldic poetry that we know today has been preserved exclusively in the form of corroborating quotations in Snorri's sagas of Norwegian kings, beginning with the poem *Ynglingatal*, with its roots in annalistic legendary obscurity, down to contemporary commentaries in verse from the twelfth century. It should perhaps be noted that the poetry that is quoted would often be very hard to identify without Snorri's prose frame. Sometimes such details as names of persons and places may help to locate the poem in place and time. But this poetry frequently presents strongly conventionalized and typical descriptions of sea battles and similar things that could have occurred anywhere at sea. Nor is the identification of the participants made easier through the frequent paraphrasing of their names by means of various heiti and kennings for kings, earls, warriors, etc.[1]

As is well known, the technique of interfoliating and verifying prose descriptions with skaldic stanzas is often employed in Icelandic family sagas, too—above all, for obvious reasons, in those that have a poet as the central figure: Egill Skalla-Grímsson, Gunnlaugur ormstunga, and others. It is a difficult and often insoluble problem for scholars to decide which of these inserted stanzas—often described as improvised on the spur of the moment—ought to be considered "genuine" and which "false." Did, for instance, the historic tenth-century poet Egill Skalla-Grímsson actually recite all those *lausavísur*, "loose *or* occasional stanzas," that the saga ascribes to him, from the age of three and into late old age, or are they at least sometimes poetic contributions from tradition or creations of the saga author himself?

Snorri's *Edda* is just as important as *Heimskringla* for our knowledge of skaldic poetry. But in his treatise on poetics the verses are quoted not primarily to confirm an event but to illustrate the manifold means of expression and artistic techniques that the poets had at their command.

The First Court Poets in Norway

The genesis and earliest history of skaldic poetry are veiled in obscurity. Several hypotheses on the subject have already been mentioned in connection with the discussion of kennings. (Cf. pp. 21 ff., above). The art of the skalds had representatives in Norway very early and probably in Sweden, too—if such conclusions may be drawn from some sparse traces of dróttkvætt: one stanza cut in the Karlevi stone (Öland), two lines on a copper case from Sigtuna. Otherwise all material comes from the west Norse area.

The first skald who is mentioned by name is Bragi Boddason, "the Old," who, according to tradition, is said to have lived in the ninth century. Snorri in his *Edda* quotes several groups of stanzas from his *drápa* about Ragnar loðbrók. A drápa can be characterized as a poem of praise with a refrain; without a refrain it was called a *flokkr* and was not considered to be quite so distinguished. Even here in the poetry of Bragi the characteristic dróttkvætt style is fully formed. But whether one should regard this as a result of a long development whose earlier stages can no longer be discerned, or—as Hallvard Lie did (cf. pp. 24 ff., above)—whether one should regard it as an ingenious new creation by Bragi, is and will probably remain a moot question.

As already stated, *Ragnarsdrápa* describes the mythologic decorations on a shield which the skald has received as a gift. In the stanzas that have been preserved one can discern four different motifs, probably corresponding to as many picture sections on the shield. One of these we have already met in the Eddic poem *Hymiskviða*: while catching fish in the giant's boat, Þór almost hauls the Miðgarður

serpent out of the depths of the sea. (Cf. p. 52, above.)
But the material is treated quite differently in Bragi's
dróttkvætt than it is in the Eddic fornyrðislag. Evidently
the poet assumes that the story itself is familiar to his audience. He makes it his task to capture in his figurative
language the dramatic moment represented by the carving
on the shield. With his dense web of heiti and kennings
he can actualize a rich, epic material from the world of
myth and legend without thereby making the poem itself
epic. To cite Lie's penetrating analysis, he can preserve
the "moment" of the picture at the same time as he evokes
an "epic background." It is not merely a matter of imi-
tating a visual impression. The poetic purpose is to recreate
the "symbolic-emotional total effect" of the carving. To this
end he encircles the two antagonists, Þór and the Miðgarður
serpent, repeatedly with ever new circumlocutions and epi-
thets. The following five verses from Bragi's *Ragnarsdrápa
loðbrókar* are provided with a reproduction in prose word
order, a literal translation, and Lee M. Hollander's verse
re-creations:

Þat erumk sýnt, at snimma	Shown is eke, how Odin's
sonr Aldaföðrs vildi	heir in times of yore did
afls við úri þæfðan	vie in strength, and stoutly
iarðar reist of freista.	strove, with the earth-engirder:

Þat erumk sýnt, at sonr Aldaföðrs vildi snimma of
freista afls við úri þæfðan iarðar reist.

It is shown to me that mankind's father's (= Óðin's) son
(= Þór) in ancient times wished to pit his strength
against the earth's sea-lashed coiler (= the Miðgarður
serpent).

Hamri fórsk í hœgri	In his right hand the hammer
hönd, þás allra landa,	heaved the thurses'-terror
œgir öflugbörðu	when he beheld the hateful
endiseiðs of kendi.	head of all-lands'-girdler.

Œgir öflugbörðu fórsk hamri í hœgri hönd, þá es of kendi endiseiðs allra landa.

The terror of the giantess (= Þór) seized the hammer with his right hand when he recognized the all-lands-encircling fish (= the Miðgarður serpent).

Vaðr lá Viðris arfa	Slack lay not on sand-floor
vilgi slakr, es rakðisk,	Sif's husband's his fish-line
á Eynæfis öndri,	up when on Thor's angle-hook
Jörmungandr at sandi.	Eormengand was lifted.

Vaðr viðris arfa lá vilgi slakr á Eynæfis öndri, es Jörmungandr rakðisk at sandi.

Viðrir's (= Óðin's) heir's (= Þór's) fishing line did not lie slack on Eynæfir's (name of a sea king) ski (= the railing) when the huge staff (= the Miðgarður serpent) was dragged over the sandy bottom.

Ok borðróins barða	And the mighty oar-struck
brautar þvengr inn ljóti	ocean's-lasher horrid
á haussprengi Hrungnis	glared up at the gods'- strong-
harðgeðr neðan starði.	guarder right balefully.

Ok inn ljóti þvengr borðróins barða brautar starði harðgeðr neðan á haussprengi Hrungnis.

And the oar-propelled ship's path's (= the sea's) ugly strap (= the Miðgarður serpent) stared defiantly from below at Hrungnir's (name of a giant) skull-crusher (= Þór).

Þá es forns Litar flotna	Then, on the hook of Hrungnir's-
á fangboða öngli	head-crusher uplifted,
hrøkkviáll of hrokkinn	wallowed Midgard's winding
hekk Völsunga drekku.	worm and spewed forth poison.

Þá es Völsunga drekku hrøkkviáll hekk of hrokkinn á öngli fangboða flotna forns Litar.

> Then the Volsungs' drink's (= the poison's) writhing
> eel (= Miðgarður serpent) hung curled on the old
> Lit's (name of a giant) seamen's (= the giant's) wrestling
> challenger's (= Þór's) hook.

The last half stanza is quoted in Snorri's *Edda* as an illustration of the legend that Sigmundur Völsungsson, the father of Sigurður Fáfnisbani, had such power of resistance that he could drink poison with impunity; that is why poison is called drink of the Völsungs. Further, the kennings for Þór are evidently intended to emphasize his descent from the Æsir and his traditional role as the adversary of the giants. The Miðgarður serpent is portrayed in a series of pictures in which the main word conveys a concrete, visual impression: *reistr*, "that which twists, coils"; *seiðr*, "a kind of fish"; *gandr*, "staff"; *þvengr*, "strap"; *krøkkviáll*, "a writhing eel." But through the attributes of these comparatively prosaic and almost belittling appellations the monster is endowed with more powerful proportions. It is a *reistr*, but one of the whole earth and "lashed" by the sea. It is a *seiðr*, but one surrounding all lands. It is a *gandr*, but a gigantic one, a *Jörmungandr*. It is a *þvengr*, but with the attribute *borðróins barða brautar*; the heavy mass of words itself with its alliterations and assonances seems to suggest the impression of something powerful, overwhelming. It is, finally, a *hrøkkviáll*, but not just any one but the one of the Völsung drink, the venomous one. In this way the poet projects his immediate observation and direct description into a broad, world-embracing perspective and thereby endows them with mythic dignity.

A contemporary of Haraldur hárfagri (ca. 860–940) was Þjóðólfur Hvinverski. Like Bragi, he has been credited with a poem in dróttkvætt with mythological themes inspired by a decorated shield. At the beginning of the poem Þjóðólfur states that he has received the splendidly colored shield from a man named Þórleifur. Twenty stanzas of this poem,

110

which treat two myths about gods, have been preserved in Snorri's *Edda*. There it bears the title *Haustlöng*; it has been suggested that this name, which means literally "autumn-long," implies that the poem was composed in the course of one autumn. It rolls on heavily, massively, laden with kennings. The thunder and fire following in the blazing trail of Þór as he drives his team of goats through space is vividly conjured up. As with the verses of Bragi, the following verses from Þjóðólf's *Haustlöng* are accompanied by a prose rendering of the text, a literal translation, and verse re-creations by Hollander:

Ók at ísarnleiki	Drove then Fiorgyn's-first-born
Iarðar sunr, en dunði,	forth to battle—wroth was
móðr svall Meila blóða,	Meili's-brother—, made the
mána vegr und hánum.	moon's-way quake down under.

Iarðar sunr ók at ísarnleiki, en mána vegr dunði und hánum; móðr svall Meila blóða.

Jörð's (i.e., the goddess's) son (= Þór) drove to the iron-game (= battle), and the moon's-way (= the sky) resounded beneath him; wrath swelled within Meili's brother (= Þór).

Knáttu öll, en, Ullar,	Flamed the firmament with
endilág, fyr mági,	fiery lightnings, and all
grund var grápi hrundin,	lands below the hail did
ginnunga vé brinna,	lash, before Ull's-kinsman,
Þás hafregin hafrar	as galloping, the goat-bucks—
hógreiðar fram drógu	gaped the earth on sudden—
(seðr gekk Svölnis ekkja	hauled the wheeled wain of
sundr) at Hrungnis fundi.	Hrungnir's-foeman thursward.

Öll ginnunga vé knáttu brinna fyr Ullar mági, en grund var endilág hrundin grápi, þá es hafrar drógu hógreiðar hafregin fram at fundi Hrungnis. Svölnis ekkja gekk seðr sundr.

111

The entire abode of hawks (= the firmament) did flame
before Ull's stepfather (=Þór); all the earth was lashed
by hail when the he-goats drew the god, borne in his
comfortable chariot, (= Þór) to his meeting with Hrungnir. Svölnir's (= Óðin's) widow (= the earth) nearly
burst asunder.

Þyrmðit Baldrs of barmi,	Nor did Baldr's-brother
berg, solgnum þar dolgi,	bate his progress 'gainst the
hristusk björg ok brustu,	fiend—then rent were forelands
brann upphiminn, manna;	flared the skies with lightnings.
mjök frák móti hrøkkva	Back did start, astonied,
myrkbeins Haka reinar,	the steeps'-rockboned-tenant,
þás vígligan, vagna	sallying when he saw the
vátt, sinn bana þátti.	slayer-stern-of-thurs-brood.

Baldrs of barmi þyrmðit þar solgnum dolgi manna;
berg hristusk ok björg brustu; upphiminn brann; ek
frá Haka vagna reinar myrkbeins vátt hrøkkva mjök
móti, þá es þátti sinn vígligan bana.

Baldur's brother (=Þór) did not spare there the vora-
cious enemy of mankind (= the giant); mountains
quaked and cliffs burst; the sky flamed. I learned that
Haki's (name of a sea king) carriages (= ships') strip-of-
land's (= the sea's) dark bony-knob's (= the cliff's) witness (= the giant; i.e., one who as a mountain inhabi-
tant is intimately acquainted with cliffs) rushed to the
attack when he caught sight of his martial slayer.

In the prologue to *Heimskringla* Þjóðólfur is also mentioned as the author of the famous genealogical poem *Ynglingatal*, and Snorri quotes it, evidently quite completely,
in his own *Ynglinga saga*. The poem was composed to fur-
nish a contemporary Norwegian provincial king, a certain
Rögnvaldur in Vestfold, with splendid ancestors; they are
traced back to the Swedish Uppsala kings, the Ynglings,
and through them to the progenitor of the line, Fjölnir,
son of the god Freyr.

To judge from what we know, *Ynglingatal* is based on

Swedish family legends; it may even be derived from an old Swedish poem of the same kind. Most of what is contained in the colorful chronicle of the Ynglings is certainly more myth or legend than history. Nevertheless, other sources seem to indicate that at least some of the kings of *Ynglingatal* existed in reality and not merely in story. The Old English poem *Beowulf* from about 700 (cf. p. 60, above), for example, mentions the rulers Onela, Ōhtere, and Ēadgils. Their names correspond exactly to Áli, Óttar, and Aðils of the Yngling dynasty, who, according to their place in the family tree, should have lived about the year 500. That date agrees very well with their counterparts in *Beowulf.* An archeologist, Birger Nerman, has maintained that three of the Uppsala mounds at Old Uppsala should contain the graves of the Yngling kings Aun, Egill, and Aðils. The so-called Óttar mound, or Utter's mound, in the Vendel parish of Uppland has been dated to the beginning of the sixth century with the help of a grave find, an east Roman coin. This is considered to coincide with Óttar Vendelcrow; the mound could be his grave. But here, of course, we are on uncertain ground.

The fact that *Ynglingatal* has been analyzed and commented on more than any other skaldic poem is due mainly to the glimpses it affords into a more or less inaccessible prehistoric time, glimpses which stir the imagination. But quite apart from its uncertain value as an historical source, the poem also has certain unique characteristics and merits as poetry. It is written in kviðuháttr, a relatively simple meter compared with dróttkvætt. (Cf. p. 17, above.) It has no regular division into stanzas of eight lines, a feature that in itself can be regarded as archaic. Each of the twenty-seven rulers who are mentioned by name are treated in passages of from eight to twenty lines. In such short space there can be no question of biographies, but throughout the poem there are descriptions of the often violent and sometimes strange endings of those rulers.

In spite of this seemingly monotonous and schematic presentation, the poem takes on color and animation through the poet's verbal art. A beautiful example of the personification of nature—otherwise very rarely found in Old Norse poetry—is given in the comments on king Yngvar's fall on the coast of Estonia:

Ok austmarr	And the sea
jöfri sænskum	a song doth sing
Gymis ljóð	in the east
at gamni kveðr.	to atheling slain.

And the East Sea (= the Baltic) sings Gymir's (= the personified sea's, the sea god's) songs for the pleasure of the Swedish ruler.

When by way of exception one of the Ynglings dies a natural death from illness or old age, the goddess of death, Hel, receives him. In such cases the situation in the presentation of the poem can acquire a slightly erotic overtone. It is said about Dyggvi that "Úlf's and Narfi's sister" (= Hel) selects him and keeps him *at gamni*, "for pleasure (often used to mean love)." And king Hálfdan is invited by "Hveðrung's maiden" (= Hel) to come from life on earth *til þings*, "to a (love) meeting" with her.

On one occasion the author of *Ynglingatal* employs an allusion to the tragic love story of Hagbarður and Signý, known from Saxo Grammaticus and Danish ballads, when he describes a death by hanging: Signý's father had Hagbarður hanged. After King Agni has fallen asleep with his golden necklace tight around his neck, his wife Skjálf has her men fasten a rope to the necklace and thus hoist him up on a tree limb. The poet says Agni was to *temja* . . . / *svalan hest* / *Signýar vers*, "to tame . . . Signý's lover's cold horse." The conventional picture of the gallows as a horse occurs also in connection with King Jörundur: "the high-

114

breasted Sleipnir (= Óðin's famous eight-legged horse) of
the rope" was to carry him.

Death by burning, which is how more than one of the
Ynglings met his end, is paraphrased in more or less original
locutions. King Visbur is burned to death in his house by
his sons: "Yelping, the dog of embers (= the fire) bit the
ruler of the ship-of-the-hearth (= the hall, the house)." The
picture of the house as a ship is varied in a stanza about
King Eysteinn; perhaps the poet here was thinking of the
custom of burning the corpse of a chieftain in a ship:

Ok bitsótt	And the fire
í brandnói	fell upon him
hlíðar þangs	in his tight-
á hilmi rann,	timbered vessel
þás timbrfastr	when the tang-
toptar nökkvi	of-slopes'-terror
flotna fullr,	overwhelmed
of fylki brann.	him and his men.

And the slope's tang's (= the heather's) biting pesti-
lence (= the fire) fell upon the prince in the hearthfire's-ship (= the house) when the homestead's-tightly-
timbered-ship (= the house), full of shipmates, burned
around the king.

The same motif undergoes an even more imaginative
shaping in the obituary of Ingjaldur illráði (the Wicked),
himself a notorious incendiary, when, finally, in a desperate
situation, he has himself burned to death indoors together
with all his men. It is said that *húsþjófr* / *hyrjar leistum* /
goðkynning / *i gögnum sté*, that is, that "the house-thief
(= the fire) trod through the man-born-of-gods (= the king)
with feet (*or* stockings, stocking feet) of fire."

Another famous Norwegian skald at the court of King
Haraldur was Þorbjörn hornklofi. Snorri cites as one of his
works *Glymdrápa*, which is written in regular dróttkvætt.

115

The title can be interpreted as something like "the sonorous poem," and probably refers to the artistry of it. The so called *Haraldskvæði*, which has also been ascribed to Þorbjörn, is appreciably simpler and more easily accessible. It is mainly in málaháttr (cf. p. 15, above). This lay has been reconstructed by scholars from several sources, primarily *Heimskringla* and another collection of Norwegian royal sagas known as *Fagrskinna*. For some portions the ascribed authorship varies between Þorbjörn hornklofi and Þjóðólfr hvinverski, both of whom, of course, were members of the circle of poets around Haraldur hárfagri.

At the beginning of *Haraldksvæði*—preserved in *Fagrskinna*—there appears a white-throated valkyrie with flashing eyes, who is unfavorably disposed toward men. She understands the speech of birds, and turns toward a raven that has greeted her with a question:

"Hvat er yðr hrafnar?	"How is it, ye ravens—
Hvaðan eruð ér komnir	whence are ye come now
með dreyrgu nefi	with beaks all gory,
at degi öndverðum?	at break of morning?
Hold loðir yðr í klóum,	Carrion-reek ye carry,
hræs þefr gengr ór munni;	and your claws are bloody.
nær hykk í nótt bjogguð	Were ye near, at night-time,
þvís vissuð nái liggja."	where ye knew of corpses?"

Hreyfðisk inn hösfjaðri	Shook himself the dunhued one,
ok of hyrnu þerði,	and dried his beak,
arnar eiðbróðir,	the eagle's oath-brother,
ok at andsvörum hugði:	and of answer bethought him:
"Haraldi vér fylgðum,	"Harold we follow,
syni Halfdanar,	Halfdan's first-born,
ungum ynglingi,	the young Yngling,
síðan ór eggi kómum.	since out of egg we crept.

Kunna hugðak þik	"That king thou
konung,	knowest,

116

þanns á Kvinnum býr
dróttin Norðmanna,
djúpum ræðr kjólum,
roðnum röndum,
rauðum skjöldum,
tjörguðum árum,
tjöldum drifnum.

him who at Kvinnar dwelleth,
the hoard-warder of Northmen,
who has hollow war-ships
with reddish ribs and
with reddened war-shields,
with tarred oar-blades
and with tents foam-be-sprinkled.

Úti vill jól drekka,
ef skal einn ráða,
fylkir inn framlyndi,
ok Freys leik hefja—
ungr leiddisk eldvelli
ok inni sitja
varma dyngju
eða vöttu dúns fulla."

"Fain outside would he
drink the ale at Yule-tide,
the fight-loving folkwarder,
and Frey's-game play there.
Even half-grown, he hated
the hearthfire cozy,
the warm women's room,
and the wadded down-mittens."

Then the raven continues its panegyric to Haraldur throughout the entire poem, interrupted only by the valkyrie's questions. It is a reasonable assumption that the poet received his surname—*hornklofi* is one of many designations, with uncertain meaning, for the black bird of the battlefield—from precisely this poem, which has also been called *Hrafnsmál*, "The Speech of the Raven."

Snorri quoted the poem most extensively in the description of the battle of Hafursfjörður, in which Haraldur finally conquered his opponents and subjected all of Norway to his rule. According to tradition this event and Harald's political policies in general are said to have been a strong incentive for the migration to Iceland. Many Norwegian noblemen preferred to escape from the tyrant and begin a new existence on the remote island. The following two stanzas from the skald's lively depiction of the battle are quoted from chapter 18 of *Haralds saga hárfagra*:

Heyrðir þú í Hafrsfirði,
hve hizug barðisk

Heard hast how the highborn one
in the Hafrsfjord fought,

117

konungr hinn kynstóri	the keen-eyed king's son,
við Kjötva hinn auðlagða.	'gainst Kjotvi the Wealthy.
Knerrir kómu austan,	Came their fleet from the east,
kapps um lystir,	eager for combat,
með gínöndum höfðum	with gaping figureheads
ok gröfnum tinglum.	and graven ship-prows.

Hlaðnir váru þeir hölða	Were they laden with franklins
ok hvíta skjalda,	and linden shields unstained,
vigra vestrœnna	with Westland spearshafts
ok valskra sverða;	and Welsh broadswords.
grenjuðu berserkir,	Their berserkers bellowed
guðr var þeim á sinnum,	as the battle opened,
emjuðu úlfheðnar	the wolf-coats shrieked loud
ok ísörn dúðu.	and shook their weapons.

It is not surprising that in answer to a question from the valkyrie the raven is given the opportunity of praising the king's magnanimity to his skalds: one can see from their garments and golden rings that they are under his protection; they wear beautiful leather cloaks, swords with silver mountings, coats of mail, engraved helmets and arm rings—all gifts from Haraldur. Material reward played an important role as a stimulus to the spiritual accomplishments of the court skalds. Their ideal of an openhanded ruler could sometimes be given very crass expression.

One of the most beautiful, although not, perhaps, most typical praise poems in skaldic style is Eyvindur skáldaspillir's poem in commemoration of Hákon Adalsteinsfóstri, who fell in the battle of Storð about 960. It is called *Hákonarmál*. The poet's strange surname can be translated "the skald destroyer," and has been considered to mean "plagiarist." For Eyvind's memorial poem has borrowed the whole idea from an earlier poem, *Eiríksmál*, about Hákon's brother Eiríkur. *Hákonarmál* describes how Óðinn sends two valkyries to the battlefield to bring the king to Valhöll. While the rest of the poem is composed in ljóðaháttr, the

battle itself is in málaháttr, as can be illustrated by the
seventh stanza:

Brunnu beneldar	Burned the wound-fires
í blóðgum undum,	in bloody gashes,
lutu langbarðar	were the long-beards lifted
at lýða fjörvi,	against the life of warriors—
svarraði sárgymir	the sea-of-wounds surged high
á sverða nesi,	around the swords' edges,
fell flóð fleina	ran the stream-of-arrows
í fjöru Storðar.	on the strand of Storth-isle.

Wound-flames (= swords) burned in bloody wounds,
long-beards (= battle axes) sank to the lives of warriors,
the sea-of-wounds (= blood) gushed over the headland-
of-swords (= shields), the flood-of-spears (= blood) fell
upon the strand of Storð.

As Hákon approaches Valhöll, Óðinn sends Hermóður
and Bragi to meet him. The king clearly shrinks somewhat
from the meeting with the father of the gods, who does
not seem to be kindly disposed toward him. This reluctance
has been interpreted as a reflection of Hákon's Christianity,
for in the sagas he is described as a Christian by virtue of
his English education, although through public opinion
in Norway he was forced to compromise and follow certain
pagan religious customs. Obviously the author of *Hákonar-*
mál intends to present the king as a good heathen and to
clear him of all suspicion of aversion toward the Æsir. It
is particularly stressed that he has never violated their
temples. Therefore he can be welcomed in Valhöll without reservations. Eyvindur rounds off the apotheosis with the
assurance that the Fenris wolf will burst its fetters—that is,
Ragnarök will erupt—before the equal of Hákon will ever
take his place on the throne. The poem ends with a stanza
that cleverly alludes to a famous passage in *Hávamál*:

Deyr fé	Cattle die
deyja frændr,	and kinsmen die,

eyðisk land ok láð;	land and lieges are whelmed;
síz Hákon fór	since Hákon fared
með heiðin goð,	to the heathen gods
mörg er þjóð um þjáð.	many a host is harried.

Icelandic Skaldic Tradition

Gradually, however, skaldic poetry became something of an Icelandic monopoly. Young, ambitious Icelanders, skilled in the use of words, were fond of visiting Scandinavian royal courts, especially the Norwegian one, where they introduced themselves with a panegyric to the monarch. Sigurður Nordal has suggested an explanation for this remarkable fact that seems very plausible.[2] He points out that no Norwegian king from Eiríkur blóðøx (d. 954) till Haraldur harðráði (d. 1066), retained the bodyguard and retinue of his predecessor because they always represented an enemy phalanx. This must have been a major obstacle to the genesis and growth of a native Norwegian skaldic court tradition. The last of the Norwegian court skalds, Eyvindur skáldaspillir at the court of Hákon góði, could not reasonably be expected without further ado to transfer his admiration and praise to his master's slayers, the sons of Eiríkur blóðøx and Queen Gunnhildur. Thus the bloody change in regime destroyed his usefulness as a court poet. Such a situation, however, need not be equally catastrophic for an Icelander. Since he was a foreigner, one could not demand of him a similarly unswerving and one-sided loyalty. Therefore, he could move among sovereigns, both outside and inside of Norway, far more freely than his Norwegian colleagues. That was a practical advantage which may have become decisive for the Icelanders' unique position as court skalds—a phenomenon that otherwise seems somewhat puzzling.

There is an Icelandic catalogue of poets, *Skáldatal*, preserved in two editions, the more extensive of which continues down to about 1300. For a period of 350 years it enumerates a total of 110 Icelandic court poets, from Egill Skalla-Grímsson to his late descendant, Jón murti Egilsson, who in 1299 sang the praises of King Eiríkur Magnússon. This panegyric was at the same time the swan song of the Nordic court skalds. Among the plethora of names in *Skálda-tal* most of them remain to us nothing but that—names. But even among those poets who really stand forth with a profile of their own in their preserved poetry, a careful selection must be made in the following presentation. The purpose in this is to concentrate interest around a few representative poets, who together can give a fairly complete picture of the stages of development and the various branches of skaldic poetry. With this kind of selection and arrangement it is also possible to devote more time to certain individual poems.

Eulogistic poems connected with contemporary events and written for reigning sovereigns are usually considered to be the most typical form of skaldic poetry, and socially they were decidedly the most important kind. But attempts have also been made to distinguish other groups of poetry within the field, even though the boundaries are sometimes difficult to draw. If, for instance, *Ynglingatal* is classified as a genealogical poem on the basis of its content, it must simultaneously be regarded as a poem in praise of a ruling monarch from the viewpoint of its purpose. Furthermore, there are skaldic poems with mythic-heroic motifs; in several of the best known the poet takes as his point of departure a series of pictures on a shield or something of that sort. But in such cases, too, there seems generally to have been some kind of immediate stimulus. Thus, for example, Bragi Boddason the Old in his *Ragnarsdrápa* treats among other things two Eddic motifs: Þór's tremendous fishing feat, when he hooks the Miðgarður serpent (see pp. 107–10, above), and Hamðir's and Sörli's attack on King Jörmunrekkur *(Hamðismál)*. The description, however, is that of the decoration of a shield that Bragi has received as a gift

121

from Ragnar. The refrain of the drápa is quoted by Snorri in his *Edda*: "Ragnar presented to me a shield with many stories." Thus the poem was also motivated by a definite situation; the poem is Bragi's way of expressing his gratitude to a generous lord. The situation is much the same in regard to Úlfur Uggason and his poem *Húsdrápa*. A few stanzas are quoted in Snorri's *Edda*; they describe, among other things, Baldur's funeral procession and Þór's fishing adventure. In *Laxdæla saga* we learn what motivated the poem. It is presented by the poet at a great feast given by the splendor-loving and generous aristocrat Ólafur pái (Peacock) in his newly erected hall, decorated with pictures (probably wood carvings) on the walls. *Húsdrápa* reproduces this pictorial art in words, and at the same time the poem represents a token of homage for the host.

Another important branch of skaldic poetry is represented by the abundance of improvisations, individual verses, *lausavísur*, composed and recited on the spur of the moment. They can treat practically any subject whatsoever and are as diversified as their countless creators. In the Icelandic sagas it is not the privilege of established poets to make a retort or comment in the pregnant form of a verse. That was an *íþrótt* whose practice was enjoyed also by ordinary men and women.

In spite of certain difficulties and unavoidable inconsistencies, it would, of course, be quite possible to go through the corpus of skaldic poetry systematically, taking up one branch after the other. But the purpose of this book will be better served if the poems of selected skalds are considered in a generally chronological order.

Egill Skalla-Grímsson

The viking, chieftain, and poet Egill Skalla-Grímsson (ca. 910–90) stands out uniquely among other men in the rank of poets. We also have the feeling that we know him especially well since his picture in the form of a full-length, unusually detailed and colorful portrait was drawn by his great descendant Snorri Sturluson; it can now be considered definitely proved that the latter really is the author of *Egils saga*.[3]

Egill takes after his grandfather Kveld-Úlfur and his father, Skalla-Grímur. Like them, he belongs to the rather gloomy and problematic side of the family. They are tall, burly men with grimly ugly facial features. Their appearance corresponds to dark strains in the depth of their souls: this is where the berserk fury and other secret powers lurk. They can be brutal, cruel, and avaricious, but also tenderly sensitive. In marked contrast to them are the men of the light side of the family, such as Skalla-Grím's brother Þórólfur and Egil's own brother of the same name. (It can probably be attributed in part to literary stylization—but perhaps also to reality—that the contrast between the light and dark sides of the family continues from one generation to the next even after the poet Egil's death.) These are stately, fair-haired men with frank and harmonious dispositions. They possess an air of calm and self-evident authority, perfectly cut out for positions of leadership at a royal court—even though their fates turn out to be otherwise.

It is significant that the saga has nothing to tell about poetic gifts among the fair-haired members of the family while at the same time providing samples of poetry from both Kveld-Úlfur and Skalla-Grímur. Perhaps it is to be interpreted as a sign that the gift of composing poetry—Óðin's mead, with its mythic origin—is in league with the obscure and mysterious within man. It is more a matter of destiny than of choice. As an example of Skalla-Grím's poetic art a stanza about a smith at his work may be quoted. After moving to Iceland, he devoted much time to forging, together with his men. When his menservants complained that they had to get up so early in the morning, Skalla-Grímur spoke this verse:

Mjök verðr ár, sás aura,
ísarns meiðr at rísa,
váðir viðra bróður
veðrseygjar skal kveðja;
gjalla lætk á golli
geisla njóts, meðan þjóta,
heitu, hrœrikytjur
hreggs vindfrekar, sleggjur.

Mjök ár verðr at rísa ísarns
meiðr, sás kveðja skal veðrs-
eyjar váðir vidda bróður
aura. Lætk sleggjur gjalla
á heitu golli geisla njóts,
meðan vindfrekar hroeri-
kytjur hreggs þjóta.

> Very early must the iron's (weapon's) tree (= warrior,
> man, ironsmith) rise who intends to demand wealth from
> the sea's brother's (the wind's) wind-sucking clothes
> (= the bellows). I cause hammers to clang on the rays-
> owner's (the smith's) hot gold, while the storm's wind-
> devouring moving enclosure (= the bellows) roars.

This is a regular dróttkvætt stanza which reveals evidence of great skill at handling the demanding meter. At
the same time it has a concrete and rustic—one is tempted
to say cheerfully vital—character, which conveys a strong
breath of the heavy work in the smith shop.

Egill, Skalla-Grím's son, who was born and grew up in
Borgarfjörður in southwest Iceland, revealed his poetic
talent quite early. At the age of three he paid a neighbor a
visit, and on this occasion he is said to have composed two
dróttkvætt stanzas for his host. In these he demonstrates
his mastery of both the very strict meter and the kenning
style with circumlocutions such as "the serpent's land" or
"the bed of the heather's-gleam-band (the serpent)" for
gold—both kennings, of course, referring to Fáfnir's gloating on his gold treasure—and "the tree of the wound gosling
(i.e., of the arrow or spear)" or "the board ground's (i.e.,
the sea's: borð, shipboard) horse's (i.e., the ship's) tree" for
man and seafarer, and "the brook grouse's favorite bed"
for duck eggs. The poet's self-confidence seems justified
when in the first of the stanzas he declares: "you will not
find a better three-year-old rhyme smith than I." Unfortunately, however, we must share the doubt of the critics

about such extraordinary poetic precociousness. It is somewhat less difficult to accept as authentic another stanza which the saga ascribes to Egill at the age of seven. The precocious lad has just slain an eleven-year-old playmate with an ax. Skalla-Grímur is displeased, but Egil's mother, Bera, declares that he has the makings of a viking and that he will certainly have a longship of his own when he is old enough. Egill said:

Þat mælti mín móðir,	This did say my mother:
at mér skyldi kaupa	that for me should be bought
fley ok fagrar árar,	a ship and shapely oars,
fara á brott með víkingum,	to share the life of vikings—
standa upp í stafni,	to stand up in the stem and
stýra dýrum knerri,	steer the goodly galley,
halda svá til hafnar,	hold her to the harbor [us.
höggva maan ok annan.	and hew down those who met

This is certainly an achievement which is considerably simpler metrically, and which one could plausibly ascribe to a boy with verbal and poetic talent. The prediction in the stanza was to come true in a very high degree. Egill traveled far and wide and became a viking. As a continuous thread throughout his entire story there is his dramatic controversy with the Norwegian king Eiríkur blóðøx and his queen, Gunnhildur. After a series of baleful intermezzos, Egill, like his father, Skalla-Grímur, before him, has to shake the dust of Norway from his feet. But before doing so, he seizes the opportunity of wreaking bloody vengeance upon the royal couple, including the slaying of a son of theirs not yet fifteen years of age. Finally, on an islet near the open sea, he raises a *niðstöng*, a libelous pole, with a runic inscription, a threatening conjuration to all the land wights in Norway to force King Eiríkur and Queen Gunnhildur to flee the land.

This pole of insult has been the subject of lively discussion by scholars. The saga does not reveal the words of

125

the text that Egill carved on the pole. But the Norwegian scholar Magnus Olsen has maintained that the text must have consisted of the two dróttkvætt stanzas that were quoted shortly before the *niðstöng* episode. They contain powerful curses on the royal couple and exhort the gods to drive the "suppressor of the people" and "murderer of brothers" out of the country. Olsen points out that these two stanzas, when cut in runes, reveal quite remarkable numerical peculiarities. For each half stanza—we recall that the half stanza often represented a marked unit in the dróttkvætt—contains exactly 72 runes. In that respect the stanzas here mentioned are quite unique in Egil's entire production. And that cannot be merely a matter of chance, Olsen maintains, but has to have some connection with the fact that they are curses. It must therefore be an expression of number magic. The older runic alphabet consisted of 24 symbols, that is 3 x 8 or 2 x 12; 3, 9, and 12 are, as we know, traditionally charged with power in the world of legend and myth. The younger runic alphabet had 16 symbols, that is 2 x 8. Where runes have demonstrably been cut for magical purposes, the number of symbols preferably equals sums or products of these numbers. In Egil's case there are, then, 72 runes in each of the half stanzas, that is 3 x 24 (the sum total of the older runic alphabet) or 8 x 9. With such an arrangement the inscription on the scorn pole would have to be filled with magic powers. Recently, however, some doubt has been expressed regarding the validity of Olsen's rune counting.[4]

However that may be—King Eiríkur and his queen were forced to go into exile within a year after Egill had raised his scorn pole, driven out by Hákon Aðalsteinsfóstri. If that had not happened, Egil's famous poem *Höfuðlausn* ("Head-Ransom") might never have been composed. After burying his father and staying on his ancestral family estate, Borg, for a time, Egill is seized by inexplicable melancholy and decides to make another journey abroad. He is shipwrecked off the coast of Northumberland, still completely ignorant of the fact that his mortal enemy, King Eiríkur, has been compelled to leave Norway and has now been made ruler of Northumberland by the English king for the purpose of protecting the boundary from Scots and Irishmen. When he learns of his enemy's presence, Egill sees no other expedient than to stake everything on one card. He chooses to appear voluntarily before King Eiríkur, under the pretext that he has felt an irresistible need to seek reconciliation with him—which seems to be as far from the truth as possible. But first he turns to his old friend Arinbjörn, who is highly trusted by Eiríkur and has faithfully accompanied him into exile. With this friend as intercessor, Egill manages to escape being slain on sight by the embittered king and his still more malevolent wife. Only by mobilizing all his authority and by virtually threatening Eiríkur can Arinbjörn have Egil's execution postponed till the following day. Then he advises his friend to utilize his brief respite to compose a panegyric, preferably a drápa of twenty stanzas, for King Eiríkur and to recite it for him the following day. That is what Arinbjörn's relative Bragi had done when he had incurred the wrath of Björn, king of the Swedes, and had received his head as a reward. Maybe fortune would be just as favorable this time. Egill says that he is willing to try for his friend's sake. "But I had not thought that *I* would write a praise poem for king Eiríkur." The saga relates that Egill—not without suspenseful obstacles—wins the race with time and recites his drápa before the monarch, who leaves him his head as a reward for the poem—albeit very reluctantly. Egill is permitted to go his way unmolested.

Höfuðlausn can scarcely be regarded as a remarkable poem, nor could one expect it to be if it was really composed under the circumstances described in the saga. Its greatest claim to fame consists in the fact that it is, as far as we know, the first Norse poem to employ end rhyme,

127

together with the traditional native alliteration. The eight short verses rhyme in pairs with masculine rhymes; a metric form with end rhymes of that kind is called *runhent*. This metric innovation certainly must have had foreign models. It is believed that Egill encountered them during earlier sojourns in England, maybe primarily in religious poetry or hymns in Latin.[5] According to the saga, he and his brother Þórólfur had themselves primsigned at the request of King Athelstan during their first sojourn in the country. The first stanza of the poem goes as follows:

Vestr fórk of ver,	I sailed to the West
en ek Viðris ber	and of Odin's breast
munstrandar mar,	bear I the sea—
svá er mitt of far;	thus is't with me.
drók eik á flot	I put out to float,
við ísa brot,	at ice-break, my boat
hlóðk mærðar hlut	freighted with load
míns knarrar skut.	of lofty ode.

I sailed westward over the sea, bringing with me Viðrir's (Óðin's) strand-of-the-mind's (the breast's) ocean (= the skaldic mead); thus is my voyage. I set the oak afloat when the ice broke up; I loaded the stern of my ship with a cargo of praise.

Thus the poet emphasizes at the outset that he has made his voyage for the sole purpose of paying homage to the king with a praise poem; this purpose is accentuated even more strongly in the following stanza. This need not conflict with the account of the saga. For, as has been pointed out, whether Eglil composed *Höfuðlausn* during a wakeful night in York or not, it was undoubtedly wisest for him to pretend to King Eiríkur that his complimentary call was well prepared.

Höfuðlausn praises primarily King Eirík's martial exploits and on the whole Egill keeps to the common ground

128

of battle kennings. For instance, the sword is called battle sun *(hjaldrröðull)*, the point of the sword is called wound digger *(bengrefill)*, the arrows, wound bees *(unda bý)*, blood is the river of the sword *(mækis á)* or sword-point billow *(oddbreki)*. The raven, the bird of the battlefield, is called the crane of battle *(hjaldrs trani)* and wound gull *(benmár)*.

In the last stanza of the poem, however, there appears a kenning that is somewhat more singular and can give rise to a substantive question. Egill finishes his praise poem with the remark that he has now presented it "from the harbor of laughter" *(ór hlátra ham)*, that is, from his breast. There are those who believe that the poet has chosen his metaphor with studied irony. By mentioning the chest as the dwelling place of laughter in this very situation, they insist, the poet finally has given a hint that the entire eulogy of King Eiríkur should be regarded as a huge joke. The kenning, in other words, should be understood as a sort of flimflam that Egill smuggles into the final summation of his drápa.

However ingenious this interpretation may appear to be, it must be regarded as less than cogent. Viewed realistically, such a play on words would have been extremely risky in Egil's situation. If Eiríkur had perceived or even suspected the locution of being ambiguous, the encomium would probably never have become a head ransom. But another point of view is more important as a matter of principle. Nowadays we do not expect a metaphor, a poetic picture, to serve a purpose of its own. We prefer to see it as a link in a larger context; it is supposed to express part of the aim and tone of the whole. Many times this is also the case in Norse skaldic poetry. But there one must often take into consideration the fact that a kenning functions, so to speak, on its own, without being especially well attuned to its surroundings. This naturally holds true primarily for such concepts as are frequently paraphrased by the poets: battle, warrior, ship, sword, and so on. This is where we come close to the formula, the cliché. As for the above-mentioned interpretation, we may become a bit more hesitant since a later poet uses the kenning "the ship of laughter *(hlátr-Ellíði)*" for the chest.[6] In any case, we must be very cautious in seeking to interpret individual kennings as an expression for a specific artistic purpose on the part of a given poet.

Höfuðlausn introduces a new meter into the genre, but it is otherwise a rather conventional laudatory poem. What really makes it deeply original is the situation of the poet: he presents a praise poem to his mortal enemy, in a game with his head at stake. Egil's two other great poems are more personal in content. They have also been preserved in connection with the saga.

Arinbjarnarkviða is closely connected to the episode at King Eirík's court in York. The object is to praise his faithful friend Arinbjörn, who played such a decisive role on that occasion. But it is typical of Egil's monumentally self-centered disposition that even so the poem mostly revolves around his own person and his appearance. It should be mentioned in this connection that the saga itself on one occasion provides a detailed and graphic portrait of Egil's appearance. He has taken part in a great battle on the side of the English king Athelstan together with his much admired older brother Þórólfur. The accomplishments of the brothers were memorable, but Þórólfur was slain. After the victory there is a feast with much drinking and merriment around the tables in the king's hall. Egill and his men have been given seats of honor opposite the king:

> He had his helmet on his head and laid his sword across his knees. He kept drawing the sword halfway out of the sheath and thrusting it back in again. He sat upright, but his head was bowed. Egill had coarse features: a broad forehead, bushy eyebrows, and a short and extremely thick nose. His long beard covered much

of his face, and his chin and jawbone were terribly broad. His neck was so thick and his shoulders so broad that he stood out from all other men. His expression was harsh and grim when he was angry. He was of great stature, being taller than anyone else. His hair was gray and thick, but he became bald quite young. But as he sat there, as written above, he alternately pulled one of his eyebrows down to his cheek and the other one up to his hairline. Egill had black eyes and eyebrows, which met above the bridge of his nose. He would not eat although he had been served, but remained sitting there, raising and lowering his eyebrows.

In part the impulse for this description may have come to Snorri from Egil's own poems, for they seem to suggest that he really had a striking physiognomy. We rather get the impression that he felt somewhat embarassed at his appearance and for that reason was strongly impelled to occupy himself with the matter. In *Arinbjarnarkviða*, at any rate, he does this in a clever and self-ironic way. He expresses his surprising decision to throw himself on King Eirík's mercy voluntarily in the third stanza with the words: "I pulled the hat of audacity over my dark forelock and called on the prince." The design is carried out to completion in the seventh stanza. This refers to the situation in which Egill, having just recited his drápa, has received his head as a reward for this poem:

Né hamfagrt	Unhandsome
hölðum þótti	to the hird did seem
skáldfé mitt	the poet's meed
at skata húsum,	in the prince's hall,
þás úlfgrátt	for Ygg's-draught
við Yggjar miði	when my ugly head,
hattar staup	wolf-gray all,
at hilmi þák.	as reward I got.

The meter is kviðuháttr and consequently comparatively simple, closely related with fornyrðislag in Eddic poetry (see p. 13 above). One of the two kennings in the stanza, *hattar staup,* "the lump of the hat," refers to the head, and the other, *Yggjar mjöðr,* "Ygg's (Óðin's) mead," refers to poetic art. The last four lines thus say that Egill received his head in exchange for the poem. One commentator, however, believes he has discovered a pun here that combines the two kennings in a clever manner. The expression *hattar staup* is usually interpreted as "the lump of the hat"; *staup* is, among other things, a lump of metal. But the word can also mean "tankard," "tumbler." So Egill pours the poetic mead out of the tankard of his head, and in return he is allowed to keep this tankard![7] It is an ingenious interpretation which seems to harmonize quite well with the taste for the complicated and the double entendre of the Norse poets—their ambiguity, to borrow one of the newer popular terms from poetic analysis. Whether this interpretation is correct is another question, and one that is impossible to decide. From the immediately preceding stanza in *Arinbjarnarkviða,* however, one can obtain completely convincing evidence that Egill has chosen a certain kenning for the purpose of having it correspond with the metaphor of skaldic mead. The poet reminds us of how he presented his *Höfuðlausn,*

svát Yggs full	Ygg's-beaker
ýranda kom	thus brimming
at hvers manns	to ear-mouth
hlusta munnum.	of every man.

This half stanza is a good illustration of how a poet freshens up a faded metaphor by exploiting the possibilities of making it concrete. The conventional phrase about skaldic mead is given new visuality—even though it is somewhat bizarre—when it is seen as a foaming drink for the open mouths of the ears. Egill is confident of his ability to make people listen when he requests silence so that he can recite his poem.

The most artistically executed—although not the most realistic—description of a face in *Arinbjarnarkviða* is nevertheless not that of the poet himself but rather that of King Eiríkur. In the fifth stanza a picture of the ruler is drawn which glares fiercely at Egill:

Vara þat tunglskin	Fearsome was 't
tryggt at líta	to face, nor flinch,
né ógnlaust	the angry glance
Eiríks bráa,	of Eric's brow-moons,
þás ormfránn	when sharply
ennismáni	they shot keen beams
skein allvalds	from under
œgigeislum.	the atheling's brows.

As we can see, it is a metaphor, consistently developed throughout the entire stanza, with the kenning *ennimáni*, "forehead moon" (= eye) as its nucleus. The choice of attributes is brought into harmony with it: *tunglskin*, "moonlight," and *œgigeislar*, "terror-rays." The epithet *ormfránn*, "serpent-gleaming" intensifies the frightening sting of the gaze. It is a series of pictures whose suggestive radiance can scarcely fail to be perceived even by the modern reader.

In *Arinbjarnarkviða* Egill speaks in a conspicuously self-centered manner about his own work as a poet; it becomes to a certain degree a poem about poetry. In several verses already quoted he calls the art of poetry Ygg's mead or Ygg's full horn; in a third stanza we encounter the same metaphor, the only difference being that Yggur has been replaced with another name for Óðinn, Viður. This kenning and similar ones are carefully explained by Snorri in his Edda. (See pp. 4 f., above). The metaphor of poetic art as Óðin's drink rather suggests that the poet was regarded as an inspired man in compact with higher powers. This is an aspect of poetry which should not have been unfamiliar to Egill, who had raised the scorn pole and was experienced in the art of rune magic. But at the same time the Norse skalds had a keen awareness of being experts and regarded themselves as a guild of professionals, who had at their command all the subtleties of their craft. Egill also stressed that sector of a poet's activity. He expresses his willingness to sing Arinbjörn's praise by saying that it is easy to smooth the boards of poetry *(mærðar efni)* with the jack-plane of the voice *(ómunlokarr)*. The raw material lies ready, but it needs an experienced, artistic hand to work it.

The meaning is not so clear in another formulation, where Egill talks about raising the song of praise over his friend in full view of many, steeply climbed with the feet of poetry *(bratt stiginn bragar fótum)*. One wonders what it may mean to mount a praise song. All things considered, it may be that the poet, as Sigurður Nordal assumes, already has in mind the metaphor that he will employ to conclude the poem. For at the end Egill calls his laudatory poem a praise pile *(lofköstr)*, and the verb "to climb" would go well with that kenning.[8] Anticipations of that kind are not improbable, and perhaps not even unusual in poetry. The final stanza reads as follows:

Vark árvakr,	Awake early,
bark orð saman	I bore words together
með málþjóns	by the tongue's
morginverkum,	timely working:
hlóðk lofköst	high I heaped
þanns lengi stendr	a hill of praise
óbrotgjarn	on song-fields,
í bragar túni.	which not soon will fall.

The voice slave or speech servant *(málþjónn)* is a kenning for the tongue. Thus Egill says that in the early hours of the morning he put his tongue to work to compose the poem about his friend. In this stanza Åke Ohlmarks believes he has found a play on words that would create an especially strong metaphorical context. Icelandic has a noun *urð*, used for rocks that have fallen down in an avalanche. In the phrase *bark orð saman* the sound resemblance *orð/urð*, Ohlmarks believes, hovered in the poet's mind. The association with such rocks would accord very well with the picture of the pile or cairn made of stones collected on the field. This would yield a well-executed parallel between the work of a poet and the rural occupation of clearing a new strip of land for plowing or for pasture.[9] But whether we accept this ingenious interpretation or not, the stanza is Egil's own counterpart to the Horatian *monumentum aere perennius*—a monument more enduring than bronze.

Egil's appreciation of the immense and the high-flown can be seen in a stanza in which he describes how people eagerly seek the help of generous Arinbjörn. His friends come streaming together, it is said, from all corners of the wide bottom of the wind tub *(á vindkers viðum botni)*. The tub of wind is space or the universe; *Völuspá* also talks about the sky as *vindheimr*, "the world of the winds." The bottom of the wind tub, then, is the wide earth. The choice of kenning lends a kind of universal touch and cosmic dimension to Arinbjörn's popularity. The locution is also a good example of the fact that the poet's figurative language was not always affected and ingeniously calculated. Sometimes, as in this case, it could be both simple and monumental.

Like *Höfuðlausn*, the poem *Sonatorrek* ("The Loss of Sons") has been given a dramatic frame in the saga, which vividly brings the whole train of events much closer to us. A son of Egill, Böðvarr, is drowned during a storm along the coast. When his corpse has drifted ashore, Egill has his father, Skalla-Grím's, grave mound opened and buries his son there. Then he goes to bed in his bed-closet

135

and remains lying there for two days without eating or drinking. On the third day his wife sends for their daughter Þorgerður, who comes without delay. She goes into Egil's bed-closet and lies down also. She intends to suffer the same fate; she does not wish to survive her father and brother. But after a while Egill notices that his daughter is chewing something and asks what it is. It is seaweed, she answers; one becomes ill from it and does not live so long. She gives her father some of it to chew on. But Þorgerður soon asks for water to drink, since seaweed makes one so thirsty. Then she passes the drinking horn to Egill, who takes a deep draught. The saga continues:

Then Þorgerður said: "Now we have been tricked; it is milk."

Then Egill bit a piece out of the horn, as big as his teeth could take, and cast the horn from him.

Þorgerður said: "What are we going to do now? This plan did not work. Now, father, I wish we could remain alive long enough for you to compose a memorial poem about Böðvar and for me to engrave it on a rune stick. Then we can die if we want to. I think that your son Þorsteinn will be very slow in completing a poem about Böðvar, but it would not be fitting for him not to be honored with a memorial poem now, because I do not think that the two of us will be present at his funeral feast."

Egill said that it was unlikely that he would be able to compose a poem now, even if he wanted to. "But I can try," he said.

If this story is true, we may be indebted to the affection and cunning of Þorgerður Egilsdóttir for a poem which is generally regarded as the first purely subjective lyric in the North. More than anywhere else Egill here reveals his egocentricity. Officially, so to speak, *Sonatorrek* is a memorial poem in honor of his favorite son, who has

136

drowned, and of another son, Gunnar, who died from illness shortly before. But most of all the poem revolves
around the poet's own desolation and around his relationship to Óðinn and the art of poetry.

The meter is kviðuháttr, the same meter as in *Arinbjarnarkviða*. Metrically *Sonatorrek* is therefore not a particularly demanding poem. Some stanzas are also unusually
bare expressions for Egil's feelings, almost completely without kennings or at best with simple, direct images without
any trace of paradox and punning. Such locutions remind
us of the life wisdom in the form of maxims in *Hávamál*:
"For my kin has nearly come to an end like storm-lashed
trees in the forest. Not happy is the man who bears the
bones of his kinsman from his house."

We gain a strong impression of how powerful a factor
kinship was even for such an individualist and original
character as Egill. In two further stanzas he broods over
the disaster which has struck both himself and his family:

Grimmt vörum hlið,
þats hrönn of braut
föður míns
á frændgarði;
veitk ófullt
ok opit standa
sonar skarð,
es mér sær of vann.

Grim the gap
which the gale did tear
in my sib's
serried ranges—
unfilled aye
and open will stand
the breach blasted
by the breaking sea.

Mjök hefr Rán
ryskt um mik,
emk ofsnauðr
at ástvinum;
sleit marr bönd
minnar ættar,
snaran þátt
af sjálfum mér.

Sorely Rán
hath smitten me—
left me bare
of bosom-friends;
the sea snapped
my sib's tight links—
a strong strand
is stripped from me.

For a moment the old warrior toys with the thought of revenge. If only he could have avenged himself with his sword; then Ægir, the god of the sea, and his henchmen would have been done with. But he resigns himself and instead creates a picture of the impotence of his desolation and old age:

En ek ekki	But strength to cope
eiga þóttumk	I could not muster,
sakar afl	so meseemed,
við sonar bana,	with my son's slayer:
þvít alþjóð	soon will it
fyr augum verðr	be seen by all
gamals þegns	how helpless
gengileysi.	the hoary warrior.

In spite of everything Egil's poetic gift provides consolation in his grief. A moment before he had wanted to die, but now he is gradually captivated by the creative and alleviating process of poetic composition. But he has to overcome considerable resistance in the beginning, as the hesitant introduction reveals:

Mjök erum tregt	Tardily takes
tungu at hrœra	my tongue to move,
eða loptvætt	and to stir
ljóðpundara;	the steelyard-of-song:
era nú vænligt	hopeless is't
of Viðurs þýfi	about Odin's-theft,
né hógdrœgt	hard to draw
ó hugar fylgsni.	from the heart's-fastness!

The steelyard of song *(ljóðpundari)* can mean either the tongue or the poetic gift, which weighs the words of the poem on a pair of scales. Viður's (Óðin's) stolen goods is poetic art itself; we recall that the god had stolen the skaldic mead from the giants. Ohlmarks comments on the stanza with empathy and enthusiasm: "The figurative language is magnificent. The tongue, paralyzed by sorrow and parched from starvation and thirst, is compared to a rusty old steelyard that will hardly tilt any longer when on a rare occasion it is used."[10] The mind's corner or the spirit's hiding place *(hugar fylgsni)* he regards as a direct correspondence to the alcove bed where Egill wanted to hide and "die in silence like a wounded animal." In content the following stanza is a pure paraphrase of the first one, with another allusion to Óðin's successful coup: poetic art is now called Frigg's husband's find of joy, taken from the world of giants in ancient times.

In the fifth stanza Egill has picked up momentum and finds two graphic kennings for his occupation: "From the temple of words I carry the planks of the praise poem, adorned with the foliage of language." The temple of words *(orðhof)* has been interpreted as mouth, but it may just as well mean the poet's mind. Whichever one prefers, the meaning is about the same. Egill compares the matter of his poem to plain boards which he carries out of the temple of words, clad in the leafage of language. This is a counterpart to the image in *Arinbjarnarkviða*, where he trims his lumber with the jackplane of the tongue.

In the first two stanzas we twice found Egill referring to the poetic art as Óðin's theft or find. This is a conventional and rather worn kenning. But at a later stage of *Sonatorrek* the relationship between Óðinn, poetry, and Egill assumes a more tangible and personal character. The poet cannot refrain from complaining about the god. Formerly he had felt that he could trust Óðin's friendship, but now the god has broken their good alliance—for he has snatched two of Egil's sons to him. But, Egill finally admits, Óðinn has at any rate given him some redress for what has befallen him: "The wolf's battle-skilled enemy gave me a flawless *íþrótt*"—i.e., the art of composing poetry.

Those words recall what Goethe has the unfortunate poet Torquato Tasso say in the drama that bears his name:

Und wenn der Mensch in seiner Qual verstummt,
gab mir ein Gott zu sagen, wie ich leide.

[While man falls silent in his torment,
A God gave me (the gift) to express my suffering.]

More than eight hundred years before Goethe wrote these words, the old viking Egill Skalla-Grímsson had had a similar experience—even though he expresses it in rougher form. The saga itself confirms the assuaging effect that the composition of the poem had on the poet and that his sensible daughter had counted on from the beginning: "Egill recovered strength gradually as the poem progressed, and when it was finished, he recited it for Ásgerður and Þorgerður and his household. Then he got out of his bed and once more took his place in the high seat. He called this poem Sonatorrek."[11]

A number of lausavísur in the saga afford a few more insights into Egil's old age. His younger colleague Einar Helgason (later on called skálaglamm) sometimes coaxes him into relating his journeys and deeds from the days of his youth and manhood—"and that kind of talk pleased Egill." On such occasions the old warrior can refresh his memory and impress Einar with a dróttkvætt stanza describing how once he fought against eight men and twice against no less than eleven; he slew them all himself and gave the corpses to the wolves. But otherwise his life curve is declining. He spends his last years with his niece Þórdis and her husband on the farm Mosfell, where he stumps around stiff-legged, hard of hearing, and almost blind, a hinderance to the young and busy people. Once he has drawn close to the fire to warm himself, and somebody asks him if he has cold feet and tells him to take care that he does not put them too close to the fire. Egill answers meekly, and then recites a simple and sadly resigned stanza. But his humor and self-irony are still there in the final word game with its somewhat ambiguous meaning; it is constructed around the word *ekkja*, which in poetic language could mean both "widow" and "heel" (just as, on the other hand, *hæll* means not only "heel" but also "widow"):

Langt þykki mér,	Long the time seems—
ligg einn saman,	all alone I lie,
karl afgamall,	an old old man—
án konungs vörnum;	without king's favor:
eigum ekkjur	two widows boast I,
allkaldar tvær,	both all chilly,
en þær konur	and these two women
þurfu blossa.	great warmth require.

These are Egil's last alliterative words in the saga. In them, as in most of what he composed, we sense the presence of a distinct and unique personality. Egill Skalla-Grímsson is subjective in a manner that is not common among Old Norse skalds.

Kormákur Ögmundarson. Egil's younger contemporary Kormákur Ögmundarson (c. 935–70) also reveals a profile of his own. He is one of the very few erotic poets in skaldic poetry, and the foremost among them. The rather brief *Kormáks saga* is above all a poet's biography. In that respect it belongs to a quite small group of Icelandic sagas. *Egils saga Skalla-Grímssonar* is in a class by itself because of both its broad scope and its excellent literary qualities. Most famous among the others is *Gunnlaugs saga orm-stungu*, and besides this saga we can also mention the stories about Björn Hítdælakappi and about Hallfreður, Ólafur Tryggvason's poet. The masterpiece *Gísla saga Súrs-sonar* could perhaps also be assigned to this category; here our attention is drawn to the outlawed Gísli's stanzas about the two contrasting "dream women"—one good and kind, the other one evil and threatening—who appear to him in his sleep.[12]

A distinctive characteristic of the sagas about skalds is the abundant interspersion of poetry, and in *Kormáks saga* it is decidedly more dominant than anywhere else. In an Icelandic edition the stanzas make up one-third of the entire number of lines; sixty-four of them are by Kormákur himself, whereas his antagonist Hólmgöngu-Bersi has been credited with fifteen. These numerous occasional verses are throughout very closely connected with definite situations in the saga; it is almost a rule that they are represented as improvisations created on the spur of the moment. The rather meager prose in *Kormáks saga* can best be regarded as a kind of binding medium for the stanzas, an endeavor to tie them into a coherent account of the poet's unrequited and unfulfilled love for Steingerður. The relationship between prose and poetry is a constant text-critical problem in the study of the sagas; it naturally becomes more difficult the greater the role is that is played by the poems. If we hope to gain a clearer idea of Kormák's image in the saga and of the place of his poetry in that image, this question cannot be circumvented. A few thoughts concerning the case in question can also serve to illustrate views and distinctions that have often been applied in a similar context.

In reality the scholar has three (or four) possibilities to choose from. First, he can regard both the stanzas and the story of the saga in principle as fully historical. In that case the poetry is an authentic product of the poet Kormákur Ögmundarson, who lived around the middle of the tenth century; the course of his life's story was faithfully preserved in oral tradition until the saga was written down during the thirteenth century. Second, he can accept the stanzas as authentic, but regard the prose text as a freely constructed biography. A third possibility would be to conceive of both poetry and prose as the creation of the author of the saga. A fourth possibility, theoretically conceivable, would be that the prose description is historically reliable but that the stanzas represent later poetic decorations. This can no doubt be disregarded in this case.

We know a few data about Kormák's poetry independently of the saga. In the Icelandic *Skáldatal* (see p. 120, above) he is mentioned as the author of laudatory poems in honor of both Sigurður Hlaðajarl and Haraldur gráfeldur. Snorri quotes one stanza from the *Sigurðar drápa* in *Heimskringla* and six half stanzas in his *Edda*. There are also two verses of Kormák's love poetry quoted in the so-called *Third Grammatical Treatise*. All things considered, nothing conflicts with the view that the stanzas in *Kormáks saga* could be authentic poetry by the skald from the tenth century. Neither their form nor their content seems to require another assumption. On the other hand, it is out of the question that the author of the saga could have written the stanzas he ascribes to his hero. For when it comes to the content, there are such striking discrepancies between poetry and prose as no author would have laid himself open to blame for if he had written both. This is an opinion that needs to be explained and illustrated.

In one of the foreign episodes in the saga, which takes place in the Brenneyjar (the Brenn Islands, situated in the mouth of the Göta Elf near present-day Gothenburg) Kormákur together with his brother saves his beloved Steingerður from a viking ship in which she has been carried off. They have to swim ashore, and the saga relates: "When Kormákur approached the shore, eels twisted around his arms and legs so that he was close to being pulled down. Kormákur quoted a stanza." In this stanza he says that the "goats of the ditch" ran against him "in herds" as he swam across the water; the word *díki* can in poetic language be used for water, probably a rather narrow body of water such as a strait. It certainly seems as if Kormák's encounter

143

with the aggressive eels could simply be the result of a misunderstanding of Kormák's stanza on the part of the saga author. It is true that in Sveinbjörn Egilsson's classic dictionary of poetic language it is stated that the kenning *dikis bokkar* here means "eels": "a jocular kenning because of the movements of the eels, which is the point of comparison." But it is probably difficult for many readers to see any essential similarity between the movements of an eel and those of a goat. And in that case they will probably not be inclined to agree with the latest Swedish translator and commentator of the stanza when he says that "the goat of the ditch (sea)" would be a "good and original" kenning for the eel.[13] Could the saga author's own explanation not have influenced the judgment of late interpreters? Maybe *dikis bokkar* does not refer to eels at all. Nor does the stanza yield the slightest intimation that they wound themselves around Kormák's arms and legs. How about letting the kenning refer to quite different animals living in water, for instance, porpoises? Those who have seen a shoal of porpoises plow along on the surface of the water will probably agree that their movements rather resemble those of springing goats. To meet a shoal like that may also have been so memorable to the poet—whether he was swimming or not; he does not mention that himself—that he has immortalized the encounter in a verse. The Icelandic word for goat, *hafr*, has been and still is a component of names for whales; in Modern Icelandic a dolphin is called *höfrungur*.

According to the saga, Kormák's last battle is fought in Scotland against a giantlike being, the Scots' *blótrisi* (a giant whom the Scots presumably worshiped). But there is no giant in the stanza which is supposed to refer to and verify that very episode. The skald says only that it was certainly not like having the woman, Steingerður, in his arms, when he wrestled with the "steerer of the rope stallion," i.e., the steersman, the viking. It would also have been rather daring of Kormákur to talk about his fight with

144

a giant in an authentic stanza when the events could be checked by his companions. But one of his later fellow countrymen gives his imagination free rein, especially since in this case the events take place far away from his home country. The words of the skald have been interpreted in a way that he could certainly never have foreseen.

On the whole this biography should probably be regarded as a freehand sketch without any appreciable support in Kormák's numerous verses. In spite of their large number they provide only a very flimsy basis for a coherent biography. Some of them employ such general applications for woman or the passage of arms, for example, that they could be applied to many different situations. And when, on the other hand, we meet a concrete episode and individuals identified by name—which often occurs in Kormák's verse—we are given extremely tenuous clues as to how they are to be fitted into a broader context. However that may be, the rather awkward presentation of a mysterious love story has succeeded in captivating poets of later times and has enticed them to endeavor to fill out and round off the picture.

As a quite young man Kormákur meets Steingerður, a farmer's daughter, and is immediately smitten with love for her. He improvises a series of stanzas on the matter. The girl's father, however, opposes his further wooing and tries to have him slain from ambush. In principle, love poetry *(mansöngr)*, addressed to women mentioned by name, was regarded as disgraceful and was punishable by law. But Steingerður reciprocates Kormák's love and urges him to become reconciled with her father and formally to ask for her hand. She becomes his betrothed and the wedding day is set. But then something strange happens: Kormákur suddenly loses all interest in the matter and simply stays away from the wedding. In the saga this turn of events is attributed to a magic spell worked upon him by a woman skilled in magic arts, whose two sons he has slain; she has threatened him previously, saying that she would take revenge by bringing it about that he would never possess Steingerð's love. The relatives of the bride naturally regard Kormák's behavior as an insult and they at once arrange a marriage between her and another man. Kormákur tries with all his might to prevent this but without success. Steingerður is married, not only now but also later, after a divorce, to a new suitor. The remainder of Kormák's life is completely dominated by his unhappy love for her. One time after another their paths cross, both in Iceland and abroad, but their meetings never lead to any intimacy between them. Steingerð's attitude is rather ambivalent: she does not really avoid the poet's courtship, but she no longer wants to accept him as a lover or husband. Kormákur has to be content with praising his beloved in his dróttkvætt stanzas and showering malicious lampoons on her husband. Finally, as already mentioned, he is killed during a battle in Scotland. While dying he composes three more stanzas, all of them addressed to Steingerður.

The author of *Kormák's saga* blames his hero's erotic misfortunes on a witch's curse. This explanation has no support in the skald's own stanzas. Only once does Kormákur mention "rík sköp," i.e., a powerful fate, in connection with his relationship to Steingerður. Modern interpreters have not been willing to accept such allusions to witchcraft or fate. According to the Norwegian author Hans E. Kinck, *Kormáks saga* deals with "the erotic phantom, the sudden dispiritedness that befalls two lovers when they are near their goal." Kormákur burns for Steingerður his whole life, but backs down every time he could possess her. It is the struggle for the beloved one and not the possession that characterizes Kormák's eroticism, Kinck maintains. He seeks the explanation for the poet's fate in his artist's nature: "He is a poet who parts with his love in his poetry about her. Through the lines of his highly wrought dróttkvætt she is gradually transformed from having been an individual whom he loved into being the celebrated object—she

146

has become his model. This is the kernel of this love relationship, which is the tragedy of the genius and the man."[14]

Other psychological or psychiatric keys that have been tried on Kormák's case are maternal fixation and psychic impotence. However one may judge these different attempts to help the old saga man with the analysis, there remains one undeniable fact: Kormák's demeanor is full of contradictions and irrational acts and reactions. There are clear evidences of irresolution, irritability, and lack of balance in his behavior. Should they perhaps be regarded as a somewhat fumbling endeavor on the part of the author to create a typical artistic and Bohemian nature?

The author of *Kormáks saga* is not a good psychologist or skillful director of his characters' fates, that is true. Hard judgment could be pronounced against him, not least of all when compared with his more successful colleagues in the saga genre. But, as Einar Ól. Sveinsson expresses it: "Whatever one may say about the saga, we certainly owe a debt of gratitude to the man who wrote down the stanzas."[15] There are still, to be sure, a few obscure points in the sixty-four stanzas that the saga ascribes to Kormákur, but that is only to be expected after an oral tradition of between two and three hundred years. Most of the poetry can be interpreted with certainty and provides a reliable picture of Kormák's qualifications as a skald.

Dróttkvætt may seem to be a meter made for pompous court poems, suitable for such grim statements as saying that the warrior gave the raven food. But for love poetry? Sometimes with Kormákur there is a strange contrast between the heavy fall of the drottkvætt stanza and the erotic mood. But all the same he manages to express a surprisingly large number of different nuances. As a love poet he is incomparably more interesting than his skaldic colleagues.

The kennings, those baroquelike ornaments of dróttkvætt poetry, are scarcely Kormák's strong point. In his

147

erotic poetry there is, of course, above all the word "woman" that has to be paraphrased. Generally he uses the name of a goddess or valkyrie as the basic word of the kenning: Eir, Freyja, Fríður, Frigg, Gná, Gunnur, Hildur, Hlín, Hrist, Ilmur, Nanna, Rindur, Sága. Otherwise þella, "pine," "fir tree," is used very often in that function. The attribute of the main word mostly refers to the woman's jewelry or dress. Thus she is "the pine of gold," "the Hlín of rings," "the Rindur of the necklace," "the pine of flax," "the Ilmur of sleeves." With "the Sága of beer" the skald, of course, refers to a young woman's task of serving drinks to thirsty men.

The attribute of the stem word of the kenning can, as we know, be another kenning. With Kormákur that is especially common with the word "gold." With reference to Fáfnir's brooding over the treasure, the beloved one is called "Gná of the serpent bed"—that is a three-storied kenning. More often the skald talks about gold as the water's gleam and the like; according to Snorri's *Edda*, Fáfnir's inheritance was finally sunk into the Rhine and never found again. Consequently Kormákur calls woman "Hildur of the billow's gleam" or "Gunnur of the strait's sun." If one wants a four-storied kenning, one can paraphrase water once more and call it, for example, "Áti's bench"—Áti was a sea king. Steingerður then becomes to Kormákur simply "Eir of the fire of Áti's bench."

Kennings of that kind, as a rule, ought certainly not to be regarded as realistic, not as descriptions of existing reality. To a large extent these are clichés. So there is hardly reason to believe that the skald's frequent references to the beloved woman's gold and jewelry must always derive from actual impressions. But according to the aristocratic conventions of skaldic poetry, a young woman ought to appear that way.

But Kormák's kenning language is not very intricate in comparison with that of some of his brother skalds. Nor does he have the same ability as Egill Skalla-Grímsson to preserve a unified pictorial vision throughout an entire stanza so that he opens a view over two worlds at the same time, that of nature and that of man. Kormákur comes closest to an achievement of that kind in a stanza which the saga associates with his very first encounter with Steingerður. He has been enchanted by her eyes and suspects that this is going to have dire consequences for both of them. He spends kennings lavishly on the young woman: "the linen-bedecked Hrist of the beer" *(lauka brims hörvi glæst Hrist)*, "Fríður of the golden necklace" *(gullmens Fríðr)*, "Hlín of rings" *(hringa Hlín)*. Her "moon of the eyelash" *(brámáni)* shines upon him beneath the "bright sky of the brows" *(ljóss brúna himinn)*; "the moons of the eyelids" *(hvarma tungl)* strike him with their ray:

Brámáni skein brúna	Brightly shone the beaming
brims und ljósum himni	brow-moons of the goodly
Hristar hörvi glæstrar	lady linen-dight, how
haukfránn á mik lauka;	like a hawk's, upon me;
en sá geisli sýslir	but that beam from forehead's—
síðan gullmens Fríðar	bright-hued-orbs, I fear me,
hvarma tungls ok hringa	of the Eir-of-gold doth
Hlínar óþurft mína.	ill spell for us later.

The leek breakers' (the spiced breakers') (= the beer's) linen-bedecked Hrist's (= the woman's) hawk-keen eyelash moon (= eye) shone toward me under the eyebrow's bright sky (= the forehead); but this ray from the gold necklace's Fríð's (= the woman's) eyelid moon (= eye) will have dire consequences for me and the Hlín of rings (= the woman).

Even the modern reader, who is completely unfamiliar with this kind of poetry, may perhaps perceive some of the poet's melancholy and fatalism behind the tightly knit verbal meshwork.

149

Kormákur is at his best in more discreet formulations or in situations that are captured in an impressionistic manner. He can present himself as "the dark squire," "Ögmund's son," "the skald," and talk about his curly hair, his black eyes, and his pale complexion. Quite often he simply mentions the woman he loves by name without circumlocutions. There is a unique charm in the scene in which the girl is curiously regarding the strange young man, leaning on some kind of half door with an opening down below so that her feet are partly visible beneath it—these ankles which at once make the poet's heart beat faster:

Brunnu beggja kinna	Brightly beamed the lights-of-
björt ljós á mik drósar	both-her-cheeks upon me—
—oss hlœgir þat eigi—	e'er will I recall it—
eldhúss of við feldan;	o'er the heaped-up woodpile;
en til ökla svanna	and the instep saw I
ítrvaxins gatk líta	of the shapely woman—
—þrá muna oss um ævi	no laughing matter, lo! my
eldask—hjá þreskeldi.	longing—by the threshold.

The maid's both cheeks' clear lights (= the eyes) burn toward me—this gives me no rest—over the sitting room door; I could see the beautifully statured maiden's ankles—our yearning will endure as long as we live—at the threshold.

Enthusiastically Kormákur estimates the worth of one eye of the adored girl at three hundred and her hair at five hundred wadmal. In all, her value is equal to the whole of Iceland, the faraway land of the Huns, Denmark, England, and Ireland combined. On another occasion the poet asserts that rocks will float on water and lands sink and the great famous mountains will fall into the sea before there will be born another woman as beautiful as Steingerður. There is strong sensualism and fervor in some stanzas, where his imagination revolves around the beloved woman's

150

bed and his union with her. There is, e.g., one memorable episode, describing Kormák's first encounter with Steingerður after his first journey abroad. They sit down under the open sky and talk until nightfall. Then they cannot find their horses and go to a small farmhouse not far away. There they are allowed to spend the night and go to sleep in their beds, which are separated only by a wooden partition. In a stanza the skald complains that they are resting each on his side of the board; powerful fate has its share in that. When shall we two be allowed joyfully to share one bed? he asks. According to an eminent specialist of skaldic poetry, Ernst Albin Kock, however, this question is expressed in a wording that has a coarse sexual hidden meaning. This applies to the final kennings for Kormákur himself and the girl he loves— if the scholar has interpreted the difficult passage correctly:

Hvílum, handar bála	Side by side we rest here,
Hlín—valda sköp sínu,	Sif-of-jewels,—I fear we're
þat séum, reið at ráði,	prey to hostile powers—
rík—tveim megin bríkar,	parted by a wall, though:
nærgi's oss í eina	when, oh, when, I wonder
angrlaust sæing göngum,	(Hild-of-silken-ribbons),
dýr Sköfnungi drafnar	shall we, free from fretting,
dúneyjar vit Freyja.	(fair one), sleep together?

We rest, arm-flame's (gold's) Hlín (= woman, Steingerður) each on his side of a wooden partition. A powerful fate rules that; we see that it is hostile. When shall we, Freyja of the down-isle (= woman, Steingerður), dear to the water-foam's Sköfnungur (= man, Kormákur), share the same bed without harm?

The metaphor "Freyja of the down islet" *(dúneyjar Freyja)* is, of course, taken from the islets where eiderdown is collected, a well-known Icelandic activity. In this case, according to Kock, the picture was intended to refer to her pubes. And when the skald talks about himself, using the name of the sword he has wielded in battle, as "Sköfnungur of the water foam" *(drafnar Sköfnungr)*, that would be a corresponding allusion to his male instrument, his *gladius seminis*.[16] This is an interpretation of Kormák's stanza that at any rate is not at odds with the skalds' penchant for the ambiguous, the linguistic picture puzzle.

Kormák's love poetry is complemented by his equally wholehearted libelous poetry. The latter is, of course, really the reverse side of the former: in the same stanza in which he praises Steingerður, he pours out the vials of his wrath upon her husband, Þorvaldur tinteinn. In a situation picture from the sea the skald can describe the contrast between his own manly labor of taking in the sails with the other man's petty concern about a broken dung sled.

Kormák's poetry has been compared to later love poetry from the Middle Ages. One scholar has pointed to the Celtic Tristan legend and called Kormákur a forerunner of the troubadours—several hundred years before a Bernard de Ventadour tuned his instrument. Troubadour is not a totally misleading designation for Kormákur Ögmundarson, but in that case he is an inimitably Norse troubadour. Light winds from sea and moorland, mountains and rivers, from Icelandic everyday life breathe on us out of his dróttkvætt stanzas. Kormák's poetry is an outstanding document on Nordic love in the eleventh century.

This opinion has recently been challenged by a young Icelandic scholar.[17] In an extensive investigation covering four typical "skald sagas"—about Kormákur, Hallfreður, Björn Hítdælakappi and Gunnlaugur ormstunga—he maintains that the cited love poetry was inspired by Continental European troubadour poetry. In other words, the verses could not have been composed by the authors to whom they are ascribed, but must be regarded as the works of the men who wrote the sagas themselves, men who had a good knowledge of the literary culture of the twelfth and thirteenth centuries in Europe. The thesis is based on a reasonable skepticism and an altogether legitimate desire to view Icelandic poetry in a broader perspective of literary history. On the other hand, it is based on a far too flimsy foundation. The similarities between the Icelandic poetry in question and the works of the minstrels are very general and can be explained on the basis of their subject matter and purpose; metrically the dróttkvætt in skaldic poetry is something absolutely original. No direct, historically corroborated points of contact have been demonstrated; these are pure assumptions. And if the love poetry of the skald sagas seems to have little in common with authentic native tradition, this may be an optical illusion because comparatively little has been preserved from personal amorous poetry. Since, as mentioned above, such poetry was punishable by law, it may have led a more hidden existence, limited to those persons or circles that were most closely involved.

Of course, research has not said its final word on the matter. Nevertheless, the burden of proof rests on those who, as a matter of principle, want to deny Kormákur and his brother skalds the creation of their amatory poetry.

Eilífur Guðrúnarson

If Eilífur Guðrúnarson deserves a place in this survey, it is not only because his *Þórsdrápa* has been considered to be perhaps the most difficult of all dróttkvætt poetry that we know. This poem also represents a certain kind of skaldic poetry and evidently also a definite era in the stylistic development of the genre. According to *Skáldatal* (see p. 120, above) Eilífur wrote about Hákon jarl—who led the defense of heathendom in Norway against the victorious missionary king Ólafur Tryggvason—and consequently must have lived during the latter part of the tenth century. In the year 1000

Christianity was adopted as the official religion of Iceland. This was a settlement of an internal struggle between the old and the new "custom" that was both peaceful and, on certain points, marked by compromise. It has been asserted that in poetry, too, indications can be found that adherents of the old faith rallied to the defense of this tradition near the end of the tenth century. There are those who have regarded even *Völuspá* from this perspective—as a grand synthesis of Nordic pagan faith in its most noble form. (See p. 36, above.)

A poem like Eilífur Guðrúnarson's *Þórsdrápa* accords in its way very well with the religious situation of the time. As its name denotes, it is a drápa dedicated to Þór—that one of the Æsir who was most often pitted against the foreigner, the White-Christ. Nineteen coherent stanzas—and probably two more half stanzas—have been preserved from *Þórsdrápa* in Snorri's *Edda*, which also furnishes the title of the poem. The poem relates that Þór, with neither his hammer nor his belt of strength, visits the giant Geirröður and with his Æsir strength thwarts all evil designs and finally kills both the giant and his two horrible daughters. This homage to the powerful god is fashioned in a kenning language which even for dróttkvætt is unprecedented in its sheer massiveness and difficulty of interpretation. It seems as though the heathen rallying of strength is reflected even in style. Furthermore, some scholars assert that a striking increase in the number of mythological kennings can be observed in skaldic poetry during this very period of time.

As a sample of the art of *Þórsdrápa* let us examine stanza 14, which describes an incident that occurred in Geirröð's cave. The giant's daughters Gjálp and Greip attempt to overcome Þór and his companion Þjálfi by surprise by suddenly pressing the bench on which the travelers are sitting up against the low roof of the cave and thus crushing their skulls. But the attack does not achieve its intended purpose:

Ok húmloga himni　　　　Lötens brunspröt de läto
hallfylvingum vallar,　　　låghemmets skumvalv klämma,
—tráðusk þar við tróði　　tryckta med brak mot taket
tungls brásalir—þrungu;　tunglens bråsalar gungat;
húfstjóri braut hváru　　svävande stormnäs' stävkarms
hreggs vafreiða tveggja　styrare läggbröt bägge
hlátr-Elliða hellis　　　grottvivens skratts skutors
hundfornan kjöl sprundi.　skorvgamla köl med böl då.

And they pressed the sky of the dusk flames with their
leaning brown staves of the field—the halls of the eyebrow moon were pushed then with a stick; the steerer
of the hull of the fluttering nesses of the storm broke
the keel of the laughter launch of both the cave crones.

This rebus perhaps requires some comment. Whereas
the meaning of the second helming, or half stanza, seems
clear, the first one presents difficulties which various scholars have attempted to solve in different ways. Åke Ohlmark's metrical interpretation of this helming is based in
part on several readings proposed by Ernst Albin Kock.
"Lötens brunspröt ("the felly's brown spokes") is a free
rendering of *vallar hall-fylvingar* ("the field's inclining
brown sticks"), that is, Þór's and Þjálfi's brown walking
staves, which they press against the roof of the dusky cave
in order to counter the sudden pressure exerted by the
giantesses from beneath the bench. The roof of the cavern,
in turn, is designated by the kenning *húm-loga himinn*
("the sky of the dusk flame"), which in the translation has
become "låghemmets skumvalv" ("the dusk-vault of the
flame-home"). The kenning *tungls brásalir* exemplifies a
kind of verbal inversion that is not unusual in dróttkvætt
poetry; it would be more logical to write *brátungls salir*.
"Moon of the eyebrow," as we have already seen, is a commonly used kenning for the eye; the hall of the eye is
the skull. All things considered, it is probably the skulls
of the giantesses that are meant here, as they press upward

from beneath the bench. But this could also refer to Þór and Þjálfi since their heads are simultaneously being shoved against the roof of the cave. The second helming contains the counterblow and the retribution. Þór is designated by the imposing kenning complex *hreggs vafr-eiða húf-stjóri: hregg* is a storm, *eið* a neck of land between two bodies of water; the storm's fluttering *(vafr-)* nesses are the storm clouds racing across the sky; *húfr* designates certain planks in the hull of a vessel, but is often used also as a *pars pro toto* for the entire ship; the vessel that sails forward among the clouds is the famous thunder chariot, and its *stjóri* is none other than Þór himself. Or in Ohlmark's Swedish version: "svävande stormnäs' stävkarms styrare" ("the steersman of the prow-railing of the soaring storm-nesses"). With the help of his staff Þór forces the bench toward the floor and breaks "the cave women's" *(hellis sprund)* backbones: "the laughter launch" *(hlátr-Elliði)* is the chest, and the keel of this boat is the curved spine. The epithet *hundforn* refers to the giants as extremely old beings, but as so often elsewhere, here too the prefix *hund-* ("dog") probably has a contemptuous connotation.

A modern reader need not feel completely unfamiliar with Eilíf's kenning language. The comparison between the ship and the chest, which was probably suggested by the similarity between the ribs of a ship and human ribs, can be found in the works of modern poets like Harry Martinson and Ragnar Thoursie.[18] And the ancient poet's development of the picture with the spine as a ship's keel is an ingenious stroke that makes it even more vivid. What may have a disturbing effect on us when we try to appreciate such a stanza esthetically—quite aside from the sheer difficulty of the language—is primarily the impression we get of a studied jigsaw puzzle. But it would be sorely anachronistic to apply to this kind of poetry what is perhaps the favorite critical criterion of our time: that of "the personal expression," "spontaneity," "genuineness"—a basis of evaluation as time-restricted and subjective as any. And it would be just as anachronistic to deny dróttkvætt skalds in general "inspiration" merely because their inspiration was expressed in forms different from those we have become accustomed to. Is it not possible to imagine that Eilífur Guðrúnarson experienced the true artistic joy of release when he succeeded in fashioning his poetic vision into the heavy harmony of the dróttkvætt stanza and in binding his sweeping view, his burlesque imagination, into the firmly riveted eight-lined verbal smithwork? And did not his contemporary audience feel any of the magic glow that we like to associate with relevant and living poetry? Cannot even a Nordic man or woman from our time feel something of this when confronted with the ancient skald's work?

Hallfreður Ottarsson, Vandræðaskáld

A contemporary of Eilífur Guðrúnarson is Einar Helgason skálaglamm (the surname, "the jingle of scales," according to tradition from a pair of gilded scales which he received as a poet's reward). He is also one of Hákon jarl's skalds. Einar is mentioned in *Egils saga Skalla-Grímssonar* as Egil's young friend and pupil. His own best-known work is an ingenious drápa to Hákon jarl, *Vellekla* ("Lack of Gold"), whose title is considered to imply a rather unvarnished admonition to Hákon to be generous to the skald. In this poem, too, scholars believe they have found reflections of the hardening religious struggle that is typical of this era: the jarl's efforts on behalf of the pagan cult are praised.

The special problems created for the skald during this time of transition are reflected in the most interesting manner in the poetry of Hallfreður Óttarsson (ca. 965–1007). To be sure, Snorri's *Edda* has preserved a half stanza by Eilífur Guðrúnarson in which Christ seems to be mentioned

157

as the king of Rome, sitting by the Urðarbrunn (the well of Urður). Even the skald of the vigorously pagan *Þórs drápa* must have heeded the signs of the times and finally also paid homage to the White Christ. But however the case may have been with Eilífur himself, the process of reorientation with its many complications is clearly seen in the case of Hallfreður. He is said to have received his surname *vandræðaskáld*, "the troublesome poet," from Ólafur Tryggvason. He became Ólaf's most prominent court poet. The little saga about Hallfreður tells us that he submitted to being baptized only on the condition that the king himself should become his godfather. Only reluctantly does the skald say farewell to the mythology that was so intimately connected with his art.[19] Everyone has written poetry so that they have enjoyed Óðin's favor, he declares in a stanza in front of Ólafur. He has himself had good experiences from Óðin's rule and is not inclined to exchange his adoration for hatred merely because he is now a servant of Christ:

Öll hefr ætt til hylli	To praise thy power, Odin,
Óðins skipat ljóðum,	poets have e'er indited
allgilda man ek aldar	sacred songs—for me 'tis
iðju várra niðja,	seemly to remember;
en trauðr, því at vel Viðris	loath I were—for well did [me—
vald hugnaðisk skaldi,	Vidrir's might aye suit [great-
legg ek á frumver Friggjar	to harbor hate 'gainst Frigg's-
fjón, því at Kristi þjónum.	husband, Christ though serve I.

All men have composed their poetry in such a way as to gain the favor of Óðinn. I remember the excellent achievements of our forebears. And unwillingly—for Viðrir's (Óðin's) power pleased me—do I turn my hatred against Frigg's husband (= Óðinn) just because I serve Christ.

The zealous king is offended, according to the saga, and tells the skald to do penance by composing another stanza. Hallfreður complies and now he expresses himself less tepidly, as befits a proselyte:

Mér skyli Freyr ok Freyja	Let then Freyr and Freya—
fjörð lét ek af dul Njarðar	the folly of Niord forsook I—
—liknisk gröm við Grímni—	wreak their wrath on me, and
gramr ok Þórr inn rammi.	wretches worship Odin:
Krist vil ek allrar ástar,	Christ's love alone will I,
erumk leið sonar reiði	loath to have His anger,
—vald á frægt und foldar	and His Father's eke; for
feðr—einn ok guð kveðja.	all the glory is Their's aye.

May Freyr and Freyja and Þór the mighty be angry with me. I have already abandoned the folly of Njörður. Let evil spirits pay homage to Grímnir (Óðinn). Christ's love alone and God's do I crave. I regret the Son's wrath. He has illustrious power under the Father of the world.

There are fragments preserved from Hallfreð's memorial drápa for Ólafur after the battle of Svoldir, at which the poet, however, was not present. If we can believe the saga, he did not feel at home anywhere after Ólaf's death, and he spent the few remaining years of his life in the shadow of his old master. In this section his biography has a touch of legend. Thus Ólafur appears to his skald in a dream and admonishes him not to kill Eiríkur jarl, one of the conspirators at Svoldir. And the last of the stanzas that have been ascribed to Hallfreður breathes not only a stoical composure in the face of death but also piety and a concern for his soul's salvation which would have pleased his godfather:

Ek mynda nú andask	Dreadless would I die now—
—ungr vark harðr i tungu—	dagger-sharp my tongue was—
senn, ef sálu minni,	nor sad, if saved I knew my
sorglaust, vissa ek borgit.	soul was with my Maker:
Veit ek at vætki of sýtik,	I shall not worry—well I

valdi guð hvar aldri   wot that some time each must
—dauðr verðr hverr—   die—hell-fire I fear, though
    nema hræðumk   —for my God will keep me.
helvíti, skal slíta.

I would now die free of apprehension if I knew that
my soul would be saved. When young I was sharp of
tongue. I know I should not be afraid—all men must
die. I fear only hell. May God rule over where I shall
pass my life (in the world beyond).

Hallfreð's dróttkvætt style is on the whole simpler than
that of his predecessors. This is due to the fact that he
refrained from the pagan mythology of the kennings out
of respect for his lord, who abhorred and assailed the worship of the Æsir in all of its manifestations.

The statement that Hallfreð's art is relatively easy to
understand holds true also for his erotic poetry. For in
Hallfreðar saga, as in *Kormáks saga*, there is a series of
lausavísur connected with a love story—but not such a
tragic and fateful one as for the older poet. Like Kormákur,
young Hallfreður sees his beloved girl, Kolfinna, given in
marriage to an older rival, Grís. But he does not seem to
take his ill fate so tragically. Later on, indeed, he has the
satisfaction of enjoying Kolfina's favors during a night spent
with her at a summer dairy. In one stanza he declares
arrogantly that he has flayed the goat skin from the pig;
i.e., he has cuckolded the husband. There is a striking contrast between the less successful Kormák's pining and heat-
edly sensual lament in a similar situation with Steingerður.
(See p. 146, above). The wording is characteristic of the
tone that Hallfreður permits himself about Kolfinna's husband, even in stanzas which, according to the saga, are
recited directly to her. In such libelous art he is superior
to Kormákur. He is fond of dwelling on the picture of
Grís as a bedfellow of the fair young woman. The man

waddles up to her bed like a seagull, his stomach distended with herring, and falls upon her with his repulsive stench, while the wife, downhearted, droops "like a swan on the water." Conventional kennings for man or warrior are used by the courier Hallfreður in parodistically rustic variations for Grís to brand him as a yokel: for instance, instead of *stála striðir*, "the breaker of steel, swords," or *linns landa þægir*, "the serpent's land's (= the gold's) devastator" ("generous man"), he is called *orfa*, "the scythe handle's," *striðir* or *orfþægir*.

On the other hand, however, Hallfreður also finds beautiful and laudatory metaphors for the woman he loves—as when he envisions her as a swan on the water. As with Kormákur, there is perhaps now and then a scabrous hidden meaning lurking in his kennings. But this certainly does not apply to the following finely executed comparison; it may remind the reader of Fröding's picture of Elsa Örn as a pleasure yacht in *Balen*:

Þykki mér, es ek þekki	When that I behold the
þunnísunga Gunni,	Hlín-of-gauzy-kerchiefs,
sem fleybrautir fljóti	't is as though between isles
fley meðal tveggja eyja;	twain a galley floated;
en þás sér á Ságu	and, when nigh a knot of
saums í kvinna flaumi,	noble maids, as though within
sem skrautbúin skríði	golden gear adight, a
skeið með gyldum reiða.	gallant ship proceeded.

It seems to me, when I catch sight of the Gunnur (name of a valkyrie) of gauzy kerchiefs (?) (= the woman, Kolfinna), as though a ship were gliding over the water between two islands. But when Sága (name of a goddess) of needlework (= the woman, Kolfinna) appears among a bevy of ladies, it is as though a warship with golden tackling were sailing forth in its splendor.

Sighvatur Þórðarson

Of no other court skald has so much poetry been pre-served as of Sighvatur Þórðarson (ca. 995–1045). Snorri quotes him copiously in *Heimskringla* and gives a very appreciative portrait of the man. According to the same source Sighvatur seems to have enjoyed high favor with Ólafur Haraldsson, later Ólafur the Saint. He held the post of a *stallari,* one of the most prominent men of the court, and he was entrusted with important diplomatic missions by the king.

Snorri relates that Sighvatur was missing from the pha-lanx of the royal army when the fatal battle of Stiklastaðir was fought in 1030; he was then on a pilgrimage to Rome. Another of Ólaf's skalds, Þormóður Kolbrúnarskáld, could not refrain from making a remark about his absence and said aloud to a companion:

"Let us not stand so closely, my brothers-in-arms, that Sighvatur skald cannot take his place when he comes. He will want to stand next to the king, nor will the king have it otherwise."

The king overheard that and replied: "You need not jibe at Sighvatur because he is not here. He has fol-lowed me often and well. Right now he will be praying for us, and that is something we really have need of."

Þormóður answered: "It may be so, Sire, that what you need most now is prayers. But the lines would be thin around your standard if your entire bodyguard were now on pilgrimage to Rome. It is also true, what we talked about that time, that nobody got near because of Sighvatur, if one wished to speak to you."

When after his return to Norway Sighvatur was told about such reproaches, he is said to have refuted them with the stanza:

Hafa láti mik heitan
Hvíta-Krist at víti
eld, ef Áleif vildak,
emk skírr of þat, firrask.
Vatnœrin hefk vitni,
vark til Rúms í háska,
öld leynik því aldri,
annarra þau manna.

Holy Christ may cast me
in quenchless fires of hellpain,
the All-seeing, if from
Olaf I fled: I am guiltless.
Witnesses have I like water:
I went to Rome as palmer,
amends to make for my
many sins—why deny it?

> May the White Christ let me suffer the hot fire if I chose
> to remain away from Ólafur. I am innocent of this. I
> have multitudes of witnesses that I was undertaking a
> perilous pilgrimage to Rome. This I will not conceal
> from people.

Also quoted is a beautiful stanza by Sighvatur in which
he has the whole Norwegian mountain landscape partici-
pate in the grief at Ólaf's death—an animation of nature
such as is rarely found in skaldic poetry:

Há þótti mér hlæja
höll um Nóreg allan
—fyrr var ek kendr á
   knörrum—
klif, meðan Ólafr lifði.
Nú þykki mér miklu
—mitt stríð er svá—hlíðir
—jöfurs hylli varð ek alla—
óblíðari síðan.

Smiled, methought, the sloping
sides of braes in Norway—
e'er close to him kept me
the king—when Olaf lived still:
gloomier now the grey fells—
my grief is heavy—with him I
sailed the seas in my time—
since the king did leave us.

> The high, steep cliffs seemed to me to laugh over all
> of Norway—I earlier sailed on a ship—as long as Ólafur
> lived. Now I think the mountain slopes—my grief is
> heavy—I enjoyed by lord's full favor—are much sterner
> since his death.

According to Snorri, Sighvatur also became a dear friend
of Ólaf's son Magnús when at an early age the latter became
the ruler of Norway. But the experienced poet and dip-

lomat does not shrink back from reminding his new lord straight out of the duties of a king. After a conference among the king's friends it is said to have fallen to Sighvat's lot to warn Magnús of the rebellious mood in his country. He solved the delicate mission by means of a poem, *Bersöglisvísur* ("Outspoken Verses"). At the same time as he assures the young sovereign of his loyalty and friendship, he urges him strongly in the poem to refrain from his policy of vengeance against his father's Norwegian adversaries. One verse runs as follows:

Hverr eggjar þik höggva,	Whoever eggs thee, atheling,
hjaldrgegnir, bú þegna?	to axe the farmers' cattle?
Ofrausn er þat jöfri	Unheard of is 't for hero
innan lands at vinna.	to harry in his own country!
Engr hafði svá ungum	Youthful king such cursèd
áðr bragningi ráðit.	counsel ne'er was given:
Rán hykk rekkum þínum,	weary of sack are thy warriors,
(reiðr er herr) konungr,	ween I, and wrathful the farmers.
leiðask.	

> Whoever eggs you, man of battle, to tear down the farmers' houses? It is arrogance for a prince to harry in his own country. No one had given the young ruler such advice. I think that your men, king,—furious are the people—are weary of plundering.

Snorri points out that after this admonition Magnús was willing to listen to reason and soon became popular and beloved of all his people and for that reason was called the Good.

What is most easily accessible in Sighvat's poetry, and most alive to people of our day, are probably his *Austrfararvísur* ("Stanzas from a Journey to the East"). Here he reproduces miscellaneous impressions from a journey to Rögnvaldur jarl in Västergötland undertaken in 1019 on behalf of King Ólafur. With his light touch—it has often been called journalistic—and his humorous comments this travel causerie is a rather unique example of skaldic poetry. There is a refreshing breath of speed and adventure in a sea-voyage stanza like the following:

Kátr var ek opt, þá er úti
örðigt veðr á fjörðum
vísa segl, í vási,
vindblásit skóf Strinda.
Hestr óð kafs at kostum,
kilir ristu haf Lista,
út þá er eisa létum
undan skeiðr at sundi.

I was often merry despite fatigue when, out in the fjords, h a r s h w e a t h e r pressed the wind-filled sail of the Strand-people's lord (= Ólafur). The sea-stallion sped splendidly; the keels cleft the waves near Listi when we let the warships rush forth from the sound.

Less merry are the comments on how the royal delegates struggle on foot through the vast forest along the borders of Värmland, sore of foot and irritable of mood:

Vara fýst, er ek rann rastir
reiðr of skóg frá Eiðum
—menn of veit at mœttum
meini—tólf ok eina.
Hykka fót án flekkum,
fell sár á il hvára,
hvast gengum þó þingat
þann dag, konungs mönnum.

Well you may know, unwilling and weary we trudged thirteen miles from Eid, nor idled, onward with much hardship: I swear, blisters and sores were on the soles of us strollers [est's as fared through the Eid Forfastness the king's men hastily.

It was not eagerly that I ran, angry, twelve miles plus one—all should know that we suffered distress—through the forest from Eið. I think there was not a foot without blisters; sores afflicted the soles of all the king's men. Yet we went our way swiftly that day.

Sighvatur also describes the company's difficulties in finding quarters for the night in Västergötland, where people generally seem to be rather inhospitable. One night he is turned away by three farmers in a row, each of whom declares that his name is Ölvir. The fourth one—who nevertheless is said to be the best of the lot—also shows him the door. The evening before he was just as unsuccessful on a farm called Hof, where the servants declared that there was a religious rite being celebrated:

Réð ek til hofs at hœfa.	At dark to Hof we drifted.
Hurð var aptr, en spurðumk,	Doors were barred; so outside
inn setta ek nef nenninn,	stood I, knocking, and stoutly
niðrlútr fyrir útan.	stuck my nose in, plucky. [us:
Orð gat ek fæst af fyrðum,	Gruffly answer they gave [ened
flögð bað ek, en þau sögðu	"Get you gone!" And threat-
hnekðumk heiðnir rekkar—	us all: 't was heathen-holy.
heilagt, við þau deila.	To hell with all those fellows!

I rode to Hof. The door was closed; I remained outside, bowed down, stuck my nose in boldly and asked questions. I got few words out of the people. They said they were performing sacred rites. The heathens drove me away. I asked the ogresses to take them.

He is met with the same information at the next farmhouse door; the pagan Västgötar do not allow strangers to attend their rites:

"Gakkattu inn", kvað ekkja.	"Wreak his wrath will Óthin, [like gammer.
"armi drengr, in lengra.	wretch," said a witch- [further
Hræðumk ek við Óðins	"Keep out," quoth she, "nor
—erum heiðin vér—reiði."	come; for we are heathen."
Rýgr kvazk inni eiga	"Also," this ancient beldame
óþekk, sú er mér hnekði,	added, she who forbade me
álfa blót, sem úlfi,	foot to set in, the slattern,
ótvín í bœ sínum.	"sacred to elves we are making."

"Don't come in any further, wretch," said a crone. I fear Óðin's wrath—we are heathen." The hideous woman who drove me away like a wolf said clearly that she was sacrificing to the elves in her house.

Of his arrival in "Rögnvald's town," Skara, Sighvatur gives a somewhat more festive picture. The riders are anxious to make a favorable impression on the fair sex as they gallop through the street and prance on their steeds just like the town's lieutenant in Fröding's poem:

	[the ladies
Út munu ekkjur líta,	Readily will look [are passing
allsnúðula, prúðar	and lasses, as we [of our riding
—fljóð sjá reyk—hvar ríðum	by the road, on the dust [castle
Rögnvalds í bý gögnum.	fast, up to Rögnvald's [our horses
Keyrum hross svá at heyri	Let us spur to speed [high-born
harða langt, at garði,	sprightly, so that maidens [us
hesta rás ór húsum	and fair from the hall may hear
hugsvinn kona innan.	whisk by as we gallop briskly.

Stately ladies will surely look quickly—the women see a cloud of dust—to where we ride through Rögnvald's town. Let us spur our horses to the courtyard so that the clever woman from inside the house may hear the horses' quick trot at a great distance.

These examples of Sighvat's dróttkvætt stanzas show that he cultivates a comparatively simple and unaffected diction; he uses kennings very moderately, and in that respect he continues the line from Hallfreður.

Some Later Court Skalds

The foremost skald in the retinue of King Haraldur Sigurðarson harðráði (d. 1066), himself a connoisseur and practitioner of the poetic art, was Arnór Þórðarson, called "jarlaskáld" because he had also served the Orkney jarls. His most famous work, however, is a praise poem to Harald's coruler, Magnús Ólafsson the Good, *Hrynhenda*. According to tradition, Haraldur is said to have declared, not without envy, that this poem—contrary to Arnór's poem to Haraldur himself—would be remembered as long as there were people living in the North. *Hrynhenda* was named for its meter, *hrynhent,* which is introduced into laudatory poetry in this poem. It can be defined as a dróttkvætt stanza, increased by two syllables per line, so that every line has four lifts instead of three. The effect is that the stanza becomes much richer and is especially appropriate for pompous eloquence. Here is an example of both the metrics and the panegyric tone in Arnór's *Hrynhenda*:

	[matter
Hefnir, fenguð yrkis efni,	Ólaf's avenger! mighty
Áleifs. Gervik slíkt at málum	makest thou for song: I seize it;
Hlakkar lætr þú hrælög drekka	dew-of-wounds to drink thou givest
hauka. Nú mun kvæði aukask.	dun-hued eagles: grows my poem!
Fjórar hefr þú randa rýrir	Magnus! Thou didst win in one short
reyrar setrs, á einum vetri,	winter—first aye wast in sword-play—
allvaldr, ert þú ofvægr kallaðr,	victories four: invincible they
örva hríðir frœkn of görvar.	vow thou art, destroyer-of-war-shields!

Ólaf's avenger (= King Magnús, Ólaf's son), you gave me the subject of a poem. I turn such into words. You cause Hlökk's (valkyrie name) hawks (= ravens) to drink corpse liquid (= blood). Now the poem will grow. In one winter, sovereign and bucklers' stem's (= the sword's) seat's (= the shield's) destroyer (= warrior)—you are called overwhelming—, you have valiantly fought four storms of arrows (= battles).

Another poet active during the twelfth century was Einar Skúlason, who paid homage in his poetry to seven different kings. He achieved his greatest success as a poet with a memorial drápa of seventy-one stanzas, still preserved, about Ólafur the Saint. This poem, *Geisli* ("Ray"), is said to have been composed at the request of King Eysteinn in Norway and recited by the skald himself in 1153, or during the winter of 1153–54, in the cathedral of Trondheim, in the presence of the three corulers of Norway, Eysteinn, Sigurður, and Ingi, together with Archbishop Jón. This is a situation, it has been said, which "marks a high point in the official recognition of skaldic art."[20]

On the other hand, the same Einar Skúlason was to learn from personal experience that the golden age of court skalds was on the decline. When during a visit to Denmark he recited a poem to King Svend Grathe, an incredible thing happened: the poet received no reward. Einar gives vent to his distress in a stanza about the king's bad taste in preferring fiddles and pipes to poetry. It is difficult to avoid the suspicion that the Danish king may not have understood very much of the poetic homage that was paid to him!

In a way Einar's triumph in the cathedral of Trondheim can also be regarded as a testimony that court poetry had come a long way from its origin. *Geisli* deals not with a contemporary sovereign, but with a monarch who had been dead for over a century; it extolls not his achievements as a breaker of golden rings or feeder of ravens, but his holiness and miracles. The atmosphere surrounding this ecclesiastical ceremony is altogether different from that of the scene in which Egill Skalla-Grímsson, under the glaring eyes of Eiríkur blóðøx, ransoms his head with a drápa, or of the scene in which, at daybreak before the battle of Stiklastaðir, Þormóður Kolbrúnarskáld inspires the army to exploits and fidelity unto death by reciting the pagan poem *Bjarkamál hin fornu*. In these two cases the skald's function within a

169

present actuality is much more direct and tangible. Gradually court poetry also lost its significance as historic documentation, as history writing in prose was introduced and grew in importance. With its concrete and more detailed descriptions it soon replaced the fixed patterns of the skalds. The court skald gave way to the royal historiographer.

During its final phase Norse court poetry receives an impress of learned renaissance. It is revealing that Snorri Sturluson's own metrically equilibristic contribution to the genre, *Háttatal*, came to be included as a model in a book on poetics. (See p. 2, above.) Some of Snorri's descendants kept the noble tradition alive for a while after his death. Two of his nephews, the brothers Ólafur Þórðarson hvitaskáld (d. 1259) and Sturla Þórðarson (1214–84)—both of them historians—cultivated the art of the court skalds, but more as epigoni than as original writers. The account in *Skáldatal* (see p. 120, above) ends with *Jón Egilsson*—son of a third nephew of Snorri's—who praised King Eiríkur Magnússon in a poem in 1299. One scholar has given the following comment on the situation: "About the year 1300 skaldic poetry came to an end at the Norwegian court, where it had been sung since viking times and probably even longer. Now foreign, romantic poetry became popular: shortly afterwards the *Eufemia vísur* were written at the request of the Norwegian queen."[21]

Notes

1. Interesting examples of misinterpretations of skaldic verse made by Snorri himself are provided by Alistair Campbell in *Skaldic Verse and Anglo-Saxon History*, the Dorothea Coke Memorial Lecture in Northern Studies, delivered at University College, London, 17 March 1970 (published for the college by H. K. Lewis and Co., Ltd., London).

2. Sigurður Nordal, *Íslenzk menning I* (Reykjavík, 1942), pp. 239 ff.

3. On Snorri's authorship of *Egils saga* the most recent study

is P. Hallberg, *Snorri Sturluson och Egils saga Skallagrímssonar: Ett försök til språklig författarbestämning,* Studia Islandica 20, (Reykjavík, 1962).

4. Olsen set forth his hypothesis in his 1916 paper "Om trollruner," which was reprinted in his *Norrøne studier* (Oslo, 1938), pp. 12–16. His interpretation of Egil's runic scorn pole as number magic was questioned by W. Morgenroth in the article "Zahlenmagie in Runeninschriften: Kritische Bemerkungen zu einigen Interpretationsmethoden," *Zeitschrift der Ernst-Moritz-Arndt-Universität Greifswald* 10 (1961): 279–83.

5. Stefán Einarsson has addressed himself to this problem in "The Origin of Egill Skallagrímsson's *Runhenda,*" *Scandinavica et Fenno-Ugrica: Studier tillägnade Björn Collinder* (Stockholm, 1954), pp. 54–60.

6. The interpretation of the expression *ór hlátra ham* as ironic is criticized by Sigurður Nordal in his edition of *Egils saga Skalla-Grímssonar,* Íslenzk fornrit 2 (Reykjavík, 1933), p. 192. On the kenning *hlátr-Elliði,* used by Eilífur Guðrúnarson, see p. 156 of the text.

7. On this see Áke Ohlmarks, *Islands hedna skaldediktning* (Stockholm, 1957), p. 313.

8. On *lofköstr,* "praise pile," see Nordal, ed. cit., p. 263.

9. Ohlmarks, op. cit., p. 320.

10. Ibid., p. 299.

11. A complete verse translation of *Sonatorrek* is found in Hollander's *The Skalds* (New York, 1945), pp. 90–98; a close English rendering in P. Hallberg, *The Icelandic Saga,* tr. Paul Schach (Lincoln, Nebr., 1962), pp. 129–30. Those who wish to study the poem more thoroughly will find Ólafur M. Ólafsson's edition and commentary *Sonatorrek* (Reykjavík, 1968) useful.

12. For additional poems by Kormákur, see *The Sagas of Kormák and The Sworn Brothers,* tr. Lee M. Hollander (Princeton, 1949). The verse of Hallfreður is found in *Heimskringla,* tr. Lee M. Hollander (Austin, 1964). See also The *Saga of Gisli,* tr. George Johnston with an essay by Peter Foote (Toronto, 1963) and *The Saga of Gunnlaug Serpent-Tongue,* tr. R. Quirk (London, 1957).

13. Ohlmarks, op. cit., p. 299.

14. Hans E. Kinck, "Kjærligheten i Kormaks saga," *Mange slags kunst* (Oslo, 1921), p. 70.

15. In the introduction to his edition of *Kormáks saga,* Íslenzk fornrit 8, (Reykjavík, 1939) p. lxxx.

16. See Kock's commentary in his *Notationes norrœnæ* (Lund, 1944). Ohlmarks makes use of this interpretation, op. cit., p. 403f.

17. Bjarni Einarsson in *Skáldasögur: Um uppruna og eðli ástaskáldasagnanna fornu* (Reykjavík, 1961). The title means "Skald sagas: Concerning the genesis and nature of the ancient love stories about poets."

18. In the final stanza of Martinson's poem "Natt i staden," published in *Spektrum* (1932); and in Thoursie's poem "Skolavslutning" in the collection *Emaljögat* (1945).

19. On Hallfreð's dilemma, see Cecil Wood, "The Reluctant Christian and the King of Norway," *Scandinavian Studies* 31 (1959): 65–72.

20. Jón Helgason, *Norges og Islands digtning* (Stockholm, 1953), p. 154.

21. Ibid., p. 131.

CHAPTER 5

Christian Poetry in the Forms of Eddic Lay and Skaldic Verse

The form and style of Eddic lay and skaldic verse have deep roots in Norse mythology. Remarkably enough, however, they were sufficiently elastic to be adapted to the new material that was brought by the change of faith. In Iceland there arose an extensive body of Christian poetry that was composed in Eddic and, especially, skaldic meters and thus continued the Norse form tradition.

Among Christian poems in Eddic style, *Sólarljóð* is incomparably the foremost. Like the Eddic poems, it is anonymous; the date of its composition has been assigned variously to the twelfth or thirteenth century. The meter is ljóðaháttr, that is, the same as in *Hávamál*. It can also be said that *Sólarljóð* combines in it characteristics both of this poem and of *Völuspá*. Like *Hávamál*, it is didactic poetry with concrete examples for man's conduct and good advice for our lives. At the same time it has apocalyptic and eschatological strains which remind us of *Völuspá*.

Sólarljóð is far from being a transparent poem. The disposition exhibits abrupt transitions, and in places the symbolism has defied the efforts of scholars to interpret it. Not until near the end of the eighty-two stanzas is it revealed that the whole poem is ascribed to a deceased person who has returned from the dead and speaks to a person close to him who is still alive—evidently it is a father speaking to his son. But otherwise the situation is veiled in obscurity, and the dead man's speech is muffled, as it were.

173

The first part of the poem gives examples of various kinds of sins and their consequences; it is practical life wisdom from the Christian point of view. Thus there is a warning against sensual pleasures and women, and a dismal story is told about two inseparable friends who become rivals for the same "fair maiden" and kill each other in a duel because of her. Furthermore, people are warned to be on their guard against pride, for it leads away from God.

"Never trust your enemies, even if they approach you with friendly words"; the warning reveals the same distrust as in *Hávamál*. What may happen if the warning goes unheeded is illustrated by a story about an assassination. But here we also see the essential difference between this poem and *Hávamál*, which completely lacks the perspective of life after death. In *Sólarljóð* the Lord sees a crime being committed, and he bids the soul of the victim to enter into the bliss of heaven; "but his evil foes / will not early be / relieved from e'erlasting pain."

Then there follow a series of seven different rules for personal behavior: "heed thou give them / nor forget them ever: / in good stead will they stand thee."

In the next section the presentation becomes more subjective, and the speaker affords several glimpses into his life history. He was happy in "the lovely world" and appeared happy in the eyes of men: "for I knew little of the future." But his enjoyment of life was of little avail against the inexorable: death's fetters were drawn ever more tightly about him. *Heljar meyjar*, "Death's hand-maidens"—possibly a kenning for illnesses or pains—beset him every night. At this point—apparently on the very threshold between life and death—there is a series of seven verses, all of which begin with the words "Sól ek sá" ("I saw the sun"); it is evidently these verses that gave the entire poem its name. The first of them reads as follows:

Sól ek sá,	The sun I saw,
sanna dagstjörnu,	the day-star in sooth,
drúpa dynheimum í;	droop in the world of din;
en Heljar grind	but Hel's gate heard I
heyrðak á annan veg	on the other hand
þjóta þungliga.	grate with grinding.

There is a painfully burning intensity in this song to the sun, this farewell to the powerful symbol of life on earth—"it seemed to me as on God Almighty I gazed"—while the portal to the kingdom of death screeches, the tongue in the mouth of the dying man turns to wood, and everything around him grows cold. Then there follows the night of death:

Öllum lengri	Longer than any
var sú in eina nótt,	lasted that night
er ek lá stirðr á stráum;	when, stiff, I lay on the straw;
þá merkir þat,	which soothly shows,
er guð mælti,	as saith our Lord,
at maðr er moldu samr.	that man is made of the mould.

Thereupon the deceased relates in an enigmatic stanza how for nine days he sat on "the chair of the Norns" and then was lifted up on a horse while "the sun of giantesses" shone cruelly from the clouded heavens. It reminds us somewhat of Óðin's description in *Hávamál* of how he hung for nine nights in a tree surrounded by sighing winds to acquire magic powers. (See p. 50, above). In *Sólarljóð*, too, this probably means some kind of initiation rite, in this case intended to prepare the adept for the journey through the different worlds of the realm of death which now begins. In the following description the Icelandic poem joins the vision literature of the Middle Ages like a sprout on the poetry that has found its most powerful expression in Dante's *Divina Commedia*. On Nordic soil there is primarily the famous Norwegian *Draumkvædet*

175

that is comparable to *Sólarljóð* as a vision poem. It is also considerably more recent according to current datings.

First the dead man is shown "the world of pain," hell, where lost souls in the guise of scorched birds fly around in swarms like mosquitoes. The punishment for different sins is differentiated in a way that is typical of the theology of the Middle Ages; this is also done in Dante's poem, but on a larger scale and more systematically. Unfaithful women, who ground mold to give to their men for food, drag around blood-stained stones and have bloody hearts hanging outside their bodies. The envious have bleeding runes cut on their chests. Those who have tampered with their neighbor's property move in groups to a place with the symbolic name Fégjarnsborg ("Castle of the Avaricious"), drooping beneath their burdens of lead. Those who have not observed religious festivals have their hands nailed to hot stones. Those who have lied about their fellow men have their eyes picked out by ravens. The verse that concludes the punishment section of the poem reads as follows:

Allar ógnir	Thou canst not ever
fær þú eigi vitat,	know all the pangs [hell;
þær er helgengnir hafa;	which the damned have in
sœtar synðir	their sweet sins
verða at sárum bótum:	turn to sore anguish: [pain.
æ koma mein eptir munuð.	is pleasure e'er followed by

Several obscure symbols in this series of pictures from hell seem to be taken from Norse mythology. And it is said about the many who have been buried without receiving the last sacrament: "pagan stars hovered above their heads, engraved with the runes of horror." In this poem the symbols of the old faith are made to witness for the devil.

On the other hand, there is a description of the reward of the blessed—although it is rather short and kept in more general terms; the blessed are those who have been good to the poor and weary, those who have starved and mortified themselves, and those who have been murdered without guilt.

Then there follows a section of five stanzas with names and motifs from pagan mythology which are difficult to interpret but, as far as one can see, without direct connection with the vision of hell. Here, too, however, ominous things are related that remind us somewhat of the foreboding of Ragnarök in *Völuspá*. The blood of Norns runs from the noses of two mythical female figures and awakes hatred among men. And "Óðin's wife" travels on "the ship of the earth," borne by the swelling sails of lust.

In the last stanza but one the poet urges his listener to recite this poem to the living. Its name is at last revealed: *Sólarljóð*. The final stanza sounds like an echo of the Latin prayer's "Requiem aeternam dona eis Domine!":

Hér vit skiljumk	Now must we part,
ok hittask munum	but shall meet again
á feginsdegi fira;	when we rise again in gladness;
dróttinn minn	may our dear Lord grant
gefi dauðum ró,	their rest to the dead,
en hinum líkn, er lifa.	and eke his love to the living.

In spite of its clearly Christian spirit *Sólarljóð* has definitely not lost all contact with the symbolic and conceptual world of the old mythology. At any rate the poem does not have a conventional theological impress. In its melancholy earnestness it has an unmistakable tone of its own. Sometimes the dead man's stanzas have a suggestive and solemnly conjuring ring, which can sound rather like the speech of the seeress in *Völuspá*.

The work that was regarded as the greatest among Christian poems during the Middle Ages in Iceland, however, was *Lilja,* a regular drápa dedicated to God, Christ, and the Virgin Mary. The poem is generally dated to the middle of the fourteenth century, and a certain "Brother Eysteinn" is mentioned as its author in a manuscript from the sixteenth century. He has generally been identified with Eysteinn Ásgrímsson, who held a leading position in the Icelandic church during the years 1349–60. Another Brother Eysteinn, who was punished in 1343 for disobedience to his abbot in the Icelandic monastery Þykkvibær, has also been mentioned in this connection. Not infrequently scholars have regarded the two namesakes as one and the same person, but it has not been possible to come to an indisputable conclusion.

The author of *Lilja* entreats the Holy Virgin that from his lips there may stream forth words as pure and sweet as though they had been refined in glowing gold. He is aware that he has now entered into contest with those poets who in the olden days praised kings in artistic songs with a pagan background. He himself is about to praise a greater king, and his poem should accord therewith:

Fyrri menn, er fræðin kunnu
forn og klók af heiðnum bókum,
slungin mjúkt af sínum kongum
sungu lof með danskri tungu.
I þvílíku móðurmáli
meir skyldumst eg en nokkur þeirra
hrærðan dikt með ástarorðum
allsvaldanda kongi að gjalda.

Men of old, who knew the ancient, clever art learned from heathen books, facilely sang the praises of their kings in the Danish tongue.[1] In this my mother tongue it b e h o o v e s me more than any of them to dedicate an inspired song with words of love to the Almighty King.

Toward the end of the poem the author returns to the matter of his artistic principles. He says that he has sometimes deviated from obscure Eddic rules, i.e., from the ancient language of the skalds; he is probably thinking here primarily of the kenning style. His own poetic ideal is a different one:

Sá, er óðinn skal vandan
 velja,
velr svo mörg í kvæði að
 selja
hulin fornyrði að trautt
 má telja,
tel eg þenna svo skilning
 dvelja.
Vel því að hér má skýr orð
 skilja,
skili þjóðir minn ljósan
 vilja,
tal óbreytilegt veitt af
 vilja.
Vil eg, að kvæðið heiti
 Lilja.

Whoever choses to write poetry in the difficult manner chooses to deliver so many veiled ancient words that they can scarcely be counted. I declare that this h a m p e r s understanding. Therefore I choose that here plain words may be discerned and language in accordance with my intention so that all people clearly understand my will. I desire that the poem be named Lily.

Otherwise *Lilja* meets all the demands that can be made of a *drápa* as an art form. It is quite possible that the poet had the ambition to eclipse all earlier poems in the genre—just as his own Lord outshines all the old pagan kings. Even the external architecture of the poem is ingenious. It consists of one-hundred stanzas, of which the first and last are identical in wording: an invocation to the Almighty. The first twenty-five stanzas, the *inngangr*, lack a refrain, or *stef*. Then there follow two different so-called *stefjamál*, each containing twenty-five stanzas and with its own regularly repeated refrain. This *stef* consists of one half stanza and occurs within its respective *stefjamál* every six stanzas: thus within the first in stanzas 26, 32, 38, 44, and 50 and within the second in stanzas 51, 57, 63, 69, and 75. The remaining twenty-five stanzas without refrain, the so-called *slæmr*, comprise the concluding counterpart to the *inngangr*.

This symmetrical arrangement corresponds to a certain extent to the distribution of the material among the various sections. The *inngangr* deals with the age of the Old Testament: the creation, Satan's rebellion, Adam and Eve's fall, the whole period up to God's decision to let Mary become the mother of his only begotten Son. The section culminates in a stanza (25) in which Mary is praised as "the flower of might," "as splendid as the reddest rose," "the fragrant rose of modesty," and "burning with the spirit of purity." The two *stefjamál* are devoted to the work of salvation, the first from Mary's annunciation to the crucifixion of Jesus and the second from the death of Jesus and the victory of the heavenly kingdom to the last judgment. The *slæmr*, finally, contains mainly appeals to God, Christ, and Mary and a greeting to the readers with the revelation of the name of the poem.

The meter is hrynhent, that is, the dróttkvætt stanza extended by two syllables per line, which had been used earlier by Arnór jarlaskáld among others (see pp. 167 f., above). After the composition of *Lilja* it became customary to call this meter *liljulag*. This form, which is very artistic in itself, is occasionally varied by the poet with even more elaborate metrical devices. Thus, for instance, in the fifty-fifth stanza he begins every line with the same word that ends the previous one; in addition, the lines are rhymed in pairs. In his Swedish interpretation Axel Åkerblom[2] has succeeded in keeping these fine points with two exceptions:

Rödd engilsins kvenmann kvaddi,	Ängelns ord Henne hälsa Hon hörde,
kvadda af engli drottinn gladdi,	hörde—och fröjd av Gud henne rörde,
gladdist mær, þá er föðrinn fæddi,	födde med glädje Frälsaren späda,
fæddan sveininn reifum klæddi,	fick den späde i lindor kläda,

klæddan með sér löngum leiddi,	klädde och med sig länge ledde;
leiddr af móður faðminn breiddi,	ledd av sin moder, Han famnen bredde,
breiddr á krossinn gumna græddi,	bredde än korsfäst; den Rene oss räddat,
græddi hann oss, er helstríð mæddi.	räddat i dödskamp, när kvalet var bräddat.

The voice of the angel greeted the woman; the Lord gladdened the woman greeted by the angel; the maid rejoiced when she gave birth to the Father; the child once born was clad in swaddling clothes; she long led the one thus clad by the hand; led by his mother, he spread out his arms; arms outspread on the cross, he saved us when the agony of death overcame him.

The name of the Virgin Mary, which plays such an important part in the poem, begins all eight lines of an invocation stanza (91); the lines are at the same time rhymed crosswise. To be able to reproduce this stanza—both here and elsewhere in the poem—the Swedish translator has used the name-form *Marja,* with the first syllable long and stressed:

María, ert þú móðir skærust,	Marja, Du är av mödrar skärast.
María, lifir þú sæmd i hárri,	Marja, prisad du evigt må- vara.
María, ert þú af miskunn kærust,	Marja, Du, för Din mildhet oss kärast,
María, léttu synda fári,	Marja, oss hjälp ur vår syndafara.
María, lít þú mein þau er váru,	Marja, lyten många vi bära,
María, lít þú klökk á tárin,	Marja, svår och bitter är tåren.
María, græð þú mein in stóru,	Marja, hela de men, som oss tära.

María, dreif þú smyrsl í
sárin.

Marja, o slå Du oss olja
i såren.

Mary, you are the purest mother, / Mary, may you live in high honor, / Mary, you are most beloved for your mercy, / Mary, lessen the peril of our sins, / Mary, behold our grief, / Mary, look with compassion on our tears, / Mary, heal our great sores, / Mary, anoint our wounds.

It is also the Mother of God who is called upon in the most effusive wording, as in the following stanzas (93–94), where the enumerations afford a good idea of the rich, baroquelike diction:

Hrærð af list þó að hvers
manns yrði
hold og bein að tungum
einum,
vindur, leiftr og grænar
grundir,
grös ilmandi, duft og
sandar,
hagl og drif, sem fjaðrir,
fuglar,
fiskar, dýr, sem holt og
mýrar,
hár og korn, sem heiðar
stjörnur,
hreistr og ull, sem dropar
og gneistar,

If marvelously transform-
ed, so that the flesh and
bone of all mankind be-
came tongues alone—
wind, lightning and green
plains,
fragrant herbs, dust and
sands,
hail and driven snow, as
well as plumage, birds,
fishes, animals, also moun-
tains and moors,
hair and grain, as well as
bright stars,
fish scales and wool, also
drops and sparks,

viðr og grjót, sem staðir og
stræti,
strengir, himnar, loft og
englar,
ormasveit og akrar hvítir,

forest and s t o n e s, also
steads and streets,
channels, heavens, air, and
angels,
serpent abode and gleam-
ing fields,

jurtir, málms og laufgir
pálmar—

herbs, metal, and leafy
palms—

augabragð þótt aldrei þegði,	though they never fell silent for a moment,
allar þær af fyrnsku væri	they would all be blotted out
máðar, fyrr en Máríu prýði	by hoary age before Mary's magnificence
mætti skýra fullum hætti.	could be expounded in full measure.

It is understandable that many persons have believed that the title *Lilja* refers only to the Virgin Mary. But even though she is praised with striking warmth of feeling, the poem as a whole has a much broader purpose. It is a majestic panorama covering the history of the world from a Christian and biblical point of view. And, as already mentioned, it begins and ends with an invocation of the Almighty and the Trinity.

In comparison with *Sólarljóð*, *Lilja* unquestionably creates a less personal impression. This is only natural, for *Lilja* is a pompous and, so to speak, official theological panegyric. Yet we cannot but admire the poet's ability to employ such a wide variety of means of expressing what is already known and well known. His deep involvement in his work is unmistakable. *Lilja* also won extraordinary recognition among the people. They learned the poem by heart and many regarded it as a religious duty to recite it, perhaps not daily, but at least once a week. A testimony of the fame of the song is the Icelandic proverb that "everybody would like to have written *Lilja*."

Notes

1. *Dönsk tunga* meant not only "the Danish language" but any or all of the Old Scandinavian tongues.

2. The Swedish quotations are from Åkerblom's "Lilja: En religös dikt från Islands medeltid," *Nordisk tidskrift*, 1899, pp. 465–81.

CHAPTER 6

Rímur: Icelandic Form Tradition

Naturally Iceland, too, was reached by the medieval poetry of southern provenance that dominated the rest of the Nordic countries: the ballad and the folk song. There are beautiful examples of this kind of poetry, for instance, in *Tristrams kvæði*[1] with its refrain "Þeim var ekki skapað nema að skilja" ("For them it was fated only to sever") or *Ólafur liljurós,* the very popular and still best-known Icelandic folk song, with the refrain "Ólafur reið með björgum fram" ("Ólafur rode along the cliffs"). The Swedish counterpart is *Herr Olov och alvorna.*

But on the whole, Iceland did not provide a fertile soil for a domestic development of the ballad. Perhaps this was due to the fact that the poem of chivalry, which is of central importance to the whole genre, completely lacked a social foothold in Iceland, where nobility and knighthood had never existed. It is also possible that purely formal considerations interfered. According to Icelandic standards the usual four-line ballad stanza without alliteration and with one single end rhyme (often, by the way, only impure rhyme) must have appeared extremely meager and vastly different from the national form tradition.

However, there originated in Iceland a kind of epic poetry, *ríma* (pl. *rímur*), which is considered to have developed from the ballad stanza, reconstructed in accordance with the Icelanders' stricter metrical demands. There are a number of metric variations for the *rímur,* too, but their most common meter is *ferskeytt*: a four-line stanza with stricter rules regarding the number of unstressed syllables than in the ballad, with end rhyme not only between the second and fourth lines but also between the first and third, and with alliteration between the first and second and the third and fourth lines. The difference can be illustrated with two stanzas from *Ebbadætrakvæði* ("The Ballad of Ebbi's Daughters") and *Ólafs rímur Tryggvasonar*, respectively; alliterative letters and end-rhymed words have been italicized in the quotations:

> Og svo svara*ð*i Ebbi,
> hann gekk í burtu *frá*:
> "Sæll er sá í heiminum er,
> sem engin börnin *á*."

And thus answered Ebbe as he left there: "Lucky is he in the world who has no children."

> *N*íutigi skipa í *n*ógum *byr*
> Nor*ð*menn létu *skriða*;
> ellifu *l*águ á *l*ægi *kyr*,
> *l*of*ð*ungs flaustr a*ð* *biða*.

The Norsemen let ninety ships sail before the wind; eleven remained in the harbor to await the ruler's ship.

The new stanza form had the future before it in Iceland. It originated during the course of the fourteenth century, and for about five centuries it constituted the major share of all poetry that was composed in Icelandic. It replaced the more exclusive and aristocratic dróttkvætt poetry which had earlier been dominant for almost as long a period of time.

The rímur are often rather lengthy epic poems, divided into several songs, each of which was called a ríma; the entire cycle, however, was designated with the plural form as rímur. As the genre developed, it became customary for each ríma to have its own metric variation. Gradually it also became customary to introduce each ríma with several lyrical stanzas that were called a *mansöngr* (love poem;

man, "maiden"). The mansöngr can be a lament about unhappy love, but also about aging, about waning poetic gifts, or about the decline of the world in general. Here some scholars believe they can discern certain echoes of troubadour poetry and *Minnesang.* This belief is used in support of the hypothesis that a form of Scandinavian lyric poetry, dependent on the German Minnesang, existed before the fourteenth century, and that this lyric poetry in turn was the model for the introduction of mansöngr into Icelandic rímur.

From the beginning the rímur have also been recited for dancing, and therefore they must have had a melody. This is also suggested by their original affinity with the ballad. But even later, long after they had ceased to serve as dance songs, the rímur were chanted *(kveða rímur)* according to certain tunes *(rímnalög)* by those who knew the art—a popular literary entertainment during the evenings on the farms, and for long periods of time perhaps the only one.

The rímur treat various subjects, but they are hardly ever original. The content of old prose stories are often versified, but this is done only rarely with the realistic family sagas (e.g., *Grettisrímur*) or the kings' sagas (e.g., *Ólafs ríma Haraldssonar*). It is done primarily with the more fantastic and exotic stories of the native *fornaldar sögur* (for example, *Friðþjófs rímur*) and the foreign chivalric poems (e.g., *Sálus rímur og Nikanórs*). There are also examples of subjects from ancient Nordic mythology: *Þrymlur,* founded on the popular Eddic poem *Þrymskviða,* and *Lokrur,* about Þór's journey to Útgarða-Loki, well known from Snorri's *Edda,* are both considered to be among the oldest members of the genre. The comical poem *Skíðaríma* is dated to the fifteenth century. It tells about a filthy and grotesque old tramp, Skíði, who in his sleep is accompanied by Ása-Þór to Valhöll to serve as an arbitrator in a controversy between two ancient kings. Unfortunately, however, he happens to mention the name of God and to make the sign of the cross, which is scarcely suitable in these surroundings. A tremendous fight breaks out among all the great ancient heroes, and Skíði receives his alloted due in this parodistic laying on of hands. He wakes up at home on his farm, his whole body black and blue, and tells the members of the household about his nocturnal adventure. In his food box, which was empty the night before, they now find extremely old butter, from the kingdom of the Æsir, and give it to the dogs: "they gave up their miserable lives / and lay dead far and wide." And as a final proof of the truth of Skíði's account, they pull out of his satchel a tooth "twenty marks in weight"—evidently a trophy from the fracas in Valhöll. The final stanza of the poem—number 199—describes how the tooth is beautifully carved and ornamented and becomes the most elegant crosier at the episcopal see of Hólar.

The rímur, as already mentioned, developed into an extremely productive and tenacious genre of poetry in the history of Icelandic literature. About 115 cycles of rímur are known from the period before 1600, and from later times approximately 900 by roughly 330 known authors.[2] This enormous body of literature is still to a large extent unpublished and will probably remain so. Little by little it absorbed more and more subjects. Thus there are five different *Ambalés rímur* by as many poets; these five rímur deal with the same material that Shakespeare was later to make famous through his *Hamlet*. The books of the Bible were also transformed into rímur. As late as the beginning of this century an Icelandic farmer-poet busied himself copying Jesus-rímur for people.

The entire genre was once exposed to a blistering attack by the great lyrical poet Jónas Hallgrímsson (1807–45), who was a pioneer in Icelandic poetry through his lighter and more personal diction. And it is true that the rímur frequently degenerate into rather mechanical and pedestrian versifying, into embroideries of inane adventures. In spite of that, their importance in literary history must be appraised very high. With their strict metrical demands, their heiti and kennings—these are, of course, generally simpler than those in dróttkvætt poetry—they constituted a school for poets and kept alive the connection with the oldest native poetry. As popular entertainment they have helped to lighten the burden of the common man and, during centuries of national impotence, to preserve the old heroic ideal—this, too, a necessary condition for a fruitful contact with the ancient poetry. Certainly the strength of the rímur lies not least of all in their deep anchorage among the people. During centuries in which there was a paucity of original, creative poetry the rímur could, for this very reason, play an important role in preserving the broad literary culture which has remained as a mark of distinction in Iceland to this very day. The indefatigable verse making, practiced by aristocrats and bishops as well as by crofters and paupers, must have been very significant in making the public well acquainted with the diction and artistic devices of poetry. The old Icelandic national sport of producing an improvised stanza without premeditation has, likely enough, seen its best days, but it still has its faithful practitioners and a loyal audience. And the classical form for such epigrams is still a *ferskeytla*, the most common stanza of the rímur.

In this way the rímur have played an essential role in the unique continuity from ancient times to the present of Icelandic poetry, even if to a certain extent they have existed as a kind of literary undergrowth. Not even a modernistic poet, an "atomic poet" in the Reykjavík of the 1970s, would wish completely to evade the demands of the ancient alliteration. Probably Jón Helgason (b. 1899), himself a learned expert in the traditions of Icelandic poetry and a splendid poet, has given the best explanation for the Icelander's unique position among his Nordic brother skalds. Within their circle, he says in one of his poems, the Icelander is the only one who disciplines his language "with the triad of alliteration"—the only one whose art constantly draws nourishment from "the word magic of pagan praise poems."[3]

The past of Icelandic poetry is the living past.

Notes

1. An English translation in the original meter is found in Jacqueline Simpson's *The Northmen Talk* (London, 1965), pp. 257–60.

2. On this see Stefán Einarsson, *A History of Old Icelandic Literature* (New York, 1957), p. 165.

3. The quotation by Jón Helgason is from his poem "Eg kom þar" ("I went there") in the collection *Úr landsuðri* ("From southwest"), 2d ed. (Reykjavík, 1948).

Text Supplement

The Icelandic text on the reverse side of this page is a reproduction of page 4 of the Codex Regius of the *Poetic Edda*, somewhat reduced from the size of the original, which measures about 13 x 19 cm. In all, the manuscript includes forty-five leaves, or ninety pages of text; following leaf 32 there is a lacuna (see p. 63, above) that probably represents a gathering of eight leaves that have been lost. Codex Regius, which has been demonstrated to be a copy of a lost original, was written by an Icelandic scribe during the second half of the thirteenth century. Otherwise the fate of the vellum is unknown until in 1643 it came under the care of the bishop of Skáholt in Iceland, Brynjólfur Sveinsson, whose monogram it bears: ⌐ (Lupus Loricatus = Byrnie-Wolf = Brynjólfur). In 1662 the bishop sent the manuscript as a gift to Frederik III, king of the Danes (and Icelanders). It is now housed in the Royal Library in Copenhagen under the signature Gl. Kgl. Sml. 2365, 4to.

Photograph by courtesy of the Royal Library, Copenhagen.

lar hæuir hat bles heimdallr horn e a lopti melir oðin
við mim hauf

ymr ið aldna tre en iotvnn losnar scelfr ydrasilz alr tt
ascmdin. Geyr nv g. hrymr ekr vstan hefir lind f sin
ýz iormvngandr iotun moði. ormr knýr vnr en ari hl
ateer sliter nai nef faulr nagl far losnar. kiol ferr af
tan koma mvno mvspellz vlag lyð en loki styr fara
fyʒlz með tī freka allr þei er bros býleipz tyoe. hvat er
tī aso hvat e tī alfo gnýr allr iotvn þeir efia yoaþin
gi styma dvgar ꝺ stein dvið ves bol vilir v. e e h. Surtr
ferr svnan tī linga leza scin a: sþi sol valtiʒa. grior bi
oeg gniota en gyʒr tita troða halir helveg en him cloʒh.

hvar er hlinar harmr aua fim en oðin ferr við ulf vega
en bani belia hartz at surei þa mvn figiar fala angan
tyr. þa kor tī mveli maigr figgiaid viðan vega at val dy
rī. lete ꝺ megi hvedrvngs mvnd v ftanða hioe t hiarta
þa e heyre iað. þa kor iz moer mvgr hloðynjar gegg
opini sol við ulf vega dreyr ꞇ aʒ mobr midgarz tyoe
mvno halir allir þei stoð flyʒia genigr ꝼet no fraskyn
tar bon neppr ꝼ naðri nolt oqvidno. Sol ter forena
figr fold mar hvza a: him keidar striœnœr geisar eimi
við alde nœra leter har hret við him stalyan. Geyr tī.

Ser ho vp koma aðro sinti ioeð oe eʒ iþa grœna. fala
fœtlar flygr orn yf. sa er afialli fifca ueiðir: finar
efte asia velli ꞇ v molð þivir markat dok ꞇ agimbvl
tyf fœrnar rvnar. þar mvno eft vnde famligar gvl
nar tavflœ igrasi finar. bort ꞇ ardaga attar honðo.

M vno ofaniti aerar vaca baitr mvn alk braena balde
tī ꞇea. bva ꝼr haꝼ ꞇ balde. hroper sigtopt vel val
tivar v. e e h. þa kna hon blat rið tnosa ꞇ byrir
byota brœðra rœeta. vind hei vidan v. e e h. Sal fer
hon ftanða solo fegra gvlli þakþan agimle. þar

The following is a diplomatic copy of the Icelandic text on the facing page, beginning with the second word of the fourth line. The manuscript abbreviations have been expanded in the customary manner, the expansions being written in italics. To expedite comparison, the division into lines of the original has been retained in the transcript. In Codex Regius, *as in other vellum manuscripts, poetry is run on like prose, without indication of line or stanza. The reading of this text, which is a very clear and distinct one, benefited from the transcription of the facsimile edition by L.F.A. Wimmers and Finnur Jónsson (Copenhagen, 1891).*

Geyr nv g. Hrymr ekr avstan hefiz lind f*yr* sn
yz iormvngandr i iotvn moði. ormr kn*ý*r vn*ir* en ari hl
accar slitr nai nef favlr nagl far losnar. Kioll fer avs
tan koma mvno mvspellz v*m*lavg lyð*ir* en loki styr*ir* fara
fifls meg*ir* me*þ* freka all*ir* þeim er broð*ir* by leipz ifor. Hvat er
me*þ* aso*m* hvat e*r* me*þ* alfo*m* gnyr allr iotvn hei*m*r ǫsir ro aþin
gi stynia dv*er*gar f*yr* stein dvro*m* veg b*er*gs visir v.e.e.h. Surtr
fer svnan me*þ* sviga lǫfi scin af sverþi sol valtifa. griot bi
org gnata en gifr rata troþa halir helveg en him*inn* clofn*ar*.
Þa cǫmr hlinar harmr anar *fr*am er oðin fer við ulf vega
en bani belia biartr at surti þa mvn frigiar falla angan
tyr. Þa kǫ*m*r in micli mavgr sigfavðvr víðar vega at val dy
ri. letr h*ann* megi hveðrvngs mvnd v*m* standa hior t*il* hiarta
þa er hefnt favðvr. Þa kǫmr in mori mavgr hloðyniar ge*n*gr
oþins so*n*r við ulf vega drepr h*ann* af moþi miðgarz ueor
mvno halir allir heim stǫð ryþia gengr fet nío fiorgyn
iar bvr neppr *fr*a naðri niðs oqviðno*m*. Sol ter sortna
sigr fold imar hv*er*fa af him*n*i heiðar stiornor. geisar eimi
viþ aldr nara leicr har hiti uið him*in* sialfan. Geyr. n.
Ser hon upp koma avdro sini iorð or ǫgi iþia grǫna. falla
forsar flygr avrn yf*ir* sa er afialli fisca ueiðir. Finaz
ǫsir aiþa velli *oc* v*m* mold þinvr matkan dǫ*m*a *oc* a fimbvl
tys fornar rvnar. Þar mvno ept*ir* vndr samligar gvll
nar tavflor igrasi finaz. þers i ardaga attar hofðo.
Mvno osanir acra uaxa bavls mvn allz batna baldr
m*vn* co*m*a. bva þ*ei*r havþr *oc* baldr hroptz sigtopt*ir* vel val
tivar v.e.e.h. Þa kna hon*ir* hlavt viþ kiosa *oc* byrir

Text Supplement

bygia brǫðra tvegia. vind heim viðan v.e.e.h. Sal ser
hon standa solo fegra gvlli þacþan agimlé. Þar

*Here is the same text divided into stanzas and written in the
normalized Old Icelandic orthography as commonly used today—
for example, in Sigurður Nordal's monograph on* Völuspá. *The
arrangement of the stanzas is that of Bugge's edition (1867),
which was followed also by Jón Helgason in* Eddadigte I *(1951).
It will be noted that Bugge, on the basis of readings in other
manuscripts, has moved stanza 48 to a place different from that
in Codex Regius.*

*Three former attempts at corrections, "conjectural readings,"
of the text, accepted by Nordal, have also been followed here
and are indicated by italics: in stanzas 55 úlf > orm and okviðnum
> ókviðinn; and in stanza 62 vel valtivar > vé valtíva. In stanza
60, as in the above-mentioned editions, two lines within paren-
theses have been added from the text of* Völuspá *in the codex*
Hauksbók.

*The following prose rendering is arranged in such a way as
to correspond line by line to the Icelandic text to the extent
that this is possible.*

49 Geyr nú Garmr mjök
fyr Gnipahelli,
festr mun slitna,
en freki renna;
fjölð veit ek frœða,
fram sé ek lengra
um ragna rök
römm sigtíva.

Now Garmur bays loudly
before Gnipahellir,
the fetter will break
and the wolf run free.
Much lore do I know,
I see further into the future
To the fate of the powers,
To the destruction of the war
gods.

50 Hrymr ekr austan,
hefisk lind fyrir,
snýsk Jörmungandr
í jötunmóði;
ormr knýr unnir,
en ari hlakkar,

Hrymur fares from the east
with uplifted shield,
Jörmungandur writhes
in giant rage.
The serpent lashes the waves
and the eagle screams,

194

slítr nái Niðfölr,

Naglfar losnar.

51 Kjóll ferr austan,
koma munu Muspells
um lög lýðir,
en Loki stýrir;
fara fífls megir
með freka allir,
þeim er bróðir
Býleists í för.

48 Hvat er með ásum,
hvat er með álfum?
Gnýr allr jötunheimr,
æsir eru á þingi;
stynja dvergar
fyr steindurum,
veggbergs vísir—
vituð ér enn, eða hvat?

52 Surtr ferr sunnan
með sviga lævi,

skínn af sverði
sól valtíva;

grjótbjörg gnata,
en gífr rata,
troða halir helveg,
en himinn klofnar.

53 Þá kömr Hlínar
harmr annarr fram,
er Óðinn ferr
við úlf vega,

the dark-grey one tears the dead,
Naglfar is loosened.

A ship sails from the east,
Muspell's host
will come over the sea,
and Loki steers it.
The sons of the giant
all sail with the wolf,
with them comes
the brother of Byleist.

How fare the Æsir,
how fare the elves?
All the giant world clamors,
the Æsir are in council;
the dwarves moan
before the doors of stone,
the wise dwellers of the cliff.
Would you know more, or what?

Surtur comes from the south
with the scourge of twigs (= fire),
from the sword shines
the sun of the battle god (= Surtur?);
cliffs crash down,
troll women collapse,
men tread the Hel-way
and the heavens are rent.

Then occurs Hlín's (= Frigg's)
second woe,
when Óðinn goes forth
to fight the wolf,

en bani Belja

bjartr at Surti;
þá mun Friggjar
falla angan.

54 Þá kömr inn mikli
mögr Sigföður,

Víðarr, vega
at valdýri;
lætr hann megi Hveðrungs
mund um standa
hjör til hjarta:

þá er hefnt föður.

55 Þá kömr inn mæri
mögr Hlóðynjar,
gengr Óðins sonr
við *orm* vega,
drepr hann af móði
Miðgarðs véurr,
munu halir allir
heimstöð ryðja—
gengr fet níu
Fjörgynjar burr
neppr frá naðri
níðs ókvíðinn.

57 Sól tér sortna,
sígr fold í mar,
hverfa af himni
heiðar stjörnur;
geisar eimi
við aldrnara,

leikr hár hiti
við himin sjálfan.

and the bright bane of Beli
      (= Freyr)
(to battle) with Surtur;
then will Frigg's
joy (= Óðinn) fall.

Then comes the mighty
son of the father-of-battle (=
      Óðinn),
Viðar, to do battle
with the wolf;
with his hand he thrusts
his sword to the heart
of the son of Hveðrungur (=
      Loki?)
then is his father avenged.

Then comes Hlóðyn's
glorious son (= Þór),
goes Óðin's son
to fight the serpent,
in wrath slays him
Miðgarð's protector (=Þór)—
all men must
flee the world—
the son of Fjörgyn (= Þór)
steps nine paces,
dying, from the serpent
without fear of blame.

The sun turns black,
earth sinks into the sea,
from the heavens disappear
bright stars;
fire rages
toward the life-sustainer
      (= the world tree Yggdrasil),
the high flames leap
toward the sky itself.

196

58　Geyr nú Garmr . . .

Now Garmur bays . . .
(Refrain; cf. verse 49 above.)

59　Sér hon upp koma
öðru sinni
jörð ór ægi
iðjagrœna;
falla forsar,
flýgr örn yfir,
sá er á fjalli
fiska veiðir.

She sees arising
once again,
always green,
the earth from the sea;
waterfalls cascade,
above them soars an eagle
that in the mountains
hunts for fish.

60　Hittask æsir
á Iðavelli
ok um moldþinur
máttkan dœma

[ok minnask þar
á megindóma]
ok á Fimbultýs
fornar rúnar.

The Æsir assemble
at Iðavöllur,
and speak of the mighty
earth-encircling band
(= the Miðgarðsormur)
[and remind each other
of signal events]
and of Fimbultý's (= Óðin's)
ancient runes.

61　Þar munu eptir
undrsamligar
gullnar töflur
í grasi finnask,
þærs í árdaga
áttar höfðu.

There will again
the marvelous
golden draughtsmen
be found in the grass
which they had owned
in the morning of time.

62　Munu ósánir
akrar vaxa,
böls mun alls batna,
Baldr mun koma;
búa þeir Höðr ok Baldr
Hropts sigtóptir,

Unsown will
fields grow,
all evils become better,
Baldur will return;
Höður and Baldur will dwell
at the site of Hropt's (= Óðin's) victory-hall (= Valhöll),

vé valtíva—

the dwelling place of the battlegods—

197

vituð ér enn, eða hvat?

would you know more or what?

63   Þá kná Hœnir
hlautvið kjósa
ok burir byggja
brœðra tveggja
vindheim víðan—

vituð ér enn eða hvat?

Then may Hœnir
choose sacrificial twigs
and two brothers'
sons dwell
in the vast wind-home (= the sky)—

would you know more, or what?

64   Sal sér hon standa
sólu fegra
gulli þakðan
á Gimlé.
Þar . . .

She sees a hall standing
more beautiful than the sun,
roofed with gold
on Gimlé.
There . . .

Bibliography

Bibliographies

Bibliography of Old Norse-Icelandic Studies, 1963–. Edited by Hans Bekker-Nielsen and Thorkil Damsgaard Olsen. Copenhagen: Munksgaard, 1964–. Annual bibliography.)

Hannesson, Jóhann S. *Bibliography of the Eddas.* Islandica 37. (A supplement to *Bibliography of the Eddas*, Islandica 13, by Halldór Hermannsson.) Ithaca, N.Y.: Cornell University Press, 1955.

Hermannsson, Halldór. *Bibliography of the Eddas.* Islandica 13. Ithaca, N.Y.: Cornell University Press, 1920.

Hollander, Lee M. *A Bibliography of Skaldic Studies.* Copenhagen: Munksgaard, 1958.

Old Norse-Icelandic Studies. A Select Bibliography. Compiled by Hans Bekker-Nielsen. Toronto: University of Toronto Press, 1967.

Schach, Paul. "Old Norse Literature." In *The Medieval Literature of Western Europe: A Review of Research, Mainly 1930–1960.* Edited by John H. Fisher. Published for the Modern Language Association of America by the New York University Press. London: University of London Press, 1966. Pp. 255–80.

Bibliographical references to Eddic and skaldic poetry can be found in the *Acta philologica Scandinavica, Arkiv för nordisk filologi, Scandinavica,* in *Germanistik* (quarterly), and in the annual bibliographies of *Íslensk tunga,* the *Publications of the Modern Language Association, Scandinavian Studies,* and *Year's Work in Modern Language Studies.* Excellent selected bibliographies are appended to the individual articles in *Kulturhistorisk leksikon for nordisk middelalder.* Additional convenient sources of bibliography are the supplements by Anne Holtsmark to the second edition of the Paasche volume (listed below in Literary History and Criticism section) and the annotated bibliography

Bibliography

in Turville-Petre's *Myth and Religion of the North*. (In Background Material Section, below.)

Editions

POETIC EDDA

Boer, R. C. *Die Edda mit historisch-kritischem Commentar.* 2 vol. Vol. 1, *Einleitung und Text.* Vol. 2, *Commentar.* Haarlem: H. D. Tjeenk Villink & Zoon, 1922.

Bugge, Sophus E. *Norrœn fornkvœði.* Christiania, 1867. Photomechanic reprint, Oslo: Aschehoug, 1926.

Detter, Friedrich, and Richard Heinzel. *Sæmundar Edda.* 2 vols. Vol. 1, Text. Vol. 2, Anmerkungen. Leipzig: Wigand, 1903.

Edda: Die Lieder des Codex Regius neben verwandten Denkmälern. Edited by Gustav Neckel. Vol. 1, Text. 4th rev. ed by Hans Kuhn. Heidelberg: Winter, 1962. Vol. 2, Kurzes Wörterbuch. 3d rev. ed. by Hans Kuhn. Heidelberg: Winter, 1968.

Eddadigte. Vol. 1, *Völuspá, Hávamál.* Nordisk filologi 4. Edited by Jón Helgason. 2d ed. Copenhagen: Munksgaard, 1962.

Eddadigte. Vol. 2, *Gudedigte.* Nordisk filologi 7. Edited by Jón Helgason. 3d ed. Copenhagen: Munksgaard, 1962.

Eddadigte. Vol. 3, *Heltedigte.* Nordisk filologi 8. Edited by Jón Helgason. 2d ed. Copenhagen: Munksgaard, 1962.

Eddic Lays. Selected and edited by Frederic T. Wood. (With glossary.) Charlottesville, Va.: Privately printed, 1940.

Eddica Minora. Edited by F. Genzmer and A. Heusler. 2 vols. Vol. 1, Heldendichtung. Vol. 2, Götterdichtung. Jena, 1912–20.

Eddukvæði (Sæmundar-Edda). Edited by Guðni Jónsson. Reykjavík: Íslendingasagnaútgáfan, 1949.

Helgason, Jón. *Kviður af Gotum og Hunum: Hamðismál, Guðrúnarhvöt, Hlöðskviða með skýringum.* Reykjavík: Heimskringla, 1967.

———. *Tvær kviður fornar: Völundarkviða og Atlakviða með skýringum.* Reykjavik: Heimskringla, 1962.

Hildebrand, Karl. *Die Lieder der älteren Edda.* Completely revised by Hugo Gering. 4th ed. Paderborn: Schöning, 1922.

Jónsson, Finnur. *De Gamle Eddadigte*. Copenhagen: Gad, 1932.

Nordal, Sigurður. *Völuspá*. Fylgir Árbók Háskóla Íslands 1922–23. Reykjavík. 1923. Rev. ed., Reykjavík: Helgafell, 1952. Danish translation, Copenhagen: H. Aschehoug, 1927.

Sijmons, Berend, and Hugo Gering. *Die Lieder der Edda*. 2 vols. Hale, Waisenhaus. 1906.

PROSE EDDA

Edda Snorra Sturlusonar. Nafnaþulur og Skáldatal. Edited by Guðni Jónsson. Reykjavík: Íslendingasagnaútgáfan, 1949.

Edda Snorra Sturlusonar udg. efter håndskrifterne. By Finnur Jónsson. Copenhagen: Gyldendalske Boghandel, 1931.

Snorri Sturluson: Edda. Edited by Finnur Jónsson. 2d ed. Copenhagen: Gad, 1926.

Snorri Sturluson: Edda. Gylfaginning og prosafortellingene av Skáldskaparmál. Nordisk filologi I. Edited by Anne Holtsmark and Jón Helgason. 2d ed. Copenhagen: Gad, 1926.

SKALDIC POETRY

Jónsson, Finnur. *Carmina scaldica: Udvalg af norske og islandske Skjaldekvad*. 2d ed. Copenhagen: Gad, 1929.

———. *Den norsk-islandske Skjaldedigtning*. 4 vols. Vols. I A, IIA, *Tekst efter håndskrifterne*; Vols. IB, IIB, *Rettet Tekst*. Copenhagen, 1912–15.

Kock, Ernst A. *Den norsk-isländska ·skaldedigtningen, reviderad*. 2 vols. Edited by Elisabeth Kock and Ivar Lundquist. Lund: Gleerup, 1936–49.

Kock, E. A., and Rudolf Meissner. *Skaldisches Lesebuch*. Vol. I, *Text;* Vol. II, *Wörterbuch*. Halle: Niemeyer, 1931.

Skjaldevers. Nordisk filologi XII. Edited by Jón Helgason. Copenhagen: Munksgaard, 1962.

OTHER

Heimskringla. Edited by Bjarni Aðalbjarnarson. 3 vols. Íslenzk fornrit 26–28. Reykjavík: Hið íslenzka fornritafélag, 1941–51.

For scholars and advanced students the facsimile editions of the *Corpus codicum Islandicorum medii ævi I–XX* (Copen-

Bibliography

hagen, 1930–56) is extremely valuable, especially the *Codex Regius of the Elder Edda* (vol. 10), edited by Andreas Heusler, and the *Codex Regius of the Younger Edda* (vol. 14), edited by Ellias Wessén.

Bilingual Editions

Das Nibelungenlied. Edited and translated by Helmut de Boor. 2d ed. Bremen: Carl Schünemann Verlag, 1959.

Das Nibelungenlied. Critically edited and translated by Ulrich Pretzel. Stuttgart: Hirzel Verlag, 1973.

Gunnlaugs saga Ormstungu: The Saga of Gunnlaug Serpent-Tongue. Edited with introduction and notes by P. G. Foote. Translated from the Icelandic by R. Quick. London: Thomas Nelson & Sons, 1957.

Lilja (The Lily). Edited with metrical translation, notes and glossary by Eiríkr Magnússon. London, 1870.

The Poetic Edda. Vol. 1, *Heroic Poems.* Edited with translation, introduction and commentary by Ursula Dronke. Oxford: Clarendon Press, 1969. (*Atlakviða, Atlamál in Grœnlenzko, Guðrúnarhvöt, Hamðismál.*)

The Saga of King Heidrek the Wise. Translated from the Icelandic with introduction, notes and appendices by Christopher Tolkien. London: Thomas Nelson & Sons, 1960.

Völsunga saga: The Saga of the Volsungs. Edited and translated with an introduction, notes, and appendices by R. G. Finch. London: Thomas Nelson & Sons, 1965.

Völuspá: The Song of the Sybil. Translated by Paul B. Taylor and W. H. Auden with the Icelandic text edited by Peter H. Salus and Paul B. Taylor. University of Iowa,˙Iowa City: Windhover Press, 1968.

Translations

The Elder Edda: A Selection. Translated from the Icelandic by Paul B. Taylor and W. H. Auden. Introduction by Peter H. Salus and Paul B. Taylor. Notes by Peter H. Salus. New York: Random House, 1970.

Icelandic Christian Classics: The Lay of the Sun, The Lily. Translated by Charles Venn Pilchner. Melbourne: Oxford University Press, 1950.

The Northmen Talk: A Choice of Tales from Iceland. Translated and with an introduction by Jacqueline Simpson. Foreword by Eric Linklater. London: Phoenix House; Madison: University of Wisconsin Press, 1965.

Poems of the Vikings: The Elder Edda. Translated by Patricia Terry with an introduction by Charles W. Dunn. Indianapolis and New York: Bobbs-Merrill, 1969.

The Poetic Edda. Translated from the Icelandic with an introduction and notes by Henry Adams Bellows. New York: The American-Scandinavian Foundation, 1923.

The Poetic Edda. Translated with an introduction and explanatory notes by Lee M. Hollander. 2d ed., rev. Austin: University of Texas Press, 1962.

The Prose Edda by Snorri Sturluson. Translated by Arthur G. Brodeur. New York: The American-Scandinavian Foundation, 1916.

The Prose Edda of Snorri Sturluson: Tales from Norse Mythology. Selected and edited by Jean I. Young. Berkeley and Los Angeles: University of California Press, 1964.

Sturluson, Snorri. *Heimskringla: History of the Kings of Norway.* Translated with introduction and notes by Lee M. Hollander. Published for the American-Scandinavian Foundation by the University of Texas Press, Austin, 1964.

Literary History and Criticism

Craigie, William A. *The Art of Poetry in Iceland.* Oxford: Clarendon Press, 1937.

Einarsson, Stefán. *A History of Icelandic Literature.* Published by the Johns Hopkins Press for the American-Scandinavian Foundation, New York, 1957.

———. *Íslensk bókmentasaga, 874–1960.* Reykjavík: Snæbjörn Jónsson, 1961.

Bibliography

Hallberg, Peter. *The Icelandic Saga*. Translated with an introduction and notes by Paul Schach. Lincoln, Nebr.: University of Nebraska Press, 1962.

Helgason, Jón. "Norges og Islands digtning." *Nordisk Kultur*, vol. VIII B. Stockholm: Bonnier. Oslo: Aschehoug. Copenhagen: Schultz, 1934.

Heusler, Andreas. *Die altgermanische Dichtung*. Berlin-Neubabelsberg: Athenaion. 1931. 2d rev. ed., Pottsdam: Athenaion, 1941.

Holtsmark, Anne. *Studier i norrøn diktning*. Oslo: Gyldendal Norsk Forlag, 1956.

Jónsson, Finnur. *Den oldnorske og oldislandske Literaturs Historie*. 3 vols. 2d ed. Copenhagen: Gad, 1920–24.

Lange, Wolfgang. *Studien zur christlichen Dichtung der Nordgermanen, 1000–1200*. Palaestra CCXXII. Göttingen: Vandenhoeck & Ruprecht, 1958.

Lie, Hallvard. *"Natur" og "Unatur" i skaldekunsten*. Oslo: Det Norske Samlaget, 1957.

Mogk, E. *Geschichte der norwegisch-isländischen Literatur*. 2d ed. Strassburg: Trübner, 1904.

Nordal, Sigurður. *Íslenzk menning I*. Reykjavík: Mál og menning. 1942. (English translation by Vilhjálmur Bjarnar forthcoming.)

———. "Three Essays on *Völuspa*." Translated by B. S. Benedikz and J. S. McKinnel. *Saga-Book of the Viking Society* 18 (1970–71): 79–135.

Noreen, Erik. *Den norsk-isländska poesien*. Stockholm: Norstedt & Söner, 1926.

Paasche, F. *Norges og Islands litteratur indtil utgangen av meddelalderen*. Oslo: Aschehoug, 1924. 2d ed. (with supplements by Anne Holtsmark), 1957.

Phillpotts, Bertha S. *Edda and Saga*. London: Butterworth, 1931.

Sveinsson, Einar Ól. *Íslenzkar bókmenntir i fornöld*. Vol. 1. Reykjavík: Almenna Bókafélagið, 1962.

Turville-Petre, E.O.G. *Origins of Icelandic Literature*. Oxford: Clarendon Press, 1953.

Vries, Jan de. *Altnordische Literaturgeschichte*. 2 vols. Berlin: de Gruyter, 1941–42. 2d ed., 1964–67.

Background Material

Bæksted, Anders. *Guder og helte i Norden*. Copenhagen: Politikens forlag, 1963.

Baetke, Walter. *Die Götterlehre der Snorra-Edda*. Berlin: Akademi-Verlag, 1950.

Boor, Helmut de. *Das Attilabild in Geschichte, Legende und Heroischer Dichtung*. Bern: A. Franke, 1932.

Brady, Caroline. *The Legends of Ermanaric*. Berkeley and Los Angeles: University of California Press, 1943.

Chadwick, H. M., and N. K. *The Growth of Literature*. Cambridge: Cambridge University Press, 1932–40. 2d ed., Göttingen, 1951.

Holtsmark, Anne. *Norrøn mytologi: Tro og myter i vikingetiden*. Oslo: Det Norske Samlaget, 1971.

———. *Studier i Snorres mytologi*. Oslo: Universitets-forlaget. 1964.

King, Cynthia. *In the Morning of Time: The Story of the Norse God Balder*. New York: Four Winds Press, 1970.

Munch, Peter Andreas. *Norse Mythology: Legends of Gods and Heroes*. In the revision of Magnus Olsen. Translated from the Norwegian by Sigurd Bernhard Hustvedt. New York: The American-Scandinavian Foundation, 1927.

Musset, Lucien. *Les peuples scandinaves au moyen âge*. Paris: Presses universitaires de France, 1951.

Ohlmarks, Åke. *Gudatro i nordisk forntid*. Stockholm: Gummesson, 1970.

Olsen, Magnus. *Fra norrøn filologi*. Oslo: Aschehoug, 1949.

———. *Norrøne studier*. Oslo: Aschehoug, 1938.

Philippson, Ernst A. *Die Genealogie der Götter in germanischer Religion, Mythologie und Theologie*. Urbana, Ill.: University of Illinois Press, 1953.

Schneider, Hermann. *Germanische Heldensage*. 3 vols. Berlin: de Gruyter, 1928–34. 2d ed., 1962.

See, Klaus von. *Germanische Heldensage: Stoffe, Probleme, Methoden: Eine Einführung*. Frankfurt/Main: Athenäum Verlag, 1971.

Strömbäck, Dag. *Sejd: Textstudier i nordisk religionshistoria*. Stockholm: H. Geber, 1935.

Bibliography

Turville-Petre, E.O.G. *The Heroic Age of Scandinavia*. London and New York: Hutchinson's University Library, 1951.

————. *Myth and Religion of the North: The Religion of Ancient Scandinavia*. New York: Holt, Rinehart and Winston, 1964.

Vries, Jan de. *Altgermanische Religionsgeschichte*. 2d rev. ed. 2 vols. Berlin: de Gruyter, 1956–57.

————. *Heroic Song and Heroic Legend*. Translated by B. J. Timmer. London and New York: Oxford University Press, 1963.

Zink, Georges. *Les Légendes héroïques de Dietrich et d'Ermrich dans les littératures germaniques*. Lyon and Paris: IAC, 1950.

Dictionaries and Miscellaneous Aids

Cleasby, Richard, and Gudbrand Vigfusson. *An Icelandic-English Dictionary*. New York: Oxford, 1874. 2d ed. with a Supplement by William A. Craigie, New York: Oxford, 1957.

Eddulyklar. Edited by Guðni Jónsson. Reykjavík: Íslendingasagnaútgáfan, 1959.

Gering, Hugo. *Kommentar zu den Liedern der Edda*. Edited by Barend Sijmons. Part 1, *Götterlieder;* Part 2, *Heldenlieder*. Halle: Waisenhaus, 1927, 1931.

————. *Vollständiges Wörterbuch zu den Liedern der Edda*. Berlin, 1903.

Gordon, E. V. *An Introduction to Old Norse*. 2d ed. revised by A. R. Taylor. Oxford: Clarendon Press, 1957.

Heusler, Andreas. *Deutsche Versgeschichte*. 3 vols. Berlin, 1925.

Jónsson, Finnur. *Lexicon poeticum antiquae linguae septentrionalis*. Ordbog over det norsk-islandske skjaldensprog oprindelig forfattet af Sveinbjörn Egilsson. 2d ed. Copenhagen: Lynge & Søn, 1931. Reprinted 1966.

Kock, Ernst A. *Notationes Norrœnæ: Anteckningar till edda och skaldedikt*. 5 vols. Lund: Gleerup, 1923–44.

Meissner, Rudolf. *Die Kenningar der Skalden*. Bonn: Schroeder, 1921.

Mohr, Wolfgang. *Kenningstudien*. Stuttgart: W. Kohlhammer, 1933.

206

Reichardt, Konstantin. *Studien zu den Skalden des 9. und 10. Jahrhunderts.* Leipzig: Meyer & Müller, 1928.

The above selected bibliography was compiled primarily with the needs of the nonspecialist in mind. That is why numerous specialized studies have been omitted. It is for this reason, too, that Jón Helgason's *Tvær kviður fornar* and *Kviður af Gotum og Hunum* as well as Nordal's *Völuspá* were listed under Editions. Advanced students will use them primarily for their scholarly apparatus and literary interpretations. Nordal's "Three Essays on *Völuspá*" were derived from the book *Völuspá*.

Index

Aðalhending, metrical term, 18
Aðalsteinn (Athelstan), Anglo-
Saxon king, 128, 130
Adam of Bremen, 59
Addacarus *(Quedlingburg Chro-
nicle)*, 94
Aðils Óttarsson, Swedish king
in ancient times, 101, 113
Agni Dagsson, Swedish king in
ancient times, 114
Álfur Hjálpreksson, 71
Áli Friðleifsson, king of Upp-
sala in ancient times, 113
Alvís, a dwarf, 38 f.
Alvíssmál, 21, 30, 38 f.
Ambalés rímur, 188
Ammius (= Hamðir?), 93
Andvari, a dwarf, 73
Angantýr Heiðreksson, Gothic
king, 97–100
Arinbjarnarkviða, 130–33, 137,
139
Arinbjörn Þórisson *(Egils saga)*,
127, 130, 134 f.
Aristotle, 1
Arnór jarlaskáld Þórðarson,
167 f., 180
Ásgarður, the world of the gods
(Æsir), 3 f., 7, 48
Ásgerður Bjarnardóttir *(Egils
saga)*, 140
Askur, the first man *(Völuspá)*,
31 f.
Áti, mythical sea king, 148
Atlakviða, 15 f., 61, 86, 88 f.,
93, 97, 99, 104
Atlamál, 16, 61, 88 f., 104

Atli, Hunnish king (= Attila),
16, 63, 83–89, 93 f.
Atli *(Helgakviða Hjörvarðssonar)*, 70
Atreus, Greek legendary figure,
87
Attila, Hunnish king, 83, 92 f.
Aun, Swedish king in ancient
times, 113
Austrfararvisur (Sighvatur Þórðarson), 164

*Baldrs draumar (= Vegtams-
kviða)*, 30
Baldur, one of the Æsir, 8, 19,
22, 32, 38, 57, 112, 122, 197
Balen (Gustaf Fröding), 161
Ballad, 185 f.
Barri, a grove *(Skírnismál)*, 58 f.
Baugi, a giant *(Prose Edda)*, 4
Beowulf, 14, 60, 94, 113
Bera Yngvarsdóttir *(Egils saga)*,
125
Bernard de Ventadour, 152
Bersi Véleifsson (Hólmgöngu-
Bersi, *Kormáks saga)*, 142
Bersöglisvísur (Sighvatur Þór-
ðarson), 164
Bible, 188
Bikki *(Guðrúnarhvöt)*, 90
Billingur, a giant? *(Hávamál)*,
49
Bjarkamál hin fornu, 95, 201–
3, 105, 169
Bjarki *(Bjarkamál hin fornu)*,
102

209

Index

Björn, Swedish king (*Egils saga*), 127

Björn Hítdælakappi, 141, 152

Boðn, a vat for the skaldic mead *(Prose Edda)*, 3f.

Borghildur (*Helgakviða Hundingsbana*), 64

Borgný (*Oddrúnargrátr*), 84

Bragi, god of skaldic art, 3–5, 69, 119

Bragi Boddason, Norwegian poet, 2, 5, 107 f., 110 f., 121 f., 127

Brálundur (*Helgakviða Hundingsbana I*), 64 f.

Brian, Irish king (*Njáls saga*), 95

Brísingamen, Freyja's necklace (*Þrymskviða*), 56

Brot af Sigurðarkviðu, 61, 78

Brünhilde (*Nibelungenlied*), 94, 95

Brynhildur, Buðli's daughter, 71, 77–83, 85, 95

Brynjólfur Sveinsson, Icelandic bishop, 27, 191

Buðli, Hunnish king (father of Atli and Brynhildur), 77 f., 81

Böðvar Egilsson (*Egils saga*), 135 f.

Böðvildur (*Völundarkviða*), 61 f.

Bölverkur, pseudonym for Óðinn (*Prose Edda*), 4

Codex Regius (of the *Poetic Edda*), 27, 30 f., 40, 61, 63 f., 70, 72, 77, 80, 86, 88, 93, 95, 101, 103 f., 191, 193 f.

Codex Regius (of the *Prose Edda*), 1

Codex Trajectinus (of the *Prose Edda*), 1

Codex Upsaliensis (of the *Prose Edda*), 1

Codex Wormianus (of the *Prose Edda*), 1

Collinder, Björn, 88, 104

Dagur (*Helgakviða Hundingsbana II*), 67

Danparstaðir (= Dnjepr-?) (*Hlöðskviða*), 99

Dante Alighieri, 175 f.

Darraðarljóð, 95 f.

Den nya Grottesången (Viktor Rydberg), 46

Deor's Lament, 14 f., 62, 94

Dietrich of Bern (= Þjóðrekur), 84

Disticha (Dicta) Catonis, 44 f.

Divina Commedia (Dante), 175

Drápa, 107, 122, 127, 129, 131, 143, 154, 157, 169, 177, 179

Draumkvædet, 175

Dróttkvætt, 17–20, 24 f., 66, 107 f., 110, 113, 115, 124, 126, 140, 146 f., 152–55, 157, 160, 167 f., 180, 186, 189

Dyggvi Domarsson, Swedish king in ancient times, 114

Dædalus, legendary Greek character, 63

Dörruður, pseudonym for Óðinn?, 96

Eadgils (= Aðils) (*Beowulf*), 113

Ebbadætrakvæði, 186

Edda (*Poetic Edda*), 5, 9, 19, 27 f., 30–32, 39, 40, 42, 46, 51, 57 f., 60, 63 f., 66, 73, 75 f., 89, 92–95, 101 f., 106 f., 110 f., 122, 133, 143, 148, 154, 157, 187, 191

Edda (*Prose Edda*), 1 f., 6, 21, 27

Egill Aunsson, Swedish king, 113

Egill Skalla-Grímsson, 17, 106, 121–41, 149, 157, 169, 171

Egils saga Skalla-Grímssonar, 123, 141, 157, 170 f.

Egilsson, Sveinbjörn, 144

Eilífur Guðrúnarson, 153 f., 156–58, 171

Einar skálaglamm Helgason, 140, 157

Einar Skúlason, 169

Eir, goddess of healing, 148

Eiríksmal, 118

Eiríkur blóðøx Haraldsson, Norwegian king, 118, 120, 125–31, 133, 169

Eiríkur Hákonarson, Norwegian earl, 159

Eiríkur Magnússon, Norwegian king, 121, 170

Embla, the first woman (*Völuspá*), 31 f.

Ermanaric (= Ermanricus, Hermanaricus, Jörmunrekkur), 94

Erpur (*Guðrúnarhvöt, Hamðismál*), 90 f.

Etzel (= Attila, Atli) (*Nibelungenlied*), 94 f.

Eufemiavísurna, 170

Euhemeros, 8

Eylimi, a king, 71

Eynæfir, a sea king, 109

Eysteinn Aðilsson, Swedish king of ancient times, 115

Eysteinn Ásgrímsson, 178

Eysteinn Haraldsson, Norwegian king, 169

Eyvindur skáldaspillir, Norwegian skald, 17, 29, 118–20

Fáfnir, a dragon, 63, 71–75, 77, 124, 148

Fáfnismál, 61, 73–75

Fagrskinna, a manuscript codex, 116

Fenja, a giantess (*Gróttasöngr*), 5, 47

Fenrisúlfur, 33, 54, 119

Ferskeytt (ferskeytla), a verse form, 185, 189

Fjalar, a dwarf (*Prose Edda*), 3 f.

Fjölnir, Swedish king in ancient times, 112

Fjölsvinnsmál, 31

Flateyjarbók, a manuscript codex, 30

Flokkur, a form of skaldic poetry, 107

Fornyrðislag, a verse form, 12–17, 19, 55, 67, 70 f., 73, 76, 84, 88, 96, 99, 103, 108, 132

Frá dauða Sinfjötla, 61

Frekasteinn, a place name, 69

Freyja, a goddess (*Þrymskviða*), 56, 59, 148, 151, 159

Freyr, one of the Æsir (*Skírnismál*), 58 f., 112, 159, 196

Fríður, name of a goddess in kennings, 148 f.

Friðþjófsrímur, 187

Frigg, Óðin's wife, 22, 139, 148, 158, 195 f.

Fróði, Danish king (*Gróttasöngr*), 5, 47 f.

Fröding, Gustaf, 161, 167

Galar, 3 f.

Galdar, a dwarf (*Prose Edda*), 49

Galdralag, a verse form, 13 f., 49

Gallehus, the Horns of, 15

211

Gangleri (*Prose Edda*), (*Grímnismál*), a cover name for Óðinn), 7 f., 21

Garmur, a dog (*Völuspá*), 32, 194, 197

Geirröður, a giant (*Þórsdrápa*), 51, 154

Geirröður, a king (*Grímnismál*), 51

Geisli (Einar Skúlason), 169

Gerður, a giant maiden (*Skírnismál*), 58 f.

Gibica (*Ger.* Gibich; Gjúki), 92

Gibich (Gibica, Gjúki), 92

Ginnungagap, 12

Gislaharius, Burgundian king, 92

Gísla saga Súrssonar, 141, 171

Gísli Súrsson, 142, 171

Gjúki, a king, 75, 77, 80, 82, 92

Gjúkungs (Gjúkungar), a royal dynasty, 63, 71, 82, 92 f.

Gjölp, a giantess (*Þórsdrápa*), 154

Glymdrápa (Þorbjörn hornklofi), 115

Gná, a goddess, 148

Gnipahellir (*Völuspá*), 32, 194

Gnitaheiði (Gnitaheiðr) (*Reginsmál*), 73

Godomarus, Burgundian king, 92

Goethe, J. W. von, 140

Grani, Sigurður Fáfnisbani's horse, 72, 78

Granmar (*Helgakviða Hundingsbana II*), 65

Greip, a giantess (*Þórsdrápa*), 154

Grettisrímur, 187

Grímhildur, King Gjúki's wife, 77 f., 83, 94

Grímnir, a pseudonym for Óðinn, 37, 51, 159

Grímnismál, 7, 14, 21, 30, 37 f., 51

Grípir, Sigurður Fáfnisbani's uncle, 71

Grípisspá, 61, 71 f.

Grís Sæmingsson (*Hallfreðar saga*), 160 f.

Grógaldr, 31

Gróttasöngr, 5, 31, 46 f., 96

Grótti, a mill, 5, 47

Guðrún, King Gjúki's daughter, 63 f., 71, 77–84, 86–91, 93 f.

Guðrúnarhvöt, 61, 89, 93

Guðrúnarkviða I, 61, 81, 87

Guðrúnarkviða II, 61, 83

Guðrúnarkviða III, 61, 84

Gundaharius, Burgundian king, 92

Gundicarius, Burgundian king, 92 f.

Gunnar, King Gjúki's son, 16, 77–80, 83–87, 89, 92 f.

Gunnar Egilsson (*Egils saga*), 137

Gunnhildur, Norwegian queen, 120, 125 f.

Gunnlaugs saga ormstungu, 141

Gunnlaugur ormstunga Illugason, 106, 152

Gunnlöð, a giant maiden (*Prose Edda*), 3 f.

Gunnur, a valkyrie, 148, 161

Gunther (*Nibelungenlied*), 92, 94

Gutþormur, King Gjúki's son, 79, 82, 92

Gylfaginning (*Prose Edda*), 2, 6–8

Gylfi, Swedish king *(Prose Edda)*, 6 f.

Gymir, a giant *(Skírnismál)*, 58

Gymir, name of the god of the sea *(Ynglingatal)*, 114

Hagbard (Hagbarður), character in a Danish ballad, 114

Hagen *(Nibelungenlied)*, 94

Haki, name of a sea king *(Haustlöng)*, 112

Hákonarmál (Eyvindur skáldaspillir), 17, 29, 118–20

Hákon Eiríksson, Norwegian earl, 18

Hákon Hákonarson, Norwegian king, 2

Hákon, inn góði Aðalsteinsfóstri, Norwegian king, 118–20, 126

Hákon Sigurðarson, Norwegian earl, 153, 157

Hálfdan Eysteinsson, Swedish king, 114, 116

Hallfreðar saga, 160

Hallfreður vandræðaskáld Óttarsson, 141, 152, 157–61, 167, 171 f.

Hallgrímsson, Jónas, 188

Hamðir, son of King Jónakur, 90–94, 121

Hamðismál, 61, 89–91, 93, 97, 121

Hamlet (Shakespeare), 188

Hár *(Bjarkamál hin fornu)*, 101

Hár High *(Prose Edda)*, 7 f.

Haraldskvæði (Þorbjörn hornklofi?), 116

Haralds saga hárfagra (Heimskringla), 117

Haraldur gráfeldr Eiríksson, Norwegian king, 143

Haraldur inn harðráði Sigurðarson, Norwegian king, 120, 167 f.

Haraldur inn hárfagri Hálfdanarson, Norwegian king, 110, 115–18

Hárbarðsljóð, 30, 51, 53, 59

Hárbarður, pseudonym for Óðinn, 51, 53

Harvaða fjöll (= Carpathian Mountains?) *(Hlöðskviða)*, 99

Hati, a giant *(Helgakviða Hjörvarðssonar)*, 70

Háttatal (Prose Edda), 2, 13, 15, 170

Haustlöng (Þjóðólfur hvinverski), 111

Hávamál, 4, 13 f., 29 f., 39–45, 48 f., 76, 104, 119, 137, 173–75

Heaþoric (= Heiðrekur?) *(Widsith)*, 99

Héðinn, Helgi Hjörvarðsson's brother, 69

Heiðreks saga (= *Hervarer saga*), 97, 99

Heiðrekur, a king *(Oddrúnargrátr)*, 84

Heiðrekur, king of the Goths *(Hlöðskviða)*, 97, 99

Heimdallur, one of the Æsir, 31, 45, 56

Heimskringla (Snorri Sturluson), 105 f., 112, 116, 143, 162, 171

Heiti, a term in poetics, 3, 6, 21 f., 106, 108, 189

Hel, the goddess and also the realm of the dead, 38, 90, 114, 175, 195

Helgakviða Hjörvarðssonar, 61, 69

Index

Helgakviða Hundingsbana I, 26, 61, 64, 66, 70

Helgakviða Hundingsbana II, 61, 67, 69

Helgason, Jón, 101, 104, 172, 189 f., 194

Helgi Hjörvarðsson, 64, 69 f.

Helgi Hundingsbani, 63–71

Heliand, 14

Helmingr, a half-stanza, 19

Helreið Brynhildar, 61, 81 f.

Hemidus (*Quedlinburg Chronicle*), 94

Herkja (*Guðrúnarkviða*), 84

Hermanaricus, a king, 93

Hermóður, a son of Óðinn (*Hákonarmál*), 119

Herr Olov och älvorna, 185

Herteitur, a pseudonym for Óðinn (*Grímnismál*), 21

Hervarar saga (= *Heiðreks saga*), 97

Hildebrandslied, 14, 60

Hildur, a valkyrie, 148, 151

Hindarfjall, 75

Hjalli, a thrall (*Atlakviða, Atlamál*), 86, 89

Hjálmar inn hugumstóri (*Heiðreks saga, Örvar-Odds saga*), 99 f.

Hjálmar's Death Song, 95, 100

Hjálmberi, a pseudonym for Óðinn, 21

Hjálprekur, a king, 71

Hjalti (*Bjarkamál hin fornu*), 102

Hjördís, King Eylimi's daughter, mother of Sigurður Fáfnisbani, 71

Hjörvarður, a king (*Helgakviða Hjörvarðssonar*), 69

Hlín, a goddess, 21, 148 f., 151, 195

Hliþe (= Hlöður?) (*Widsith*), 99

Hlöðskviða, 95, 97, 99, 104

Hlöður (*Heiðreks saga, Hlöðskviða*), 97–99

Hlökk, a valkyrie, 168

Hnitbjörg, a mountain (*Prose Edda*), 3 f.

Hofgarða-Refur (= Skáld-Refur), 19

Hollander, Lee M., 108, 111, 171

Hrafnás, a peudonym for Óðinn, 19

Hrafnsmál (*Haraldskviða*) (Þorbjörn hornklofi), 117

Hreiðmar (*Reginsmál*), 73

Hrímgerðarmál, 70

Hrímgerður, a giantess (*Helgakviða Hjörvarðssonar*), 70

Hrist, a valkyrie, 148f.

Hrólfur (*Bjarkamál hin fornu*), 101

Hrólfur kraki, Danish king, 6, 102

Hrungnir, a giant, 109, 111 f.

Hrynhenda (Arnór jarlaskáld Þórðarson), 168

Hrynhent, a verse form, 168, 180

Huginn, one of Óðin's ravens, 37, 66

Hugsvinnsmál, 45

Hundingur, a king, 65, 73

Húsdrápa (Úlfur Uggason), 122

Húskarlahvöt, 102 f.

Hveðrungur, name of a giant, 114, 196

Hvergelmir, a well (*Grímnismál*), 38

Hymir, a giant (*Hymiskviða*), 53–55

Hymiskviða, 26, 30, 53, 55, 107

214

Hyndluljóð, 30
Hænir, (Hœnir), one of the
Æsir, 73
Höðbroddur (*Helgakviða Hun-
dingsbana I*), 65
Höfuðlausn (Egill Skalla-Gríms-
son), 126–28, 130, 132, 135
Höfuðstafr, a metrical term, 12
Högni, Helgi Hundingsbani's
father-in-law, 68, 94
Högni, King Gjúki's son and
Gunnar's brother, 77, 79, 83–
86, 88 f., 94

Iðavöllur (*Völuspá*), 31, 34, 197
Iðunn, a goddess (*Prose Edda*),
3
Ilmur, a goddess, 148
Incgenþeow (= A n g a n t y r ?)
(*Widsith*), 99
Ingibjörg, K i n g I n g j a l d's
daughter (*Heiðreks saga, Ör-
var-Odds saga*), 99 f.
Ingi Haraldsson, Norwegian
king, 169
Ingjaldur inn illráði Önundar-
son, Swedish king of ancient
times, 115
Inngangr, a term in poetics,
179 f.

Jafnhár (Equally High) (*Prose
Edda*), 7
Jónakur, a king, 63 f., 89
Jón Birgersson, N o r w e g i a n
archbishop, 169
Jón Egilsson, 121, 170
Jón Loptsson, 9
Jónsson, Finnur, 88, 104, 193
Jordanes, 93
Jörð, a goddess, Þór's mother,
111

Jörmunrekkur, a king (*Guðrúnarhvöt, Hamðismál*), 90 f.,
93, 121
Jötunheimur, the world of the
giants, 56

Karlevi stone, a runic inscrip-
tion, 107
Kenning, 5 f., 8 f., 19, 21–24,
26, 39, 55, 66, 106–8, 110,
124, 129 f., 132–35, 137, 139,
144, 147–49, 154–56, 160 f.,
171, 174, 179, 189
Kenniorð, a term in poetics, 22
Kinck, Hans E., 146, 172
Kjötvi (*Haraldskvæði*), 118
Knéfröður (*Atlakviða*), 16
Kock, E. A., 151, 155, 172
Kolfinna Ávaldadóttir (*Hall-
freðar saga*), 160 f.
Kormáks saga, 141–43, 146 f.,
160, 172
Kormákur Ögmundarson, 21,
141–53, 160 f., 171
Kriemhilde (*Nibelungenlied*),
94
Kvasir (*Prose Edda*), 3–5
Kveld-Úlfur Brunda-Bjálfason
(*Egils saga*), 123
Kviðuháttr, a verse form, 17,
113, 132, 137

Lausavísa, a term in poetics,
106, 122, 140, 160
Laxdæla saga, 122
Lie, Hallvard, 20, 24–26, 107 f.
Lilja (E y s t e i n n Ásgrímsson),
177–80, 183
Liljulag, a verse form, 180
Litur, name of a giant, 110
Ljóðaháttr, a verse form, 12–
14, 17, 37 f., 58, 70, 73, 76,
118, 173

Index

Ljóðatal (Hávamál), 49
Loddfáfnir (Hávamál), 49
Logafjöll (Helgakviða Hundingsbana I), 65
Lokasenna, 14, 30, 59 f.
Loki, 8, 56 f., 59 f., 73, 195 f.
Lokrur, 187

Magnús Ólafsson, Norwegian king, 163 f., 168
Málaháttr, a verse form, 15 f., 88, 116, 119
Mansöngr, a term in poetics, 145, 186 f.
Martinsson, Harry, 156, 172
Meili, Þór's brother, 111
Meissner, Rudolf, 22, 26
Menja, a giantess (Gróttasöngr), 5, 47
Miðgarður (Völuspá, Grimnismál), 31, 37 f., 54, 107–10, 121, 196
Miðgarðsormurinn, 52, 197
Mímir, a giant, 51, 55
Minnesang, a form of poetry, 187
Móði, a son of Þór, 55
Muninn, one of Óðin's ravens, 38

Nanna, Baldur's wife, 148
Nerman, Birger, 113
Nibelungenlied, 92, 94 f.
Niðhöggur, a serpent (Völuspá, Grímnismál), 34, 38
Niðuður, a king (Völundarkviða), 61 f.
Niflungs (Niflungar), a royal dynasty, 19, 87
Njáls saga, 95
Njörður, a god, one of the Vanir, 59, 159

Nordal, Sigurður, 35 f., 120, 134, 170 f., 194
Oddrún (Oddrúnargrátr), 84–86
Oddrúnargátr, 61, 84, 86
Óðinn, one of the Æsir, 4–7, 21 f., 33, 37 f., 40, 48–51, 53–55, 59, 66 f., 73, 76, 82, 96, 104, 108, 112, 115, 118 f., 123, 128, 132 f., 137–39, 158 f., 166, 175, 177, 193, 195–97
Óðrerir (Óðrørir), a kettle for the skaldic mead (Prose Edda), 3 f.
Ohlmarks, Åke, 136, 138, 155 f., 171 f.
Óhtere (= Óttar) (Beowulf), 113
Ólafs ríma Haraldssonar, 187
Ólafs rímur Tryggvasonar, 186
Ólafs saga helga (Heimskringla), 101–3
Ólafur hvítaskáld Þórðarson, 170
Ólafur inn helgi Haraldsson, Norwegian king, 18, 101, 105, 162–65, 168 f.
Ólafur liljurós, 185
Ólafur pái Höskuldsson (Laxdæla saga), 122
Ólafur Tryggvason, Norwegian king, 141, 153, 158 f.
Olsen, Magnus, 126
Onela (= Áli) (Beowulf), 113
Óttar vendilkráka Egilsson, Swedish king of ancient times, 113
Otur, Regin's brother, 73

Ragnar loðbrók Sigurðarson, 107, 122
Ragnarsdrápa (Bragi Boddason), 25, 107 f., 121

Ragnarök, 7 f., 33, 36, 119, 177
Rán, goddess of the sea, Ægir's wife, 137
Randvér, son of King Jörmunrekkur (*Guðrúnarhvöt*), 90
Ratatoskur, a squirrel (*Grímnismál*), 38
Refur. *See* Hofgarða-Refur
Reginn, Sigurður Fáfnisbani's fosterer, 72–75
Reginsmál, 61, 73
Rigsþula, 31, 45 f.
Rígur, pseudonym for Heimdallur (*Rigsþula*), 45 f.
Rímur, a poetic genre, 57, 185–89
Rindur, a goddess, 148
Runhent, a verse form, 128
Rydberg, Viktor, 46
Rögnvaldur Ólafsson, Norwegian provincial king, 112
Rögnvaldur Úlfsson, Swedish earl, 164, 167
Rök stone, a runic inscription, 15

Sága, a goddess, 148, 161
Salgófnir, a rooster (*Helgakviða Hundingsbani*), 68
Sálus rímur og Níkanórs, 187
Sanngetall, a cover name for Óðinn (*Grímnismál*), 21
Sarus (= Sörli-?), 93
Saxo Grammaticus, 102 f., 114
Serila (= Sörli), 94
Shakespeare, William, 188
Síbil, a seeress (*Prose Edda*), 6
Siegfried (*Nibelungenlied*), 94
Sif, Þór's wife, 5 f., 22, 55, 109, 151
Sifecan (= Sifka?) (*Widsith*), 99
Sifka (*Heiðreks saga*), 97, 99

Sighvatur Þórðarson, 18, 162–65, 167
Sigmundur, father of Helgi Hundingsbani and Sigurður Fáfnisbani, 63, 65, 69, 71, 110
Signe (Signý), a Danish ballad character, 114
Sigrdrífumál, 61, 75, 77 f., 82
Sigrún, a valkyrie, 65–69
Sigurðarkviða hin skamma, 61, 81
Sigurdrífa, a valkyrie, 75–78, 82
Sigurður Fáfnisbani, 5, 63, 70–83, 86 f., 90, 92
Sigurður Haraldsson, Norwegian king, 167–69
Sigurður Hlaðajarl, 143
Sigurlinn, a queen (*Helgakviða Hjörvarðssonar*), 69
Sinfjötli, brother of Helgi Hundingsbani, 66, 70 f.
Skáldatal 120 f., 143, 153, 170
Skáld-Refur (= Hofgarða-Refur), 19
Skáldskaparmál (*Prose Edda*), 2, 5 f., 8
Skalla-Grímur Kveld-Úlfsson (*Egils saga*), 123–25, 135
Skiðaríma, 187
Skíði, a vagabond (*Skiðríma*), 187 f.
Skírnir, a servant of the god Freyr (*Skírnismál*), 26, 58
Skírnismál, 13 f., 30, 58 f.
S k j ö l d u n g s (Skjöldungar) a royal dynasty, 7
Skothending, a metrical term, 18
Skuld, a norm, 32
Skúli Bárðarson, Norwegian earl, 2
Sleipnir, Óðin's horse, 7, 115
Slæmr, a term in poetics, 179 f.

Index

Snorri Sturluson, 1–3, 5 f., 8 f., 13, 15f., 19, 21 f., 27, 31 f., 46 f., 57–59, 101–3, 105–7, 110–12, 115, 117, 122 f., 131, 133, 143, 148, 154, 157, 162–64, 170 f., 187

Sólarljóð, 173–77, 183

Són, a container for the skaldic mead, 3 f.

Sonatorrek (Egill Skalla-Grímsson), 17, 135–37, 139 f., 171

Stef, a metrical term, 179

Stefjamál, a term in poetics, 179 f.

Steingerður Þorkelsdóttir (*Kormáks saga*), 142–46, 148–52, 160

Stofn, a term in poetics, 22

Stuðlar, a metrical term, 12

Sturla Þórðarson, 170

Sunilda (= Svanhildur), 93

Suttungur, a giant (*Prose Edda*), 3–5, 13 f., 48

Svanhildur, daughter of Sigurður Fáfnisbani and Guðrún, 90 f., 93

Sváva, a valkyrie, 69 f.

Sveinsson, Einar Ól., 26, 104, 147

Sven Grathe, Danish king, 169

Svipall, a pseudonym for Óðinn, 21

Svíþjóð (the Swedish realm), 7

Svölnir, pseudonym for Óðinn, 112

Sæhrímnir, a boar (*Grímnismál*), 38

Sæmundur inn fróði Sigfússon, 27

Sörli, a son of King Jónakur, 90–94, 121

Tasso, Torquato, 140

Theodoric the Great (= Þjóðrekur, Þiðrekur af Bern), 15, 84

Third Grammatical Treatise, 143

Thoursie, Ragnar, 156

Thrace, 6

Thyestes, Greek legendary character, 87

Tristan legend, 152

Tristrams kvæði, 185

Troy (*Prose Edda*), 6

Týr, one of the Æsir, 53–55

Tyrfingur, a magic sword (*Heiðreks saga, Örvar-Odds saga*), 98 f.

Úlfur Uggason, 122

Ullur, Þór's stepson, 111 f.

Urður, a norn, 32, 158

Útgarða-Loki, a giant, 8, 59, 187

Vafþrúðnir, a giant, 38

Vafþrúðnismál, 7, 14, 30, 37 f.

Valhöll (Valhalla), 29, 37 f., 68, 118 f., 187 f., 197

Vegtamskviða (= *Baldrs draumar*), 30

Vellekla (Enar skálaglamm Helgason), 157

Verðandi, a norm, 32

Viðrir, a pseudonym for Óðinn, 109, 128, 158

Viður, a cover name for Óðinn, 133, 138, 196

Vilmundur (*Oddrúnargrátr*), 84

Virgil, 14, 60

Vísbur Vanlandason, Swedish king of ancient times, 115

Vísuhelmingur, a half-stanza, 19

218

Völsungasaga, 63, 77 f.
Völsungs (Völsungar), a royal dynasty, 7, 110
Völundarkviða, 15, 30, 61–63
Völundur, 30, 61–63
Völuspá, 7, 12, 28–31, 34–36, 38 f., 45, 48, 104, 135, 154, 173, 177, 194

Widsith, 14, 94, 99

Yggdrasill, the universe tree, 32 f., 38, 50, 196
Yggur, a pseudonym for Óðinn, 132 f.
Ymir, a giant (Grímnismál), 37
Ynglinga saga (Heimskringla), 112
Ynglingatal (Þjóðólfur Hvinverski), 17, 106, 112–14, 121
Ynglings (Ynglingar), a royal dynasty, 7, 112–16
Yngvar Eysteinsson, Swedish king of ancient times, 114

Þekkur, pseudonym for Óðinn *(Grímnismál)*, 21
Þjálfi, Þór's servant, 154–56
Þjazi, a giant *(Prose Edda)*, 3
Þjóðólfur Hvinverski, Norwegian skald, 17, 110–12, 116
Þjóðrekur (= Theodoric, Dietrich of Bern), 84
Þór, one of the Æsir, 6, 8, 22, 38 f., 48, 51–57, 59, 107–12, 121 f., 154–56, 159, 187, 196
Þóra Hákonardóttir *(Guðrúnarkviða)*, 83

Þorbjörn hornklofi, Norwegian poet, 115 f.
Þórdís Þórólfsdóttir *(Egils saga)*, 140
Þorgerður Egilsdóttir *(Egils saga)*, 136, 140
Þormóður Berason, 101
Þórólfur Kveld-Úlfsson *(Egils saga)*, 123
Þórólfur Skalla-Grímsson *(Egils saga)*, 123, 128, 130
Þórsdrápa (Eilífur Guðrúnarson), 153 f., 158
Þorsteinn Egilsson *(Egils saga)*, 136
Þorvaldur Eysteinsson *(Kormáks saga)*, 152
Þriðji (Þriði; The Third) *(Prose Edda)*, 7
Þrúðheimur, Þór's abode *(Prose Edda)*, 6
Þrymlur, 187
Þrymskviða, 30, 55–58, 104, 187
Þrymur, a giant *(Þrymskviða)*, 55–57
Þundur, a pseudonym for Óðinn, 21

Åkerblom, Axel 180, 183

Ægir, the god of the sea, 3–5, 53, 59, 66, 138
Æsir, 3 f., 6–8, 31 f., 34 f., 48, 51, 53, 55 f., 59, 110, 119, 154, 160, 188, 195, 197

Ögmundur Kormáksson *(Kormáks saga)*, 150
Örvar-Odds saga, 99 f.